# Crack the Books

ACCOUNTING FOR NON-ACCOUNTANTS

Published in 2008 by the Institute of Chartered Accountants in Ireland
CA House, Pembroke Road
Ballsbridge, DUBLIN 4


Designed and typeset by Compuscript, Shannon, Ireland
Printed by Turner Print Group, Longford, Ireland

The paper used in the printing of this book was produced from managed, renewable
plantation forests.

ISBN 978-0-903854-13-9

The opinions expressed in this publication are those of the author and do not necessarily
represent the views of ICAI. The text is designed to provide accurate and authoritative
information in regard to the subject matter covered. It is sold on the understanding that ICAI
is not engaged in rendering professional services. If professional advice or other expert
assistance is required, the services of a competent professional should be sought.

© *Crack the Books: Accounting for Non-Accountants*
The Institute of Chartered Accountants in Ireland, 2008

# Crack the Books

ACCOUNTING FOR NON-ACCOUNTANTS

## June Menton
## Chartered Accountant

Institute of Chartered Accountants in Ireland

# CONTENTS

# INTRODUCTION

This book is for the huge number of people who are not sure about Bookkeeping and Accounts. Whether you are an accountant, sole trader or are working in a small company, you will find this book useful as a reference book or just for explaining accountancy in simple terms.

There is no such thing as a job for life. People change jobs frequently. With the proliferation of computers, jobs have become less defined. Internet, email and spreadsheets place the emphasis on empowering the individual to take on more responsibility.

Non-financial employees are expected to have a grasp of accounting terms or concepts. Just about everything can be measured in monetary terms. Financial reporting enables the activities of any business to be evaluated. Understanding these terms and concepts is also important for self-employed people or people thinking of setting up their own business. The aim of this book is to provide a guide on basic bookkeeping and accounting requirements. The book can be used by sole traders, small companies, treasurers, accountants—in effect, everyone who is involved in managing and operating the financial aspects of a business. It is hoped that this book will provide an accessible and comprehensive view of the most important aspects of financial good practice, including bookkeeping, budgeting and reporting.

## ❏ Acknowledgements

I would like to thank Kieran Lyons, Director of Publishing with the Institute of Chartered Accountants in Ireland. Without Kieran's expert guidance and support, this book would not have been written. I would also like to thank my colleague Tanya Connolly in the Irish Sports Council for all her suggestions and comments. Rosemary Wilson for proof reading the book. Mr Cecil Donovan, former President of the Institute of Chartered Accountants in Ireland deserves a special mention for peer-reviewing this publication. I would like to thank Niall McCormack for the creative book cover and my family and friends for their support and concern about "how the book was going". Finally I would especially like to thank my husband Eoin O'Shea for his patience together with his maddening red pen and the book's name (inspired, ironically, by the dialogue between Mr Tony Soprano and his son AJ who was told to "crack the books").

June Menton
Chartered Accountant

# BOOKKEEPING BASICS — Chapter 1

## ❑ Role of the Bookkeeper

The bookkeeper's work is never done; as soon as the purchase invoices are recorded then the sales invoices have to be issued and the bank reconciled and so on. Particular skills and attitudes are needed to be successful as a bookkeeper. The following are some of the qualities needed:

- Honesty and integrity.
- Interest in finance.
- Good organisational skills.
- An eye for detail.
- A capacity to work in a logical and orderly manner.
- An ability to allocate regular time periods (eg weekly or monthly) to keep the books up to date.
- An ability to maintain clear and accurate records.
- An understanding of procedures for handling cash, cheques and other monetary transactions.
- Enthusiasm to learn new skills and proficiencies, if necessary.

## ❑ Accounting Stationery

As a minimum, the bookkeeper needs the following books and records:

- Cheque books.
- Bank deposit books.
- A cash book or a general ledger.
- Cheque requisition forms.
- A petty cash book and petty cash vouchers.
- A file for payments to suppliers.
- A file for creditors' statements.
- A file to store receipts from customers.
- A file of purchase orders placed with suppliers.
- A file for bank statements.

All of the stationery listed above should be available. The bookkeeper will be responsible for setting up systems to collect and record the details of financial transactions, most of which will be receipts and payments. Understanding bank accounts, the cash book, receiving funds, making payments, bank reconciliation, petty cash and managing creditors and debtors are essential.

## ❏ Manual v Computerised Bookkeeping

A decision is required as to whether to keep the books and records manually or to use a computerised accounting package. Most organisations now use computer packages to manage their accounts. Accounting software packages are relatively inexpensive. It is useful to consult the supplier of the software to be certain that the package suits the organisation in terms of size and complexity. Deciding on the appropriate means of keeping accounting records will depend on the circumstances and activity of the business. The cost–benefit principle holds that the benefits deriving from an accounting information system must be equal to or greater than the cost. In addition to performing routine tasks—preparing payroll, VAT returns, financial statements and maintaining internal control—the accounting system may be called upon to provide other management information. Some examples of accounting software packages are SAGE,[1] TAS Books[2] and Take 5.[3]

---

[1]  www.sage.ie
[2]  www.tassoftware.ie
[3]  www.takefive.ie

# BUSINESS STRUCTURE     Chapter 2

Businesses can be carried out under three different categories based on their structure: Sole trader, partnership or company. This chapter sets out the advantages and disadvantages of each of the three structures together with Companies Registration Office and Revenue requirements.

## ❑ Sole Trader

### *Structure*

The simplest business structure is that of a sole trader where the person who owns the business also runs and manages it. There are relatively few rules regarding how the business should be run. This is a simple form of business structure but can involve risk, as the sole trader is personally responsible for business debts and has unlimited liability. All the profits belong to the sole trader. There is no separation between ownership and management; the owner is the manager/employee. In a company, there is a legal separation between ownership and management. A sole trader is both the legal and actual owner of his/her own enterprise.

### *Capital Account*

When someone invests in their own business, the amount of the investment is recorded in the person's own "capital account". Because there is no legal separation between the owner and the sole trader, it is not necessary to make formal declarations of a withdrawal of funds as would be required when a company declares a dividend. In sole traders' accounts the original capital contributed by the sole trader and the retained profits are merged into a combined capital account that is reduced by any "personal drawings". The capital account is increased by the owner's investment in the business and business profits. It is decreased by losses and withdrawals of assets from the business for personal use by the owner. Set out in Figure 2.1 is an example of a capital account.

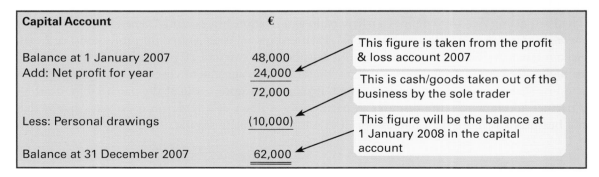

| Capital Account | € | |
|---|---|---|
| Balance at 1 January 2007 | 48,000 | |
| Add: Net profit for year | 24,000 | ← This figure is taken from the profit & loss account 2007 |
| | 72,000 | This is cash/goods taken out of the business by the sole trader |
| Less: Personal drawings | (10,000) | This figure will be the balance at 1 January 2008 in the capital account |
| Balance at 31 December 2007 | 62,000 | |

Figure 2.1

**Note:** Brackets around a figure are used to indicate that the amount is being deducted from the figure above it.

## *Taxation*

As income tax is levied on the owner personally, taxation is not shown in the business accounts but is treated as part of "drawings" when the tax is paid. For income tax reporting, the law requires that the capital and the drawings account be separated from the profit & loss account. The capital account represents the owner's interest in the assets of the business. The drawings account is used to record monies and other assets taken out of the business by the owner for personal use, which can include cash, stock etc. These "drawings" are not described as "salaries or wages", although the owner may think of the money as such. Companies do not have a drawings account.

## *Advantages of Sole Trader Status*

- Less paperwork than a company but financial statements have to be prepared at the year end for tax purposes.
- Tax losses can be used to reduce an individual's other income, eg rental income, for tax purposes.
- A sole trader can be converted to a company if required at a later stage.

## *Disadvantages of Sole Trader Status*

- There is no Companies Office protection for a chosen business name.
- The sole trader is personally responsible for the debts of the business.
- A sole trader may have more difficulty borrowing money; banks prefer to lend to incorporated businesses.
- May lack credibility. Customers often prefer to buy from a company which has an image of greater permanence.

# ❑ Partnership

## *Structure*

The Partnership Act 1890 defines a partnership as a relationship existing "*between persons carrying on business in common with a view to profit*". Partnerships are usually used for professions, eg Legal, Accountancy, Architects. A partnership can exist between two and 20 people but the number may be higher for certain professions. Partners should have an agreement covering areas such as profit and loss sharing, interest on funds invested, management duties, sale of the partnership, death of a partner and how to settle disputes. A partnership is like a sole trader in most ways except that the business has more than one owner. It is not a legal entity separate from the owners; it is an unincorporated association that brings together the talents and resources of two or more people. Partners share the profits and losses of the partnership according to an agreed formula called the profit-sharing ratio.

## Partnership Agreement

Central to the success of a partnership is the partnership agreement. The partnership agreement does not have to be in writing but it is good business practice to have a written document that clearly states the details of the partnership, including name, location, purpose, partners' respective duties, the method of distributing the profit or loss and procedures for the admission and withdrawal of partners. The partnership agreement or, in its absence, the Partnership Act 1890, may allow for interest on the original capital and for the payment of salaries to partners.

## Advantages of Partnerships

- Partnerships are easy to form.
- Each partner can learn from the expertise of the other partners and expand their skills.
- Sharing start-up costs and providing ongoing working capital.
- Sharing the business workload.

## Disadvantages of Partnerships

- Lack of long-term compatibility: a partnership agreement should be in place from the start.
- Financial problems: lack of money can cause one partner to walk away and the partnership collapses.
- Uneven workload: one partner may do more work than the other(s) and get disgruntled.
- It has a limited life. It may be dissolved when a new partner is admitted, when a partner withdraws, goes bankrupt, retires, dies or when the terms of the agreement are met.
- Each partner is an agent of the partnership within the scope of the business. Because of this mutual agency, any partner can bind the partnership to a business agreement as long as they are acting within the normal scope of the business's activities.
- Each partner has personal unlimited liability for all of the debts of the partnership. If a partnership cannot pay its debts, creditors must first satisfy their claims from the assets of the business. If these assets are not enough to pay all debts, the creditors can seek payment from the personal assets of each partner. Unlimited liability means that potential responsibility for debts is not limited to the initial investment as it is in a company. Each person is personally liable for all debts of the partnership including those arising from uncertain liabilities such as lawsuits.

## Capital Account

The owner's interest in a partnership is referred to as "capital". It is necessary to maintain separate capital and drawings accounts for each partner and to divide the profit and loss of the business among the partners according to the profit-sharing ratio. The partnership capital account is listed separately in the accounts as set out in Figure 2.2.

| Partners' Capital | € |
|---|---|
| John Murphy Capital | 20,000 |
| Peter Owen Capital | 25,000 |
| Maria Reynolds Capital | 5,000 |
| | 50,000 |

Figure 2.2

## Distribution of Partnership Profits and Losses

Partnership profits and losses can be distributed according to whatever methods the partnership specifies in the partnership agreement. Income in partnerships normally has three components:

1. Interest on capital accounts (monies invested by the partners).
2. Partners' salaries.
3. Partnership profits.

Reference to "salaries" and "interest" is not the same as salaries and interest in a company situation. "Salaries" and "interest" in a partnership are not deductions in the profit & loss account to arrive at net profit, rather they are a means of apportioning the profit among partners based on the time and effort each partner invests in the business. Partners may decide to share the profits in any ratio they choose. Even if two partners contribute the same capital it does not necessarily mean that they will receive the same amount of profit. Salaries allow for difference in services that partners provide to the partnership. Provision can be made for interest on capital accounts (monies invested) if partners invest different capital amounts.

**Example:**
John Murphy, Peter Owen and Maria Reynolds are in partnership. The profit for the year was €200,000, so how is this divided among the partners? See Figure 2.3.

Step 1. Assume that partners are entitled to a salary based on their contribution to the running of the partnership.
Step 2. Interest is provided based on 10% of their capital contributed.
Step 3. The remaining profit is divided equally.

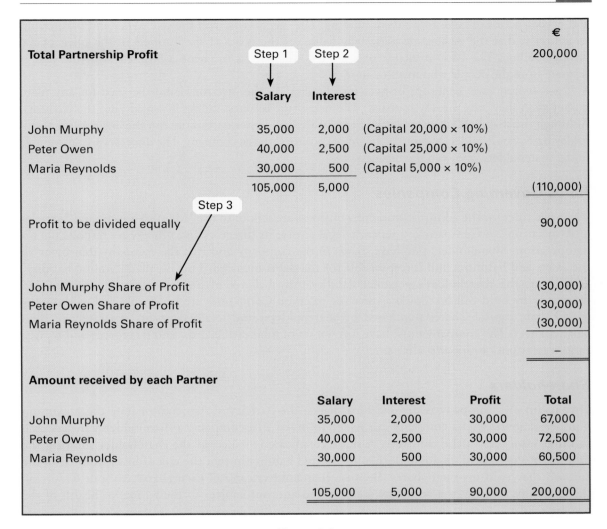

Figure 2.3

If the partnership agreement allows for the distribution of salaries and interest or both, the amount must be allocated to the partners even if the profits are not enough to cover the salaries or interest. In fact even if the business has a loss these allocations must still be made. After the allocation of salaries and interest, the negative balance must be distributed according to the profit-sharing ratios and in the absence of a partnership agreement the losses must be shared equally.

## ❑ Company

### *Structure*

Limited companies are one of the most common business structures. The history of limited companies dates back to mid-Victorian times when it was realised that businesses were expanding and needed access to large amounts of funding. The biggest risk with the sole trader and partnership structures is that the owners are personally liable for the debts of the business in the event of the business failing. The basic principle of a limited company is to create a business structure that is separate from the people who invested in it.

If a company goes bankrupt or goes into liquidation the investor cannot be sued for any more money than they have already invested. The risk of the business failing is passed onto the creditors. Although the shareholders own a limited company they do not necessarily run the business on a day-to-day basis. Shareholders appoint a "board of directors" to the company. The directors are answerable to the shareholders who own the business.

## Rules Governing Companies

The basic rules for the administration of a business are set out in the "Memorandum" and "Articles of Association". A Company is a separate legal entity; its directors and officers are responsible for its operation. Shareholders purchase shares in the company and it is the company that owns all the assets and liabilities and is responsible for the debts incurred. This is called "limited liability" as it limits the shareholder's personal liability. Any balance of profit remaining after tax and dividends are paid will be shown as revenue reserves. Companies are legally obliged to show the issued share capital (shares purchased by shareholders) and retained profits separately in their balance sheet. The company must have its own set of financial records, and its records and reports should refer only to its own affairs.

## Shareholders

Ownership of a company is divided into shares; the Articles of Association state the maximum number of shares that a company can issue. To invest in a company, a shareholder transfers cash or other resources to the company. A share certificate is issued to the shareholder showing the number of shares held. Shareholders enjoy limited liability in that the risk of loss is limited to the amount they paid for their shares. Because shareholders can sell their shares without dissolving the company, the life of a company is unlimited and not subject to the whims or health of the owners.

## Board of Directors

The duties of directors include authorising contracts, setting salaries, arranging loans with banks and declaring dividends. Dividends are distributions of resources in the form of cash to shareholders. Paying dividends is one way of rewarding shareholders for their investment when the company has been successful in earning a profit.

## Management

A management team is appointed by the board of directors to carry out corporate policies and run day-to-day operations. The operating officers usually include a chief executive officer, a chief financial officer and a chief operating officer.

Management has the duty of reporting the financial results of its administration to the board of directors which subsequently reports to the shareholders. See Figure 2.4.

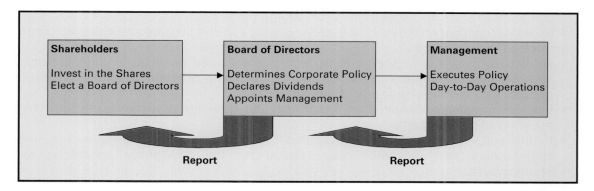

Figure 2.4

## *Capital Account*

The capital section of the balance sheet of a sole trader or partnership is very different from the capital section of a company's balance sheet. In a sole trader's accounts there is no legal separation between the owner and the business; there is no need to separate contributed capital from earnings retained for use in the business. In the financial statements of a company, the retained earnings and the share capital must be kept separate. Once the net profit for the year is calculated, companies have to provide for corporation tax and may declare dividends; the remaining profit is transferred to retained earnings. Set out in Figure 2.5 is an extract from a company profit & loss account.

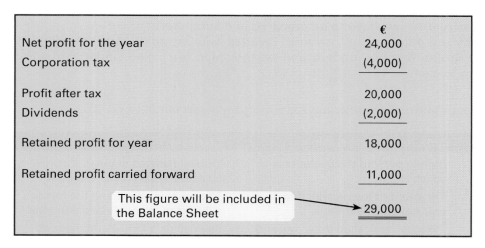

|  | € |
|---|---|
| Net profit for the year | 24,000 |
| Corporation tax | (4,000) |
| Profit after tax | 20,000 |
| Dividends | (2,000) |
| Retained profit for year | 18,000 |
| Retained profit carried forward | 11,000 |
| This figure will be included in the Balance Sheet → | 29,000 |

Figure 2.5

## Advantages of Companies

- Borrowing money: lending institutions may look more favourably on incorporated companies rather than sole traders for lending purposes.
- Separate legal entity: they can buy, sell property, sue and be sued and enter into contracts in their own right.
- Limited liability: many people form limited companies in order to limit liability. The company's creditors can only satisfy their claims against the assets of the company, not the personal property of the shareholders.
- Ease of transfer of ownership: shares can be transferred without affecting the activities of the company.
- Centralised authority and responsibility: the board of directors represents the shareholders and delegates responsibility for the day-to-day operations to management.
- Growth and tax planning: the company structure allows for additional shareholders to be included should the company grow.
- Corporate tax benefits: pension contributions can be made by the company on behalf of the directors.
- The company can continue indefinitely, unlike sole traders and partnerships.

## Disadvantages of Companies

- Higher set-up costs such as legal fees.
- Companies must follow company law and regulations.
- Double taxation: company profits are first charged to corporation tax. Dividends then suffer income tax when paid to shareholders.
- Higher accounting costs and additional paperwork. An audit may be required. Corporation tax returns will have to be prepared and submitted.
- Payroll records are required, as owners' salaries will be paid under the PAYE/PRSI system. Profits for sole traders and partnerships are taxed under the self-assessment tax system.

The difference between a sole trader/partnership and a company are set out in Figure 2.6.

|  | Sole Trader/Partnership | Company |
| --- | --- | --- |
| Shareholder's loan and equity | Money put into the business is called capital. | Money invested in the business is called share capital. |
| Profits/Losses | The profit or loss is added to capital and called net earnings. | The profit is added and the loss is subtracted from retained earnings. |
| Wages Structure | "Wages" are called drawings and are not business expenses or taxed; instead the profits are taxed. | Salaries paid to a shareholder as an employee of the company are a deductible business expense. |
| Shares | No shares are issued. | A share structure is decided by the shareholders. |

Figure 2.6

## Company Formation

Company formation is the process by which a company is legally formed. It involves drawing up the Memorandum and Articles of Association (internal rules of the company), obtaining a certificate of incorporation from the Companies Registration Office, issuing shares and appointing directors. Prior to setting up a company, information should be obtained from the Companies Registration Office (CRO), Parnell House, 14 Parnell Square, Dublin 1 or the CRO website.[4] Once a company is registered, it is a separate legal entity from the persons who formed it. The companies acts impose strict obligations on directors to comply with company law. This places important responsibilities on directors to ensure that company affairs are conducted in a proper manner and that returns are made correctly and on time to the CRO.

## Memorandum and Articles of Association

The authorised share capital of a company is a statement of the maximum number and classification of the shares that the firm is legally empowered to issue. If a company wishes to increase its issued share capital beyond its stated authorised capital, then it must first increase the authorised capital.

The Articles of Association govern the internal management of the company and will state explicitly the rights of the various classes of shareholders.

Set out in Figure 2.7 is an example of what is contained in the Memorandum and Articles of Association.

| Memorandum of Association | Articles of Association |
|---|---|
| • Governs the relationship of the company with third parties<br>• Name of the company<br>• Object of the company<br>• Details of the share capital | • Internal rules and regulations<br>• Powers of directors<br>• Procedures for conduct of meetings<br>• Dividend rights<br>• Voting rights |

Figure 2.7

## Private v Public Companies

Companies can be set up as private limited companies or public limited companies (PLCs). Most companies in Ireland are private companies. PLCs may be quoted and traded on public stock exchanges where investors can buy and sell shares on an open market. Set out in Figure 2.8 is a summary of the differences between private limited companies and public limited companies.

|  | Private Company | Public Limited Company |
|---|---|---|
| Minimum number of members | 1 | 7 |
| Maximum number of members | 99 | No limit |
| Transfer of shares | Restricted | Not restricted |
| Subscription by public for shares/debenture | Prohibited | Not restricted |
| Included at the end of the company name | Limited | Public Limited Company |

Figure 2.8

---

[4] www.cro.ie

The issue of whether to set up as a sole trader/partnership or company is a matter of choice and depends on the goals of the new business. A business may start as a sole trader and then be formed as a partnership or a company. Certain businesses cannot set up as a company, eg solicitors. Set out in Figure 2.9 is a comparison of the three structures.

### Summary of the Three Structures

| | Sole Trader | Partnership | Company |
|---|---|---|---|
| Legal status | Not separate | Not separate | Separate |
| Risk | Owner personally liable | Owners personally liable | Limited to actual investment |
| Duration | Fixed duration/life of sole trader | Fixed duration/life of partners | Infinity |
| Transferability of ownership | Sale by owner | New partnership/sale by partners | Transfer of shares |

Figure 2.9

## ❑ Company Registration Office Compliance Requirements

The companies acts impose a number of obligations on companies to make returns, including annual accounts. The CRO must be notified whenever there is a change in the company's directors, secretary or to the company's details, eg change of address. The following paragraphs outline some of the principal post-incorporation requirements of companies.

### CRO Forms that Have to be Completed

Listed below are some of the forms that must be filed by a company under certain circumstances, eg a change of company name. It is essential that these submissions be made on time.

| Form | B2 | B10 | G1Q | B1 |
|---|---|---|---|---|
| Purpose | Change of registered address | Appointment/cessation of directors (change of name/address) | Change of company name | Annual return |

## ❑ The Annual Return

Every company, whether trading or not, is required to file an annual return (Form B1) with the CRO. This form sets out certain prescribed information in respect of the company. Accounts must be filed with the annual return, except in the case of the first annual return of a new company made up to a date, that is six months after its date of incorporation. A company's annual return date (ARD) in future years is 12 months from its previous year's ARD. This, however, can be altered by bringing the ARD forward to an earlier date or extending the ARD to a later date.

### Bringing the ARD Forward to an Earlier Date

If a company wishes to alter its ARD to an earlier date, it may submit its annual return in advance of its current ARD and, whilst doing so, indicate on the Form B1 that it wishes to elect its ARD to be the anniversary of the date on which its current return has been made up to.

### Extending the ARD to a Later Date

If a company wishes to alter its ARD to a later date, it can do so by filing a Form B73. The procedure for doing so is as follows:

- The company delivers an annual return to the CRO not later than 28 days after its existing ARD, to which no accounts need to be attached.
- The company nominates on the Form B73 the new ARD; that date may not be later than six months after the existing ARD.

## ❑ Revenue Requirements

### Tax Registration

When a business starts it must be registered for tax. This can be done by completing one of the following forms:

- Registration Form TR1[5] (Sole Traders/Partnerships) or TR2[6] (Companies).
- PREM Reg.[7] – Employer (PAYE/PRSI) Tax Registration Form.

### Registration Forms

| Form | TR1 | TR2 | PREM Reg. |
|---|---|---|---|
| Tax | • Income tax<br>• PAYE/PRSI<br>• VAT | • Corporation tax<br>• PAYE/PRSI<br>• VAT | • PAYE/PRSI<br>(Payroll taxes) |
| Status | • Individuals<br>• Partnerships<br>• Trusts<br>• Unincorporated bodies | • Limited company | • Persons/companies already registered for income/corporation tax |

---

[5] www.revenue.ie/forms/formtr1.pdf

[6] www.revenue.ie/forms/formtr2.pdf

[7] www.revenue.ie/forms/premreg.pdf

A company that is incorporated in Ireland or that commences to trade in Ireland must deliver to the Revenue Commissioners particulars relating to the company. The details required include general details about the company, type of business, directors' details etc.

Shortly after registration the business may receive a visit or may request a visit from a Revenue official to assist in operating the tax system. Any difficulties or queries will be dealt with and general assistance will be given to help the business comply with its tax obligations. The Revenue Commissioners' website (www.revenue.ie) contains all the taxation compliance information required by any business; Revenue also has a **_Revenue Online Service (ROS)_** (www.ros.ie) where relevant taxes can be submitted and paid online.

# SETTING UP/BUYING A BUSINESS

## Chapter 3

The first two years are traditionally the most difficult in a new business. A client base, viable products or services and a reputation within the community takes time to establish. Knowledge and support can be gained by attending seminars, workshops, trade shows and conferences. This chapter sets out some accounting factors to be considered when buying or setting up a new business, including the preparation of a projected profit & loss account and cash flow forecast, calculation of the breakeven point for a business and funding a business.

## ❑ Buying a Business

If an existing business is being purchased, an accountant should be employed to review the past two years' financial statements. The following questions should be asked when looking at a potential business:

- Is the business profitable?
- Can the business support your salary requirements? If a business is not incorporated, the financial statements may not show the salary paid to the owners; instead the business should reflect a bottom line net profit sufficient to satisfy the salary that you as the owner would like to take from the business. If the business is a company, the owner's salary will be shown in the accounts.
- Are sales seasonal, increasing or decreasing? Sales should be broken down monthly for two years in order to identify trends and seasonal sales.
- Are you paying too much for the business? The sale price will reflect the value of the fixed assets, stock and goodwill, but there may be room for negotiation.
- Are the assets worth what is being asked? Equipment is rarely worth more than its book value. Buying stock usually requires knowledge of the saleability and condition of the stock.
- Is the goodwill price realistic? "Goodwill" is a term used to refer to the value of the business's reputation, stability and ability to generate profits.
- Do you have enough experience to keep the business profitable?
- Could the business be expanded? Can additional goods or services be introduced?
- What mistakes did the existing owners make that you should avoid? Perhaps they kept too much stock or were unable to collect debts.
- Are your own cash flow projections realistic? Projections should be based on past performance taking into account trends and the economic climate.

Detailed analysis should be carried out to assess the non-financial aspects of the potential business:

1. Review the history and the detailed operations of the business.
2. Review the business's key employees. How long are they working for the business?
3. What is the growth potential?
4. Who are your competitors?
5. What is the asking price and terms of payment? Will payments be staged?
6. What is the life cycle of the business's current products or services?

## ❏ Setting Up a Business

When setting up a business, the first financial requirement is to develop a business plan. Many banks and large accounting firms have publications or CD-ROMs to assist start-up businesses prepare their business plan. The main topics that need to be covered in a business plan are:

- An executive summary. This should be written last, after the document has been completed.
- A general business overview, including a description of the business and where it fits into the marketplace; an outline of the corporate structure, a list of shareholders and partners; a brief profile of key personnel, including expertise and business qualifications; goals and objectives, both long-term and short-term; strengths and weaknesses of the business; the company's philosophy.
- A description of the product or service, including potential customers; cost of sales, including a breakdown of the cost of raw material, freight packaging etc and how the manufacturing/distribution process works; future projections for research and development; legal protection, including patents and trademarks.
- A marketing strategy, including market research, anticipated consumer profiles and projected market share.
- The current and future competition in the market. Promotional and media strategies.
- An operational plan, such as overheads and the breakeven point. A list of major suppliers and their credit terms.
- A description of how the products will be distributed/delivered.
- A list of staff positions and job descriptions.
- A list of assets and equipment, including the asset cost and life expectancy.
- Insurance risks and policies, including fire, theft and key man insurance.
- Financial information, including projected profit & loss account on a month-by-month basis (including start-up costs). Projections beyond Year One can be included on a quarterly or annual basis. Cash flow forecasts for the corresponding periods should be prepared. A cash flow forecast is similar to the projected profit & loss account except that the cash flow will set out when income will be received (cash in) and when expenses will be paid (cash out).

**Quick Tip**

When developing a projected profit & loss account, be conservative in terms of expected income and realistic in relation to what expenses need to be paid. This will ensure that the profit figure is not over optimistic.

## ❑ Funding Requirements

Before a business commences, the entrepreneur will generate a profit & loss projection which shows whether or not it is sensible to go ahead with the business. If good profits are predicted, the business will go ahead. If the profit is too low or if losses are anticipated, the business should not proceed. Before a bank will lend money to the business they will need to see a profit & loss projection. The projections and cash flow forecasts should indicate how much money the business needs to raise. The cash flow forecast will include the total loan repayment (capital and interest), whereas only the loan interest will appear in the projected profit & loss account.

Working out the cash flow implications at the start of a business tells you exactly how much cash will be needed to start the business and keep it going. If business transactions are based on credit, the date of receipt of money for goods and services will not coincide with the date of the sale or purchase. The cash flow forecast highlights the fact that cash payments for fixed assets will normally be required at the time of purchase, whereas the profit & loss projection will spread the cost of the asset over several years. Consequently, the cash flow forecast does not include depreciation. Cash flow forecasts are important in assessing the amount of cash or the extent of a bank overdraft that a business may require.

A business with poor cash flow will have trouble paying its bills. Planning cash flow means projecting when and how money will come into the business and where and when it will be spent.

## ❑ Preparation of Projected Profit & Loss Account

When developing the projected profit or loss, start with the sales figure. Your projections for sales will be based on consumer demand and seasonal variations. Next, calculate the amount you need to spend to acquire the goods to support the level of projected sales; also estimate the amount of stock on hand at the end of each month. List out all the overheads and include estimates for monthly expenditure. Set out in Figure 3.1 is an example of a projected profit & loss account. It is important to set out the assumptions so that anyone looking at the projected profit & loss will be aware of the factors taken into account.

### *Assumptions*

- Sales are based on a forecast of demand for the product.
- The gross profit margin is 50%; therefore cost of sales will be 50% of sales.
- Salaries will be €2,500 per month.
- Travel and subsistence figures are estimates based on the required amount of travel to generate sales.
- An advertisement will be put in a trade magazine in January.
- Insurance must be paid immediately.

- Printing is estimated to cost €3,000 for advertising brochures and flyers in April.
- Postage, telephone and courier expenses are estimated.
- Rent is payable at the start of each quarter.
- Rates are levied once a year, payable immediately.
- General repairs will be carried out during the year.
- Bank interest on the loan will be €150 at the end of each quarter.
- Fixed asets costing €1,200 are depreciated at 20% straight line. The depreciation calculation is as follows:
  €1,200 × 20% = €240/12 months = €20 per month

| Profit & Loss Projections | Jan | Feb | Mar | Apr | May | Jun | Jul | Aug | Sep | Oct | Nov | Dec | TOTAL |
|---|---|---|---|---|---|---|---|---|---|---|---|---|---|
| | € | € | € | € | € | € | € | € | € | € | € | € | € |
| Sales | 1,000 | 2,000 | 3,000 | 6,000 | 7,000 | 8,000 | 9,000 | 11,000 | 13,000 | 18,000 | 22,000 | 25,000 | 125,000 |
| **Cost of Sales** | | | | | | | | | | | | | |
| Opening Stock | 0 | 100 | 150 | 75 | 200 | 100 | 50 | 50 | 50 | 50 | 200 | 400 | 0 |
| Purchases | 600 | 1,050 | 1,425 | 3,125 | 3,400 | 3,950 | 4,500 | 5,500 | 6,500 | 9,150 | 11,200 | 12,150 | **62,550** |
| Closing Stock | (100) | (150) | (75) | (200) | (100) | (50) | (50) | (50) | (50) | (200) | (400) | (50) | **(50)** |
| | 500 | 1,000 | 1,500 | 3,000 | 3,500 | 4,000 | 4,500 | 5,500 | 6,500 | 9,000 | 11,000 | 12,500 | 62,500 |
| Gross Profit | 500 | 1,000 | 1,500 | 3,000 | 3,500 | 4,000 | 4,500 | 5,500 | 6,500 | 9,000 | 11,000 | 12,500 | 62,500 |
| **Expenditure** | | | | | | | | | | | | | |
| Salaries | 2,500 | 2,500 | 2,500 | 2,500 | 2,500 | 2,500 | 2,500 | 2,500 | 2,500 | 2,500 | 2,500 | 2,500 | 30,000 |
| Travel & Subsistence | 100 | | 100 | | 100 | | 150 | | 150 | | 100 | | 700 |
| Advertising | 2,000 | | | | | | | | | | | | 2,000 |
| Insurance | 7,500 | | | | | | | | | | | | 7,500 |
| Printing | | | | 3,000 | | | | | | | | | 3,000 |
| Postage | 100 | 100 | 100 | 100 | 100 | 100 | 100 | 100 | 100 | 100 | 100 | 100 | 1,200 |
| Telephone | 250 | 250 | 250 | 250 | 250 | 250 | 250 | 250 | 250 | 250 | 250 | 250 | 3,000 |
| Courier | 300 | 300 | 300 | 300 | 300 | 300 | 300 | 300 | 300 | 300 | 300 | 300 | 3,600 |
| Rent | 1,000 | | | 1,000 | | | 1,000 | | | 1,000 | | | 4,000 |
| Rates | 3,000 | | | | | | | | | | | | 3,000 |
| Repairs | | | | | 1,000 | | | | | | | | 1,000 |
| Bank Interest | | | 150 | | | 150 | | | 150 | | | 150 | 600 |
| Depreciation | 20 | 20 | 20 | 20 | 20 | 20 | 20 | 20 | 20 | 20 | 20 | 20 | **240** |
| Total Expenditure | 16,770 | 3,170 | 3,420 | 7,170 | 4,270 | 3,320 | 4,320 | 3,170 | 3,470 | 4,170 | 3,270 | 3,320 | 59,840 |
| Profit/(Loss) | (16,270) | (2,170) | (1,920) | (4,170) | (770) | 680 | 180 | 2,330 | 3,030 | 4,830 | 7,730 | 9,180 | 2,660 |
| Accumulated Profit/(Loss) | (16,270) | (18,440) | (20,360) | (24,530) | (25,300) | (24,620) | (24,440) | (22,110) | (19,080) | (14,250) | (6,520) | 2,660 | |

Figure 3.1

# ❏ **Preparation of Projected Cash Flow Forecast**

Set out in Figure 3.2 is an example of a projected cash flow forecast.

## *Assumptions*

- A loan of €10,000 has been obtained from the bank. This is included as a cash receipt in January.
- 50% of customers will pay for sales after 30 days; 50% will settle their account within 60 days.
- 30 days' credit is taken to pay for purchases, advertising, telephone and courier.
- 60 days' credit is taken to pay for printing.
- The following expenses are paid for in the month which the expenditure is incurred — salaries, travel & subsistence, insurance, postage, rent, rates and repairs.
- The amount invested by the owners in cash is €25,000. This is included as the opening cash balance in January.
- The bank loan repayments are €250 capital and €150 interest per quarter, totalling €400.

**Note:** depreciation does not appear in the cash flow as it is not a cash outflow. The purchase of the asset will be included in the cash flow as expenditure in the month when purchased.

| Cash Flow Forecast | Jan | Feb | Mar | Apr | May | Jun | Jul | Aug | Sep | Oct | Nov | Dec | TOTAL |
|---|---|---|---|---|---|---|---|---|---|---|---|---|---|
| **Per Profit & Loss** | € | € | € | € | € | € | € | € | € | € | € | € | € |
| Sales | 1,000 | 2,000 | 3,000 | 6,000 | 7,000 | 8,000 | 9,000 | 11,000 | 13,000 | 18,000 | 22,000 | 25,000 | **125,000** |

| **Cash Receipts In** | | | | | | | | | | | | | |
|---|---|---|---|---|---|---|---|---|---|---|---|---|---|
| Cash received within 30 days (50%) | | 500 | 1,000 | 1,500 | 3,000 | 3,500 | 4,000 | 4,500 | 5,500 | 6,500 | 9,000 | 11,000 | **50,000** |
| Cash received within 60 days (50%) | | | 500 | 1,000 | 1,500 | 3,000 | 3,500 | 4,000 | 4,500 | 5,500 | 6,500 | 9,000 | **39,000** |
| Bank Loan | 10,000 | | | | | | | | | | | | 10,000 |
| **Total Cash In** | 10,000 | 500 | 1,500 | 2,500 | 4,500 | 6,500 | 7,500 | 8,500 | 10,000 | 12,000 | 15,500 | 20,000 | 99,000 |

| **Per Profit & Loss Expenditure (credit taken)** | | | | | | | | | | | | | |
|---|---|---|---|---|---|---|---|---|---|---|---|---|---|
| Purchases | 600 | 1,050 | 1,425 | 3,125 | 3,400 | 3,950 | 4,500 | 5,500 | 6,500 | 9,150 | 11,200 | 12,150 | 62,550 |
| Advertising | 2,000 | | | | | | | | | | | | 2,000 |
| Printing | | | | 3,000 | | | | | | | | | 3,000 |
| Telephone | 250 | 250 | 250 | 250 | 250 | 250 | 250 | 250 | 250 | 250 | 250 | 250 | 3,000 |
| Courier | 300 | 300 | 300 | 300 | 300 | 300 | 300 | 300 | 300 | 300 | 300 | 300 | 3,600 |

*(Continued)*

| Cash Flow Forecast | Jan | Feb | Mar | Apr | May | Jun | Jul | Aug | Sep | Oct | Nov | Dec | TOTAL |
|---|---|---|---|---|---|---|---|---|---|---|---|---|---|
| **Cash Paid Out** | | | | | | | | | | | | | |
| Purchases paid after 30 days | | 600 | 1,050 | 1,425 | 3,125 | 3,400 | 3,950 | 4,500 | 5,500 | 6,500 | 9,150 | 11,200 | 50,400 |
| Advertising paid after 30 days | | 2,000 | | | | | | | | | | | 2,000 |
| Printing paid after 60 days | | | | | | 3,000 | | | | | | | 3,000 |
| Telephone paid after 30 days | | 250 | 250 | 250 | 250 | 250 | 250 | 250 | 250 | 250 | 250 | 250 | 2,750 |
| Courier paid after 30 days | | 300 | 300 | 300 | 300 | 300 | 300 | 300 | 300 | 300 | 300 | 300 | 3,300 |
| **Expenditure (no credit taken)** | | | | | | | | | | | | | |
| Salaries | 2,500 | 2,500 | 2,500 | 2,500 | 2,500 | 2,500 | 2,500 | 2,500 | 2,500 | 2,500 | 2,500 | 2,500 | 30,000 |
| Travel & Subsistence | 100 | | 100 | | 100 | | 150 | | 150 | | 100 | | 700 |
| Insurance | 7,500 | | | | | | | | | | | | 7,500 |
| Postage | 100 | 100 | 100 | 100 | 100 | 100 | 100 | 100 | 100 | 100 | 100 | 100 | 1,200 |
| Rent | 1,000 | | | 1,000 | | | 1,000 | | | 1,000 | | | 4,000 |
| Rates | 3,000 | | | | | | | | | | | | 3,000 |
| Repairs | | | | | 1,000 | | | | | | | | 1,000 |
| Bank loan repayments | | | 400 | | | 400 | | | 400 | | | 400 | 1,600 |
| Fixed Asset | 1,200 | | | | | | | | | | | | **1,200** |
| Total Cash Out | 15,400 | 5,750 | 4,700 | 5,575 | 7,375 | 9,950 | 8,250 | 7,650 | 9,200 | 10,650 | 12,400 | 14,750 | 111,650 |

| **Summary** | | | | | | | | | | | | | |
|---|---|---|---|---|---|---|---|---|---|---|---|---|---|
| Opening Cash Balance | **25,000** | 19,600 | 14,350 | 11,150 | 8,075 | 5,200 | 1,750 | 1,000 | 1,850 | 2,650 | 4,000 | 7,100 | 25,000 |
| Total Cash In | 10,000 | 500 | 1,500 | 2,500 | 4,500 | 6,500 | 7,500 | 8,500 | 10,000 | 12,000 | 15,500 | 20,000 | 99,000 |
| Total Cash Out | (15,400) | (5,750) | (4,700) | (5,575) | (7,375) | (9,950) | (8,250) | (7,650) | (9,200) | (10,650) | (12,400) | (14,750) | (111,650) |
| Closing Cash Balance | 19,600 | 14,350 | 11,150 | 8,075 | 5,200 | 1,750 | 1,000 | 1,850 | 2,650 | 4,000 | 7,100 | 12,350 | **12,350** |

Figure 3.2

In order to check that the figures are correct, a reconciliation should be done between the cash flow forecast and the profit & loss projections, see Figure 3.3.

| Balance Sheet | Account | € | € | Source of Information |
|---|---|---|---|---|
| **Fixed Asset** | Equipment Cost | 1,200 | | Cash Flow Forecast |
| | Accumulated Depreciation | (240) | 960 | Profit & Loss Projections |
| **Current Assets** | | | | |
| Cash Balance at year end | | | 12,350 | Cash Flow Forecast |
| Stock (closing stock in December) | | | 50 | Profit & Loss Projections |
| Debtors (money owed to the business) | Sales | 125,000 | | Profit & Loss Projections |
| | Cash Received | (89,000) | 36,000 | Cash Flow Forecast |
| | (Total Cash In less Bank Loan) | | | |
| **Current Liabilities** | | | | |
| Creditors (money owed by the business) | Purchases (Cost of Sales) | 62,550 | | Profit & Loss Projections |
| | Overheads (excl Depreciation) | 59,600 | | Profit & Loss Projections |
| | Cash Paid (excl Fixed Asset & capital repayment of loan) | (109,450) | (12,700) | Cash Flow Forecast |
| Total Assets less Current Liabilities | | | 36,660 | |
| **Financed by** (how the business is funded) | | | | |
| Capital Contributed | | | 25,000 | Cash Flow Forecast |
| Bank Loan (€10,000 less capital repaid €250 x 4) | | | 9,000 | Cash Flow Forecast |
| Profit for year | | | 2,660 | Profit & Loss Projections |
| | | | 36,660 | |

Figure 3.3

**Note:** even though the projected profit & loss results in a profit of €2,660, the business has cash in the bank at the year end of €12,350 as it has taken credit from suppliers instead of paying for expenses immediately.

## ❑ Calculation of Breakeven Point

The breakeven point occurs when enough sales are generated to cover the cost of purchasing the product and cover overheads. When starting a new business, it is important to know the breakeven point. If you are not confident that the business can reach breakeven point over two to three years, you should reconsider commencing the business.

## Step 1 List the Overheads

| Overhead Costs | € |
|---|---|
| Salaries | 10,000 |
| Accounting | 2,000 |
| Light & Heat | 560 |
| Courier | 50 |
| Rent | 4,000 |
| Telephone & Fax | 390 |
| Insurance | 2,000 |
| Bank Charges | 150 |
| Bank Interest | 360 |
| Advertising | 750 |
| Bad Debts | 100 |
| Stationery | 275 |
| Repairs | 350 |
| Motor Expenses | 1,500 |
| **Total Overheads** | **22,485** |

Figure 3.4

## Step 2

Assuming that the gross profit is 35% on all sales, how much has to be generated in sales to cover these overheads?

€22,485 divided by 35 and multiplied by 100 = €64,242.

| Calculation of Breakeven Point | € |
|---|---|
| Sales required | 64,242 |
| Purchases for resale (65% of sales) | (41,757) |
| Gross profit (35% of sales) | 22,485   See Figure 3.4 |
| Less overheads | (22,485) |
| Profit | NIL |

Figure 3.5

If the profit margin decreases or expenses increase, a loss will occur. If a target profit of €10,000 is required then the calculation will be as follows:

|  | € |
|---|---|
| Overheads | 22,485 |
| Target Profit | 10,000 |
| Total | 32,485 |

€32,485 divided by 35 and multiplied by 100 = €92,814.

| Calculation of sales required to generate €10,000 profit | € |
|---|---|
| Sales required | 92,814 |
| Purchases for resale (65% of sales) | (60,329) |
| Gross Profit (35% of sales) | 32,485 |
| Less Overheads | (22,485) — See Figure 3.4 |
| Profit | 10,000 |

Figure 3.6

## ❑ Funding a Business

The first principle in funding a business is that the long-term assets of a business, eg the fixed assets, buildings, etc, must be funded by long-term capital. Medium and short-term assets, eg stock, can be funded by medium and short-term debt. A business's working capital (debtors + stock − creditors) may have to be funded by short-term debt, eg a bank overdraft, due to seasonal fluctuations in sales.

When lending to a business a bank will hold a "fixed charge" over the assets. If the business ceases, the bank will be able to sell the fixed assets to pay off the loan. Alternatively, the bank may obtain a "floating charge" over a certain class of assets, eg debtors. If the business fails, the floating charge will crystallise and attach itself to those assets.

When a business is well established and generating good profits, it can use its own money to meet expenditure and to pay for new assets or expansion. This is referred to as internal funding. If a business wishes to expand more rapidly than it can afford to by reinvesting its own profits, it will have to seek external funding or other sources of finance.

The "Accounting Equation" refers to a company's economic resources such as cash, stock and buildings and the claims against those resources at a particular time. The "Accounting Equation" must always balance. This chapter sets out the "Accounting Equation" in graphical form and goes through an example of typical transactions undertaken by a business showing the effect on the "Accounting Equation."

The Accounting Equation can be presented as follows:

Net Assets means assets less liabilities.

Alternatively the equation can be considered graphically as set out in Figure 4.1

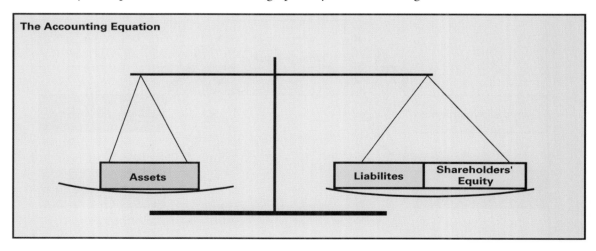

Figure 4.1

## ❏ Assets

Assets are the economic resources of a company that are expected to benefit the company's future operations. Assets include cash, debtors, stock, land, buildings, patents and copyrights.

## ❑ Liabilities

Liabilities are a business's present obligations to pay cash, transfer assets or provide services to other entities in the future. Among these obligations are amounts owed to suppliers for goods and services (creditors) and borrowed money.

## ❑ Shareholders' Equity

Shareholders' equity represents the claims by the owners of a company to the assets of the business. It is what would be left over if all the assets were sold and the liabilities paid. Shareholders' equity is made up of capital subscribed through shares by the shareholders and the amount of profits generated by the business through trading activities.

| Capital | + | Retained Earnings | = | Shareholders' Equity |

There are four types of transactions that can affect owner's equity. Two of these relate to assets that the owner puts in or takes out of the business. When the owner invests in the business or the business generates revenue, this has a positive effect on owner's equity. Alternatively, when the owner takes money out of the business or the business incurs an expense, this has a negative effect on owner's equity. See Figure 4.2.

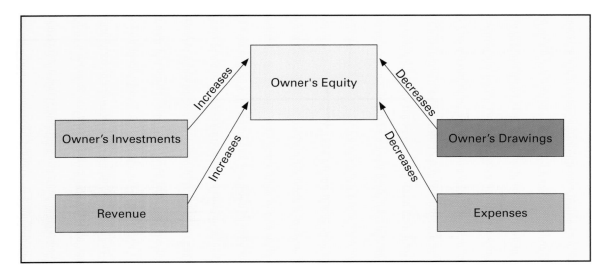

Figure 4.2

Revenue is the increases in owner's equity resulting from selling goods, rendering services or performing other business activities. Revenue are inflows, usually of cash from debtors in exchange for goods or services. When a business delivers a product or provides a service to a customer, it usually receives either cash or a promise to receive cash in the near future. The essence of revenue is that something has been earned through the sale of goods or services. This why cash received through a loan is not considered revenue.

Expenses are the costs of goods and services used up in the course of earning revenues, eg salaries, rent, advertising and telephone costs.

Retained earnings represent owner's equity that has been generated by the revenue-producing activities and kept for use in the business. Revenue and expenses are the increase and decrease in owner's equity that result from operating a business. For example, the amount a customer pays in return for a product or service is revenue to a business. The business's assets increase as does its owner's equity in those assets. On the other hand, the business must make payments so that it can provide goods and services; in this case the asset "cash" decreases or the liability "creditor" increases and owner's equity decreases. See Figure 4.3.

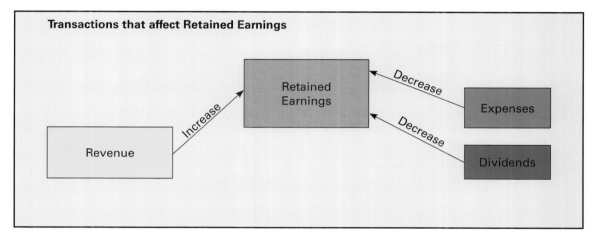

Figure 4.3

A company is successful if its revenue exceeds its expenses. When revenue exceeds expenses the difference is called "net profit". When expenses exceed revenue the difference is called "net loss". Dividends are distributions to shareholders. It is important not to confuse expenses and dividends, both of which reduce retained earnings. Retained earnings are the accumulated net profit less dividends over the life of a business.

## ❑ Accounting Equation Example

The accounting equation can be extended to show how to record various transactions of a business from the initial set-up to the ongoing trading activities. An example is set out below.

1. **Owner's investment. John decided to set up his own business with €40,000 in cash that he inherited from his aunt. He lodges the money into the business bank account. The asset "bank" and the "owner's equity" account increase by €40,000.**

| Asset | = | Owner's Equity |
|-------|---|----------------|
| Bank | | John's Capital Account |
| 40,000 | = | 40,000 |

2. John purchases equipment for €25,000, which he pays for by cheque. The asset "**bank**" decreases by €25,000 and the asset "**equipment**" increases by €25,000. There is no effect on "**owner's equity**" since one asset has been exchanged for another.

| Asset | | = | Owner's Equity |
|---|---|---|---|
| Bank | Equipment | | John's Capital Account |
| 40,000 | | | 40,000 |
| (25,000) | 25,000 | | |
| 15,000 | 25,000 | | 40,000 |
| 40,000 | | = | 40,000 |

3. John purchases €1,000 worth of stock on credit. The asset "**stock**" increases by €1,000 and the liability "**creditors**" increases by €1,000. There is no effect on "**owner's equity**" since no income has been earned.

| Asset | | | − | Liabilities | = | Owner's Equity |
|---|---|---|---|---|---|---|
| Bank | Stock | Equipment | | Creditors | | John's Capital Account |
| 40,000 | | | | | | 40,000 |
| (25,000) | | 25,000 | | | | |
| | 1,000 | | | 1,000 | | |
| 15,000 | 1,000 | 25,000 | | 1,000 | | 40,000 |
| 41,000 | | | − | 1,000 | = | 40,000 |

4. John makes a payment of €500 to the supplier from whom he purchased €1,000 worth of stock. There is a decrease of €500 in the asset "**bank**" and a decrease of €500 in the liability "**creditors**". There is no effect on "**owner's equity**" since no income has been earned.

| Asset | | | − | Liabilities | = | Owner's Equity |
|---|---|---|---|---|---|---|
| Bank | Stock | Equipment | | Creditors | | John's Capital Account |
| 40,000 | | | | | | 40,000 |
| (25,000) | | 25,000 | | | | |
| | 1,000 | | | 1,000 | | |
| (500) | | | | (500) | | |
| 14,500 | 1,000 | 25,000 | | 500 | | 40,000 |
| 40,500 | | | − | 500 | = | 40,000 |

5. John receives €5,000 from a customer for a cash sale. The asset "**bank**" is increased by €5,000 and the "**owner's equity**" is increased by €5,000. €5,000 was earned and will be included in the profit & loss account, and will ultimately be added to owner's equity. When making sales for cash or making a sale on credit the profitability will be the same in both situations. If a sale is made on credit the business must wait to receive payment. When a sale is made for cash the company has immediate cash to pay bills and make purchases.

| Asset | | | − | Liabilities | = | Owner's Equity |
|---|---|---|---|---|---|---|
| Bank | Stock | Equipment | | Creditors | | John's Capital Account |
| 40,000 | | | | | | 40,000 |
| (25,000) | | 25,000 | | | | |
| | 1,000 | | | 1,000 | | |
| (500) | | | | (500) | | |
| 5,000 | | | | | | 5,000 |
| 19,500 | 1,000 | 25,000 | | 500 | | 45,000 |
| | 45,500 | | − | 500 | = | 45,000 |

6. John makes a sale of €1,000 on credit. He will not receive this money for 30 days. The asset "**debtors**" increases by €1,000 and "**owner's equity**" increases by €1,000 since €1,000 has been earned and will be included in the profit & loss account which is ultimately added to owner's equity.

| Asset | | | | − | Liabilities | = | Owner's Equity |
|---|---|---|---|---|---|---|---|
| Bank | Debtors | Stock | Equipment | | Creditors | | John's Capital Account |
| 40,000 | | | | | | | 40,000 |
| (25,000) | | | 25,000 | | | | |
| | | 1,000 | | | 1,000 | | |
| (500) | | | | | (500) | | |
| 5,000 | | | | | | | 5,000 |
| | 1,000 | | | | | | 1,000 |
| 19,500 | 1,000 | 1,000 | 25,000 | | 500 | | 46,000 |
| | 46,500 | | | − | 500 | = | 46,000 |

7. John collected €500 from the debtor. The asset "**bank**" increases by €500 and the asset "**debtors**" decreases by €500. There is no effect on "**owner's equity**" since one asset has been exchanged for another.

| | Asset | | | – | Liabilities | = | Owner's Equity |
|---|---|---|---|---|---|---|---|
| Bank | Debtors | Stock | Equipment | | Creditors | | John's Capital Account |
| 40,000 | | | | | | | 40,000 |
| (25,000) | | | 25,000 | | | | |
| | | 1,000 | | | 1,000 | | |
| (500) | | | | | (500) | | |
| 5,000 | | | | | | | 5,000 |
| | 1,000 | | | | | | 1,000 |
| 500 | (500) | | | | | | |
| 20,000 | 500 | 1,000 | 25,000 | | 500 | | 46,000 |
| | 46,500 | | | – | 500 | = | 46,000 |

8. Expenses are recorded when they are incurred. If expenses are going to be paid later, a liability will be incurred. The "**owner's equity**" will be reduced. Assume John pays equipment rental of €2,000 and wages of €500. The asset "**bank**" will be reduced by €2,000 and €500 respectively and "**owner's equity**" will be reduced by €2,500 since expenditure has been incurred which will be included in the profit & loss account which is ultimately deducted from **owner's equity**.

| | Asset | | | – | Liabilities | = | Owner's Equity |
|---|---|---|---|---|---|---|---|
| Bank | Debtors | Stock | Equipment | | Creditors | | John's Capital Account |
| 40,000 | | | | | | | 40,000 |
| (25,000) | | | 25,000 | | | | |
| | | 1,000 | | | 1,000 | | |
| (500) | | | | | (500) | | |
| 5,000 | | | | | | | 5,000 |
| | 1,000 | | | | | | 1,000 |
| 500 | (500) | | | | | | |
| (2,000) | | | | | | | (2,000) |
| (500) | | | | | | | (500) |
| 17,500 | 500 | 1,000 | 25,000 | | 500 | | 43,500 |
| | 44,000 | | | – | 500 | = | 43,500 |

9. Assume that John takes drawings of €500 from the business. The asset **"bank"** will be reduced by €500 and **"owner's equity"** will be reduced by €500 since he has taken money out of the business.

| Asset | | | | – | Liabilities | = | Owner's Equity |
|---|---|---|---|---|---|---|---|
| Bank | Debtors | Stock | Equipment | | Creditors | | John's Capital Account |
| 40,000 | | | | | | | 40,000 |
| (25,000) | | | 25,000 | | | | |
| | | 1,000 | | | 1,000 | | |
| (500) | | | | | (500) | | |
| 5,000 | | | | | | | 5,000 |
| | 1,000 | | | | | | 1,000 |
| 500 | (500) | | | | | | |
| (2,000) | | | | | | | (2,000) |
| (500) | | | | | | | (500) |
| (500) | | | | | | | (500) |
| 17,000 | 500 | 1,000 | 25,000 | | 500 | | 43,000 |
| 43,500 | | | | – | 500 | = | 43,000 |

Set out in Figure 4.4 is a graphical presentation of the "Accounting Equation" showing how owner's investment and trading activities have an effect on owner's equity.

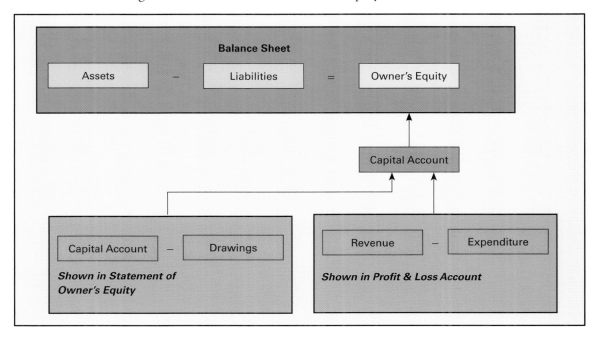

Figure 4.4

Accounting is the classification and recording of monetary transactions. It also includes the presentation and interpretation of those transactions to assess performance over a period and the financial position at a given date. Manual or computerised systems are used to record all monetary transactions throughout the year. These transactions are grouped and classified before presentation in the two key financial statements, which are the profit & loss account and balance sheet. The profit & loss account measures financial performance over the year whilst the balance sheet states the financial position as at the year end. Management will prepare for their own internal use, a budgeted profit & loss account and balance sheet, based on a set of projected financial transactions for the coming year. Accounting is an information system that measures, processes and communicates financial information about a business.

The following groups will be considered users of accounting information:

- Shareholders of limited companies will be influenced in their decision to remain investors or to increase/decrease their shareholding by receiving information about the financial performance and financial status of their company.
- Management require accounting information to help them in their roles. Supervisors are concerned with operating costs. Directors need to control the overall performance of the company and middle management need feedback on whether they are meeting their financial targets.
- Suppliers need to assess the creditworthiness of potential and existing customers when setting the amount and period of credit allowed. This will be based on the financial history of each customer. The supplier's accountant will assess the customer's latest profit & loss account and balance sheet.
- Customers need to be reassured that orders for stock will be fulfilled.
- Employees have a vested interest in the financial health and future prospects of the business.
- Lenders need to be assured that their capital is safe and that the borrowing company can service the loan or overdraft.

Accounting includes the design of an information system that meets users' needs and its major goals are the analysis, interpretation and use of information. Bookkeeping, on the other hand, is mechanical and repetitive. It is the processing and recording of financial transactions and keeping financial records. It is a small but important part of accounting.

There are a number of branches of accounting, which are set out below.

| Accounting | | |
| --- | --- | --- |
| **Financial Accounting** | **Management Accounting** | **Financial Management** |
| Focus | Preparation of financial statements | Planning, control and decision-making | Raising finance |
| Timeframe | Past events | Current & future events | Future |
| Statements | Profit & loss account and balance sheet | Budgets and comparison to actual costs | Costs of capital |
| Users | Submission of tax return, investors, loan providers and suppliers | Internal management | Internal management |

- Financial accounting generates reports and communicates them to decision-makers so they can evaluate how well the business has achieved its goals.
- Management accounting provides internal decision-makers who are charged with achieving the goals of profitability and liquidity with information about financing, investing and operating activities. Managers and employees who conduct the activities of the business need up-to-date information telling them how they have done in the past.
- Financial management provides internal decision-makers with information about raising capital in the future and how much it will cost using debt or equity (or a combination of both).

## ❑ Financial, Investing and Operating Activities

Each business must engage in financing activities to obtain adequate funds needed to begin and continue operating. Financial activities include obtaining capital from owners and from creditors such as banks and suppliers. They also include repaying creditors and paying a return to owners. Each business must engage in investing activities to spend the capital it receives in ways that are productive and will help the business achieve its objectives. Each business must engage in operating activities. In addition to selling goods and services to customers, operating activities include such actions as employing managers and staff, buying and producing goods and services and paying tax. See Figure 5.1.

An important function of accounting is to provide performance measures, which indicate whether managers are achieving business goals and whether the business activities are well managed.

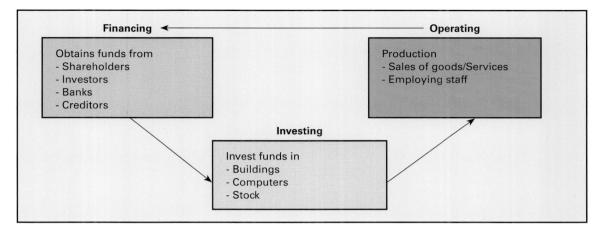

Figure 5.1

- Financing activities involve obtaining adequate funds. These activities include obtaining capital from creditors such as banks, suppliers and loans.
- Operating activities include selling goods and services to customers and employing managers and staff.
- Investing activities involve spending the capital in a productive way. These activities include buying buildings, equipment etc.

The two major goals of any business are liquidity and profitability. Profitability is the ability to earn enough income to attract and hold investment capital. Liquidity is the ability to have enough cash to pay debts when they are due. If a company is to survive and be successful it must meet both goals; all businesses pursue the goals by engaging in financial, operating and investing activities.

Set out in Figure 5.2 is a list of the direct and indirect users of financial information.

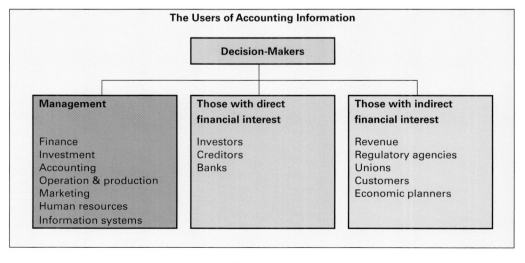

Figure 5.2

## ❑ Principles

Businesses should adopt financial policies and procedures in order to minimise their financial risk. Financial risks are the risk of failing to safeguard company assets, financial impropriety, financial misreporting or failure to achieve value for money.

## ❑ Internal Control

Internal controls are the financial policies and procedures adopted by a business. They form an important part of managing the organisation's finances. The members of the board have an important role in the development and communication of ethical financial values for the company. Staff, in turn, have a professional responsibility to understand, comply with and implement the policies and procedures on a day-to-day basis.

The board and senior management should ensure that there is a strong focus on the role of the finance function to ensure that financial staff are aware of all developments and best practice in this area. This includes all the policies and procedures needed to ensure the reliability of financial reporting, compliance with laws and regulations and the effectiveness and efficiency of operations. Management must safeguard the firm's assets, ensure reliability of its accounting records, see that its employees comply with all legal requirements and operate the firm to the best advantage of its owners.

An internal control system attempts to ensure that the following objectives are achieved:

| Internal Controls | Objective |
|---|---|
| • Safeguarding of assets | • Assets are safeguarded on behalf of their rightful owners. |
| • Segregation of duties | • Staff responsibilities must be organised to ensure that key tasks are segregated.<br>• Staff-specific responsibilities to separate custody, authorisation and approval, recording and execution of a specific transaction.<br>• Error and fraud are minimised, prevented and are likely to be detected if they do occur. |
| • Physical access controls | • Only authorised personnel should have access to the records and assets of a business. |

*(Continued)*

| Internal Controls | Objective |
|---|---|
| • Authorisation and approval limits | • Responsible persons should have appropriate authorisation or approval limits for transactions to ensure that the business can reasonably limit its exposure. |
| • Management control | • Information (including financial information) is prepared and disclosed in a timely, efficient and informative manner. |
| • Arithmetical and accounting controls | • Complete and accurate accounting records are kept so that financial transactions can be recorded and disclosed in an informative manner.<br>• Procedures are in place to ensure the reliability of data processing and information reports.<br>• Complete and accurate accounting records and non-financial information are submitted to stakeholders. |
| • Supervision and periodic reconciliation | • Variances between actual and budgeted performance are managed and monitored.<br>• Checks that provide effective supervision of the control activities are conducted on a regular and structured basis. |
| • Human resource control | • Staff adhere to policies and procedures.<br>• The recruitment, training and remuneration of appropriately qualified and experienced staff are managed properly. |

## *Components of Internal Control*

1. Control environment: The control environment is created by management's overall attitude, awareness and actions. It encompasses a company's ethics, philosophy and operating style.
2. Risk assessment: This involves identifying areas in which risk of loss of assets or inaccuracies in accounting records are high so that adequate controls can be implemented.
3. Information and communication: This relates to the accounting system established by management to gather and process information about the company's transactions.
4. Control activities: These are the procedures management puts in place to see that its policies are carried out.
5. Monitoring: This involves regular assessment of the quality of internal controls, including periodic review of compliance with all policies and procedures. Large companies often have a staff of internal auditors who review the company's system of internal control to determine if it is working properly.

## Control Activities Include the Following:

1. Managers should authorise certain transactions and activities, eg issuing a refund.
2. All transactions should be recorded; for example, if a retail shop uses a cash register to record sales, the cashier must be accountable for the cash received during his/her shift.
3. Documentation and records—well-designed documents ensure that transactions are properly recorded; eg using pre-numbered invoices and other documentation is a way of ensuring that all transactions are recorded.
4. Physical control—managers should specify who has access to assets; for example, in a retail shop only cashiers should have access to the cash register.
5. Periodic independent verification—someone other than the person responsible for the accounting records and assets should periodically check the records against the assets held; for example, at the end of a shift, the manager should count the takings of the day and compare it against the amount recorded on the cash register.
6. Separation of duties—no one person should be in charge of authorising transactions, handling assets and keeping records of assets; for example, a sales person takes an order and creates an invoice, another employee receives the cash and issues a receipt and a third person obtains the goods from the warehouse.
7. Good personnel policies—personnel practices would include supervision of staff, rotation of key personnel, reference checking of staff prior to recruitment and insisting that staff take their annual leave.

## Limitations on Internal Controls

No system of internal control is without weaknesses. An internal control system will always be vulnerable to human error. Errors can arise from misunderstandings, mistakes of judgment or carelessness. Separation of duties can be defeated by collusion of staff who agree to deceive a company. Controls that were once effective may become ineffective if changes are made in processes. No internal control can guarantee the prevention of theft; however the more procedures that are in place, the less likely a theft will occur.

## Internal Control and Management Goals

When a system of internal control is applied effectively it can achieve important management goals. It can prevent losses of cash and stock due to fraud or theft and it can ensure that transactions and account balances are accurate.

## Control of Cash

One control that managers use to meet their broad goals is the cash budget, which projects future cash receipts and payments. By maintaining adequate cash balances, a company is able to take advantage of discounts on purchases and borrow money only when necessary. A more specific control is the separation of duties involving the handling of cash. Such separation makes theft without detection unlikely unless two or more employees conspire. The separation of duties is easier in large businesses than in small ones where one person may have to carry out several duties.

1. Separate the functions of authorisation, record keeping and the holding of cash.
2. Limit the number of people who have access to cash and control who those people are.
3. Keep the amount of cash on hand to a minimum by lodging money in the bank as soon as possible.
4. Physically protect cash on hand by using a safe.
5. Record and lodge cash receipts promptly. Use cheques rather than cash for purchases.
6. Have a person who does not handle or record cash make unannounced audits of cash on hand.
7. Have a person who does not authorise, handle or record cash reconcile the cash to the cash account each month.

## Control over Stock

Assets are especially vulnerable when they enter and leave a business. When sales are made, cash or other assets enter a business and goods or services leave. Controls must be set up to prevent theft at this time.

## Control of Cash Receipts

Cash payments for the sale of goods or services can be received by post or over the counter in the form of cheques, cash or credit cards. Monies received should be recorded immediately upon receipt.

Cash received by post is vulnerable to theft by the employees who handle it. Companies generally ask customers to pay by cheque, credit card or bank transfer. When cash is received in the post, two or more employees should handle it. The employee who opens the post should make a list in triplicate of the money received. The list should contain each customer's name, the purpose for which the money was sent and the amount. One copy goes with the cash to the cashier, who lodges the money. The second copy goes to the accounts department for recording. The person who opens the post keeps the third copy. Errors can easily be caught because the amount deposited by the cashier must agree to the amount received and the amount recorded in the bank lodgement.

Cash registers are used to control cash received over the counter. The amount of cash sales is recorded on the cash register at the time of the sale. Each cash register should have a locked-in mechanism to record the day's transactions. At the end of the day, the cashier counts the cash in the register and turns it in to the cashier's office. Another employee records the cash receipts for the day in the cash receipts book. The amount of cash turned in and the amount recorded on the register should agree. Any differences must be explained immediately.

## Control over Cash Purchases and Disbursements

Cash payments should be made only after they have been authorised and supported by documentation that establishes the validity and amount of the claim. A company should separate the duties involved in purchasing goods and services and the duties involved in paying for them.

1. A formal request for a purchase is made using a "purchase requisition form", eg requesting office supplies.
2. The purchase requisition is forwarded to the purchasing department which prepares a "purchase order". This is addressed to the seller and contains a description of the item code, quantity, expected price, etc. The purchase order is sent to the seller.
3. After receiving the purchase order, the seller sends the goods and an invoice. The invoice shows the quantity of goods purchased, the unit price and terms of payment.
4. When the goods are delivered, the company checks the physical goods delivered against the delivery docket issued by the selling company. The quantity and reference numbers should be checked. The person checking the physical goods does not have a copy of the purchase order form and so does not know how many were ordered, so the employee does not know what should be received or its value.
5. The delivery docket is sent to the accounts department where it is checked against the invoice and purchase order. If everything is correct, the accounts department will prepare a cheque requisition and attach the supporting documentation. The accounts department has access to all the documentation relating to the purchase transaction but does not have access to the asset purchased.
6. The accountant examines all the documentation and signs the cheque made payable to the seller. If a seller is not paid the correct amount they will complain—this is a form of control that is outside the company. Suppliers will issue creditor statements, which should be checked monthly to ensure that the records agree with the supplier's records. Any difference should be investigated. In the above process every transaction is checked by at least one person.

# BOOKKEEPING

## Chapter 7

Bookkeeping refers to the record keeping aspect of accountancy work. The process of recording and classifying business transactions is related to bookkeeping, whereas the procedures used to interpret the results moves towards the whole area of accountancy—therefore, accountancy includes bookkeeping.

How well do you keep your books and records? Do you let invoices pile up and ignore envelopes with windows? This situation can change by introducing a few procedures that will save time, headaches and money.

What is your filing system like? All it takes is a few lever arch folders and dividers to set up an efficient system. It will save time later.

## ❑ Bookkeeping Folders

- Sales folder—this should contain a copy of the sales invoices sent to your customers. They should be filed in numerical sequence, with a separate section for credit notes.
- Purchase invoices to be paid folder—this includes all invoices received by the business but not yet paid.
- Paid invoices—this should contain all the invoices paid and kept for reference. Divide them into months and keep a schedule at the front of all invoices included.
- Fixed asset folder—keep a copy of the invoices that have included in the fixed asset register.
- Payroll/Tax folder—records must be kept of tax deduction cards/payslips/payroll records/P30, P60, P35, etc.
- Bank folder—this should include correspondence with the bank, a copy of lodgement slips and the cheques lodged. Direct debit mandates, and bank statements should also be included.
- VAT folder—include workings used for the VAT return, such as purchase listings and sales listings, together with VAT3s and the annual VAT return.
- Creditor statement folder—all statements should be filed alphabetically.
- Petty cash folder—this will include receipts for the amount of petty cash expenses. A schedule should be kept of all the payments filed monthly.

All records relating to the current accounting year should be kept together. When a new accounting year is started, new folders should be opened and the old folders kept for six years for Revenue and company law purposes.

It is recommended to set out a plan for weekly and monthly tasks.

## ❑ Weekly

- Open all post.
- Date-stamp invoices received.
- Record purchase invoices (manually/accounts package).
- Record a reference number on the purchase invoice linked to the manual purchase book or a reference generated by the accounts package.
- Write cheques for any bills that need to be paid and reconcile invoices outstanding to creditor statements. Disputes must be raised promptly with the supplier.
- Record the cheque number on the cheque requisition form and file in sequence so that if there is a query it can be retrieved quickly.
- Stamp invoices "paid" once a cheque has been issued.
- File "paid" invoices.
- Record cheque payments made to suppliers.
- Record any cheques received against individual debtor accounts.
- Review the debtors listing and identify slow—paying accounts.
- Telephone debtors to remind them that they have not paid their account.
- Any expenses that are paid "out of pocket" should be reimbursed. Keep the receipts and reimburse those expenses by cheque/petty cash. Make sure to keep all receipts.
- Reconcile the bank, recording any direct debits and standing orders.
- Pay salaries if salaries are paid weekly.

## ❑ Monthly

- Issue sales invoices.
- Record any sales invoices (manually/accounts package).
- Record a reference number on the sales invoice linked to the manual sales book or to a reference generated by the accounts package.
- Go through credit card statements. Identify what each expenditure item relates to and attach the receipt. Allocate the expenditure according to the type of expenditure, eg entertainment.
- Pay salaries if salaries are paid monthly.
- Calculate tax due and pay by the due date, eg VAT and PAYE/PRSI.

By keeping accounting records updated, problems can be quickly resolved. If left for a few months, important details will be forgotten and you will be operating in the dark. If the records are up to date, accounts can be prepared quickly.

**Quick Tip**

Make sure to keep credit card receipts and transaction slips as this is akin to a purchase invoice.

## ❏ Single-Entry Bookkeeping

A receipts and payments accounting system is an example of a single-entry bookkeeping system. Many small businesses use this type of system. A bookkeeping book with 16 columns can be used to analyse all the receipts and expenditure. When a statement of cash receipts and payments is prepared, it will **not** disclose the amount of money still owing to suppliers (creditors) or the amount owed by customers (debtors). Nor is any distinction made between expenditure on running costs that have not been used up in the period, as opposed to expenditure on such assets as equipment, which still have value remaining for future use.

## ❏ The Theory of Double-Entry Bookkeeping

|  | Debits | Credits |
|---|---|---|
| Balance Sheet | Assets | Liabilities |
| Profit & Loss | Expenses | Income |
| Result | Losses | Profits |

The system is based on the principle that every economic event has two aspects—effort and reward, sacrifice and benefit—which offset or balance each other. In the double-entry bookkeeping system:

1. Each transaction must be recorded with at least one debit and one credit.
2. The total amount of the debits must equal the total amount of the credits.

Because of the way it is designed, the whole system is always in balance. All accounting systems, no matter how sophisticated, are based on this principle—the principle of duality.

## ❏ Accounts

Accounts are the storage units for accounting data and they are used to accumulate amounts from similar transactions. A separate account is required for each figure that appears in the profit & loss account and balance sheet. An accounting system has a separate account for each asset, each liability and each component of shareholders' equity, including revenue and expenses. Whether a company keeps records by hand or by computer, managers must be able to refer to accounts so that they can review their company's financial history and plan for the future. A very small company may only need a few dozen accounts.

## T Accounts

The T account is so called because it resembles capital letter "T"; it is used to analyse transactions and looks like Figure 7.1.

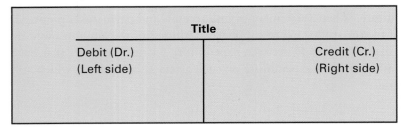

Figure 7.1

Any entry made on the left side of the account is a **debit** and any entry made on the right side is a **credit**. The term debit is abbreviated to Dr. and credit is abbreviated to Cr.

The T account is a good place to begin the study of the double entry system. Such an account has three parts:

- Title—which identifies the asset, liability or shareholders' equity account.
- A left side—which is called the debit side.
- A right side—which is called the credit side.

Suppose a company had several transactions that involve receipts and payments of cash. These transactions can be summarised in the cash account by recording receipts on the left (debit) side of the T account and payments on the right (credit) side. See Figure 7.2.

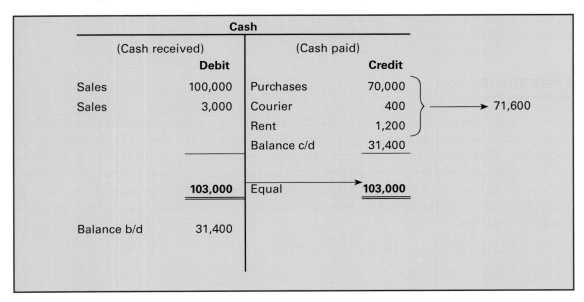

Figure 7.2

The cash receipts on the left side total €103,000; the cash payments on the right side total €71,600. These figures are simply the total of the figures on the left and right side. The difference between the total debits of €103,000 and total credits of €71,600 is called the balance. If the balance is a debit it is written on the left side; if it is a credit it is written on the right side. The cash account has a debit balance of €31,400. This is the amount of cash the business has on hand at the end of the month. The balance of €31,400 is "carried down" to the next accounting period; this is abbreviated to "balance c/d". In the next accounting period the balance is "brought down"; this is abbreviated to "balance b/d".

## Double-Entry Bookkeeping

The name "double entry" derives from the fact that each individual transaction is entered twice, recognising two aspects referred to as debits and credits.

| Debits Represent | Credits Represent |
|---|---|
| An expense | Income |
| An increase in an asset | An increase in a liability |
| A decrease in a liability | A decrease in an asset |
| Cash received | Cash paid out |

Assets received are entered on the left side of the account (known as the debit side) and the corresponding liability or reduction in asset is entered on the right-hand side. When a transaction is recorded there are two entries. This process is known as "double-entry bookkeeping".

- Any cash received into a business is recorded in the cash account as a **debit**. A corresponding **credit** is made in the account of the person, company or item that paid the cash.
- Any cash paid out of the business is recorded in the cash account as a **credit**. A corresponding **debit** is made in the account of the person, company or item that is being paid the cash.

Double-entry bookkeeping recognises that every financial transaction involves the simultaneous receiving and giving of value. Every financial transaction will involve a debit and a corresponding credit to be recorded in the appropriate accounts within the accounting system.

### Example

Wages of €200 are paid on 2 August 2007 with money from the bank account. The two accounts involved are the "**wages account**" and the "**bank account**" Wages are an expense so the entry goes on the **debit** side of the wages account. Money paid out for any reason is always a **credit** entry in the bank account. The name of the other account involved is always given as a cross-reference and as an explanation of what happened. The date is also included. Set out in Figure 7.3 is an example.

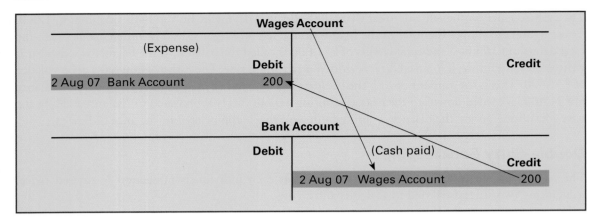

Figure 7.3

**Example**

The purchase of €900 goods on credit from a supplier on 5 August 2007. The two accounts involved are the purchases account (expense account) and the creditor account (liability). Purchases are an expense so the entry goes on the **debit** side of the purchases account. Since the purchases were not paid for immediately, a liability needs to be recorded by **crediting** a creditor account. On 29 August 2007 a part payment of €600 was made. The two accounts involved are the creditor account which will be **debited** to reduce the liability and the bank account which will be **credited** for the cash paid out. See Figure 7.4.

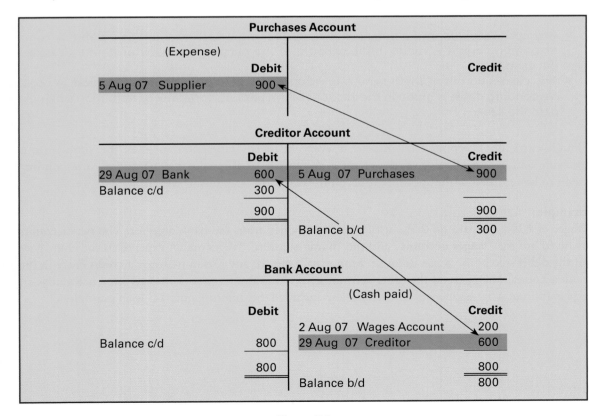

Figure 7.4

## ❑ Trial Balance

At the end of an accounting period, each account is totalled. If the entries are only on one side of the account, as in the case of wages, the entries are totalled to arrive at the balance on the account. All accounts are balanced off at the end of the month (year). All accounts with a balance are then listed in what is called a trial balance. The trial balance for the above T accounts would be as set out in Figure 7.5.

**Trial Balance**

|                  | Debits | Credits |
|------------------|--------|---------|
| Purchases        | 900    |         |
| Wages            | 200    |         |
| Bank Account     |        | 800     |
| Creditor Account |        | 300     |
| TOTAL            | 1,100  | 1,100   |

Figure 7.5

The trial balance is a list of all the debits and credits in the accounts in a double-entry bookkeeping system. The trial balance must always balance because every entry has been entered on the opposite side; this is proof of the numerical accuracy but it does not prove that every transaction has been entered in the correct account.

## ❑ Sales Daybook

The sales daybook is a book used to record details from invoices issued to customers. This information is subsequently entered in the debtor account of each person or in the cash sales account. The debtor ledger holds the account of all customers who are allowed to buy goods or services on credit as opposed to paying cash. Debtors are those who owe money to the business. Until a customer pays or clears their account, there is a debit balance showing how much is owed.

The sales daybook is used to record and summarise all credit sales and cash sales made by the business. A credit sale is a sale for which payment will not be received immediately.

The "dr" and "cr" sign under the headings denote debit and credit entries. When the columns are added across the page, the total debits must equal credits, as in Figure 7.6.

| Date | Invoice No. | Account Debtor | A/c Ref. | Total | VAT @ 21% | Football Boots | Soccer Jerseys | Runners | Tracksuits | Cash Sale |
|------|-------------|----------------|----------|-------|-----------|----------------|----------------|---------|------------|-----------|
|      |             |                |          | Dr+   | Cr–       | Cr–            | Cr–            | Cr–     | Cr–        | Cr–       |
| 1 Dec | 1 | ABC Ltd | ABC01 | 217.80 | 37.80 | 180.00 | | | | |
| 6 Dec | 2 | Sport Ltd | SPO01 | 242.00 | 42.00 | | 200.00 | | | |
| 8 Dec | 3 | M. Smith | SMI01 | 121.00 | 21.00 | | | 100.00 | | |
| 18 Dec | 4 | ABC Ltd | ABC01 | 605.00 | 105.00 | | 500.00 | | | |
| 18 Dec | 5 | Gee Ltd | GEE01 | 18,004.80 | 3,124.80 | 1,500.00 | 10,400.00 | 2,300.00 | 680.00 | |
| 18 Dec | 6 | Cash | — | 1,210.00 | 210.00 | | | | | 1,000.00 |
| | Total at 31/12/07   € | | | 20,400.60 | 3,540.60 | 1,680.00 | 11,100.00 | 2,400.00 | 680.00 | 1,000.00 |
| | | | | = | + | + | + | + | + | + |

| Recorded in Debtors in the Balance Sheet | Recorded in VAT Nominal in the Balance Sheet | Recorded in Sales Nominal in the Profit & Loss Account |
|---|---|---|

Figure 7.6

Information can be used from the sales daybook to determine the sales profile.

**Example**

$$\frac{\text{Soccer Jersey sales}}{\text{Total net sales}} = \frac{€11,110}{€20,400.60 - €3,540.60} \times 100\% = 66\%$$

The sale of soccer jerseys represents approximately two thirds of the total sales in December 2007.

## ❏ Sales Returns Daybook

This daybook is used in circumstances when a customer subsequently returns goods previously sold on credit. On 20 December, ABC Ltd returned the football boots and the soccer jerseys, as the logo printed on them was incorrect. Goods were taken back and a credit note issued for the full value of the sales invoice. The sales and VAT due will have to be reduced as the original sales are now cancelled. The transactions will be the opposite of a sale in that the debtors will be **credited** and the sales nominal and VAT nominal will be **debited**, as in Figure 7.7.

| Date | Credit Note No. | Debtor | A/c Ref. | Total | VAT @ 21% | Football Boots | Soccer Jerseys | Runners | Tracksuits |
|------|------|------|------|------|------|------|------|------|------|
| | | | | Cr– | Dr+ | Dr+ | Dr+ | Dr+ | Dr+ |
| 20 Dec | 1 | ABC Ltd | ABC01 | 217.80 | 37.80 | 180.00 | | | |
| 20 Dec | 2 | ABC Ltd | ABC01 | 605.00 | 105.00 | | 500.00 | | |
| | Total at 31/12/07 | | € | 822.80 | 142.80 | 180.00 | 500.00 | | |

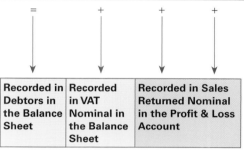

Figure 7.7

## ❏ Purchases Daybook

The purchases daybook is a book used to record invoices received from suppliers (see Figure 7.8). The information is subsequently entered into the individual account of each supplier in the purchase ledger. The purchases ledger is the ledger that holds the accounts of all suppliers who sell to the business on credit as opposed to paying cash. Creditors are people or organisations that are owed money by the business. Until the supplier is paid there is a credit balance showing how much the business owes. The purchases daybook is used to record and summarise all credit purchases made by the business. Purchases are divided up for VAT purposes between "purchases for resale" (such as stock) and "purchases not for resale" (such as overheads). The information is required for the annual "VAT Return of Trading Details".

Cash purchases are recorded and summarised in a book called the cash purchases book, which is similar to the one below except that there will not be a column for "creditors" and "A/c ref".

| Date | Invoice No. | Creditor | A/c Ref. | Total | Purchases not for resale VAT @ 21% | Purchases not for resale VAT @ 13.5% | Purchases for resale VAT @ 21% | Electricity | Stationery | Telephone | Accountancy Fees | Purchase of sports wear |
|---|---|---|---|---|---|---|---|---|---|---|---|---|
| | | | | Cr− | Dr+ | Dr+ | Dr+ | Dr+ | Dr+ | Dr+ | Dr+ | Dr+ |
| 01 Dec | 19550 | ESB | ESB01 | 227.00 | | 27.00 | | 200.00 | | | | |
| 05 Dec | 123 | Murphy Stationery | MUR01 | 151.25 | 26.25 | | | | 125.00 | | | |
| 06 Dec | 200153 | Vodafone | VOD01 | 181.50 | 31.50 | | | | | 150.00 | | |
| 08 Dec | 136 | Pens Ltd | PEN01 | 3,025.00 | | | 525.00 | | | | | 2,500.00 |
| 11 Dec | 145 | C&G Accountant | CG01 | 726.00 | 126.00 | | | | | | 600.00 | |
| 13 Dec | 189571 | Smart | SMA01 | 66.55 | 11.55 | | | | | 55.00 | | |
| 18 Dec | 0046SD | J Stein | STE01 | 913.55 | | | 158.55 | | | | | 755.00 |
| 20 Dec | 56195G | Chow | CHO01 | 1,331.00 | | | 231.00 | | | | | 1,100.00 |
| 22 Dec | 12964 | Fair | FAI01 | 842.16 | | | 146.16 | | | | | 696.00 |
| Total at 31/12/07 € | | | | 7,464.01 | 195.30 | 27.00 | 1,060.71 | 200.00 | 125.00 | 205.00 | 600.00 | 5,051.00 |
| | | | | = | + | + | + | + | + | + | + | + |
| | | | | Record in Creditors in Balance Sheet | Record in VAT Nominal in Balance Sheet | Record in VAT Nominal in Balance Sheet | Record in VAT Nominal in Balance Sheet | Record in Light & Heat Nominal in Profit & Loss | Record in Stationery Nominal in Profit & Loss | Record in Telephone Nominal in Profit & Loss | Record in Accountancy Nominal in Profit & Loss | Recorded in Purchases for resale Nominal in Profit & Loss |

Figure 7.8

## ❏ Purchases Returns Daybook

The purchases returns daybook is maintained to record credit notes received from suppliers as a result of faulty goods, overcharging, etc. A credit note is received from Murphy Stationery because folders costing €50 excluding VAT were returned. The goods bought from J Stein had to be returned as they were defective. The supplier issued a credit note for the full amount of the purchase invoice. See Figure 7.9.

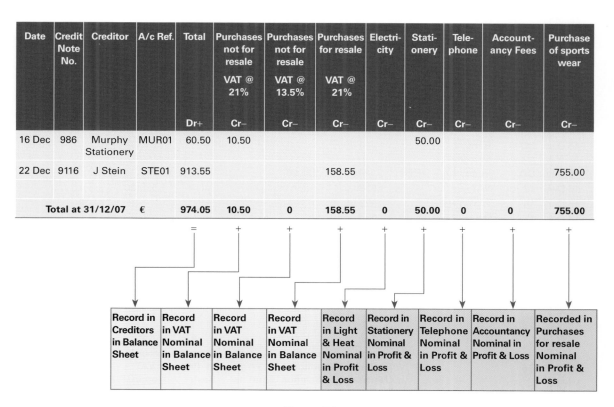

| Date | Credit Note No. | Creditor | A/c Ref. | Total | Purchases not for resale VAT @ 21% | Purchases not for resale VAT @ 13.5% | Purchases for resale VAT @ 21% | Electri-city | Stati-onery | Tele-phone | Account-ancy Fees | Purchase of sports wear |
|------|------|----------|---------|-------|------|------|------|------|------|------|------|------|
| | | | | Dr+ | Cr– | Cr– | Cr– | Cr– | Cr– | Cr– | Cr– | Cr– |
| 16 Dec | 986 | Murphy Stationery | MUR01 | 60.50 | 10.50 | | | | 50.00 | | | |
| 22 Dec | 9116 | J Stein | STE01 | 913.55 | | | 158.55 | | | | | 755.00 |
| | **Total at 31/12/07** | | € | 974.05 | 10.50 | 0 | 158.55 | 0 | 50.00 | 0 | 0 | 755.00 |

Figure 7.9

## ❑ Cheque Payments Book

The cheque payments book records all payments made by a business which are processed through the bank account. These payments would include cheques drawn on the business bank account and also bank interest charges, standing orders and direct debits. Every cheque written and every direct debit that goes though the bank account needs to be recorded. Using the cheque book stub, write up the cheque payments book; this should be checked against the bank statement and any additional direct debits added on. Once this has been completed, the cheque payments book should be totalled and closed off for the month, as in Figure 7.10.

| Date | Cheque No. | Payee | A/c Ref. | Total | Payments to Creditors | Wages | Petty Cash | VAT | PAYE/ PRSI | Bank Charges |
|---|---|---|---|---|---|---|---|---|---|---|
| | | | | Cr– | Dr+ | Dr+ | Dr+ | Dr+ | Dr+ | Dr+ |
| 2 Dec | 15 | ESB | ESB01 | 227.00 | 227.00 | | | | | |
| 13 Dec | 16 | Petty Cash | | 400.00 | | | 400.00 | | | |
| 15 Dec | DD | Bank Charges | | 20.00 | | | | | | 20.00 |
| 16 Dec | DD | Vodafone | VOD01 | 181.50 | 181.50 | | | | | |
| 16 Dec | 17 | VAT | | 1,535.00 | | | | 1,535.00 | | |
| 16 Dec | 18 | PAYE/PRSI | | 270.00 | | | | | 270.00 | |
| 17 Dec | 19 | Wages | | 1,000.00 | | 1,000.00 | | | | |
| 20 Dec | 20 | C&G Accountant | CG01 | 726.00 | 726.00 | | | | | |
| | Total at 31/12/07 € | | | 4,359.50 | 1,134.50 | 1,000.00 | 400.00 | 1,535.00 | 270.00 | 20.00 |
| | | | | = | + | + | + | + | + | + |

| Record in Bank Nominal in Balance Sheet | Record in Creditors in Balance Sheet | Record in Wages Nominal in Profit & Loss | Record in Petty Cash Nominal in Balance Sheet | Record in VAT Nominal in Balance Sheet | Record in PAYE/ PRSI Nominal in Balance Sheet | Record in Bank Charges Nominal in Profit & Loss |
|---|---|---|---|---|---|---|

Figure 7.10

## ❑ The Cash Receipts Book

The cash receipts book is used to record all cash receipts of the business, whether in relation to receipts from customers to whom sales were previously made on credit or receipts in respect of cash sales. A record should be kept of the origin of the money as income may be received that is not related to sales. If there is more than one bank account, a separate sheet should be used and a column included for transfers from the other bank account. The cash receipts book should be checked against the bank statement to ensure that all lodgements have been included in the cash receipts book. Some customers may transfer the money directly into the bank account and this will only be recorded in the cash receipts book once the bank statement is received. Once this has been completed the cash receipts book should be totalled and closed off for the month, as in Figure 7.11.

| Date | Lodgement No. | Name | A/c Ref. | Total | Receipts from Debtors | Bank Interest Received | Transfer from Deposit account | Cash Sales | Other Income |
|------|------|------|------|------|------|------|------|------|------|
| | | | | Dr+ | Cr– | Cr– | Cr– | Cr– | Cr– |
| 9 Dec | | Sport Ltd | SPO01 | | 242.00 | | | | |
| 9 Dec | 4 | M Smyth | SMI01 | 363.00 | 121.00 | | | | |
| 12 Dec | | Bank Interest | N/A | 5.00 | | 5.00 | | | |
| 15 Dec | 5 | Gee Ltd | GEE01 | 5,000.00 | 5,000.00 | | | | |
| 18 Dec | 6 | Cash Sales | N/A | 1,210.00 | | | | 1,210.00 | |
| 20 Dec | | Transfer from Deposit Account | N/A | 500.00 | | | 500.00 | | |
| | Total as at 31/12/07 € | | | 7,078.00 | 5,363.00 | 5.00 | 500.00 | 1,210.00 | 0 |
| | | | | = | + | + | + | + | + |

| Record in Bank Nominal in the Balance Sheet | Record in Debtors in the Balance Sheet | Record in Interest received Nominal in Profit & Loss | Record in Deposit Account Nominal in Balance Sheet | Record in Cash Account in the Balance Sheet |
|------|------|------|------|------|

Figure 7.11

Gee Ltd paid €5,000 as a deposit for the order, which was lodged on 15 December and allocated against the total amount that they owe (€18,004.80). Receipts should be listed separately and a total included because the bank statement will only list the total lodgement, eg lodgement number 4 for €363 includes receipts from Sport Ltd (€242) and M Smyth (€121).

**Quick Tip**

If the books do not balance, the following remedies are useful:
- Check the cheque payments book, cash receipts book, sales book and purchases book to ensure that the extension across the page line by line agrees to the total column.
- If the amount of the difference is divisible by 9 then one of the figures may have been transposed incorrectly, eg if €325 is written as €352 the difference is 27 (which is divisible by 9).
- Check the tots for each column.
- Check the balance carried forward total to the next page and re-add the total across the top of the new page to ensure it balances.

The flow of transactions in the double-entry system can best be shown by way of a diagram as set out in Figure 7.12.

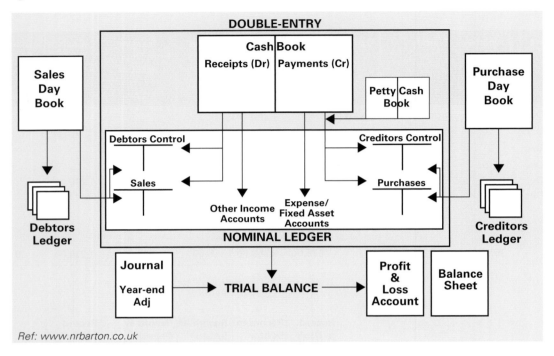

Ref: www.nrbarton.co.uk

Figure 7.12

## Using Double-Entry Accounting

For every transaction, one or more accounts must be debited and one or more accounts must be credited. The total of the debits must equal the total of the credits.

| Asset | – | Liability | = | Owner's Equity |

If a debit increases assets, then a credit must be used to increase liabilities or owner's equity. Likewise, if a credit decreases assets, then a debit must be used to decrease liabilities or owner's equity. The rule can be shown as set out in Figure 7.13.

| Assets | | – | Liabilities | | = | Owner's Equity | |
|---|---|---|---|---|---|---|---|
| Debit for Increase (+) | Credit for Decrease (–) | | Debit for Decrease (–) | Credit for Increase (+) | | Debit for Decrease (–) | Credit for Increase (+) |

Figure 7.13

Steps to be used when recording a transaction:

1. Analyse the transaction to determine its effect on assets, liabilities and owner's equity.
2. Apply the rules of double entry—increases in assets are recorded as debits and increases in liabilities are recorded as credits.
3. Record the entry—transactions are recorded in chronological order.
4. Post the entry—the entry is posted to the general ledger by transferring the date and amount to the proper accounts.
5. Prepare the trial balance to confirm the balance on accounts. Periodically, accountants prepare a trial balance to confirm that the accounts are still in balance after recording and posting transactions.

Set out below are examples of how the transactions in a business are recorded using T accounts and journal entries.

## ❏ Purchase of Shares

On 1 January, Joe Ryan and his wife set up a company. They invested €40,000 in cash in return for 40,000 €1 ordinary shares.

Using T accounts, the amounts would appear as follows:

| Bank | | Ordinary Share Capital | |
|---|---|---|---|
| 01 Jan   Capital   40,000 | | | 01 Jan   Bank     40,000 |

Transactions can be shown in journal form by recording the transaction with the date, account name, the amount of the debit on one line and the same details relating to the credit side of the transaction on the next line.

Using journals, the amounts would appear as follows:

| Date | Account | Statement | Debit | Credit |
|---|---|---|---|---|
| 01 Jan | Bank | Balance Sheet | 40,000 | |
| | Ordinary Share Capital | Balance Sheet | | 40,000 |

## ❏ Payment of Rent in Advance

On 3 January rent of €3,200 is paid in advance for two months. The rent paid is a prepayment that will increase assets "prepaid rent" and the asset "bank" will be decreased. A prepayment is an asset because the expenditure now will benefit future accounting periods. This transaction does not affect the totals of assets or liabilities and owner's equity because it simply trades one asset for another asset.

Using T accounts, the amounts would appear as follows:

| Bank | | | | Prepaid Rent | | |
|---|---|---|---|---|---|---|
| 01 Jan Capital 40,000 | 3-Jan Rent 3,200 | | | 03 Jan Bank 3,200 | | |

Using journals, the amounts would appear as follows:

| Date | Account | Statement | Debit | Credit |
|---|---|---|---|---|
| 03 Jan | Prepaid Rent | Balance Sheet | 3,200 | |
| | Bank | Balance Sheet | | 3,200 |

## ❏ Purchase of Stock on Credit

On 5 January stock was purchased on credit, which was invoiced for €5,200. The purchase of stock increases the asset "stock" with a **debit** and increases the liability "creditors" with a **credit**. A creditor is used when there is a delay between the time of the purchase and the time of payment.

Using T accounts, the amounts would appear as follows:

| Stock | | | | Creditors | | |
|---|---|---|---|---|---|---|
| 05 Jan Creditor 5,200 | | | | | 05 Jan Stock 5,200 | |

Using journals, the amounts would appear as follows:

| Date | Account | Statement | Debit | Credit |
|---|---|---|---|---|
| 05 Jan | Stock | Balance Sheet | 5,200 | |
| | Creditors | Balance Sheet | | 5,200 |

## ❏ Purchase of Asset

On 6 January, an asset was purchased which was partly paid for by cheque and partly on credit. The equipment cost €16,320. €13,320 will be paid by cheque and the balance (€3,000) the following month. The purchase of equipment by cheque and on credit increases the asset account "equipment" with a **debit**, decreases the asset "bank" with a **credit** and increases the liability account "creditors" with a **credit**.

Using T accounts, the amounts would appear as follows:

| Bank | | | | Creditors | | |
|---|---|---|---|---|---|---|
| 01 Jan Capital 40,000 | 03 Jan Rent | 3,200 | | | 05 Jan Stock | 5,200 |
| | 06 Jan Equipment | 13,320 | | | 06 Jan Equipment | 3,000 |

| Equipment | | |
|---|---|---|
| 06 Jan Creditor 3,000 | | |
| 06 Jan Bank 13,320 | | |

Using journals, the amounts would appear as follows:

| Date | Account | Statement | Debit | Credit |
|---|---|---|---|---|
| 06 Jan | Equipment | Balance Sheet | 3,000 | |
| | Equipment | Balance Sheet | 13,320 | |
| | Creditors | Balance Sheet | | 3,000 |
| | Bank | Balance Sheet | | 13,320 |

## ❑ Payment of a Liability

On 9 January, a partial payment of €2,600 was made for the amount owed for the stock. The payment of a liability decreases the liability account "creditors" with a **debit** and decreases the asset account "bank" with a **credit**.

Using T accounts, the amounts would appear as follows:

| Bank | | | Creditors | | |
|---|---|---|---|---|---|
| 01 Jan Capital 40,000 | 03 Jan Rent 3,200 | 09 Jan Bank 2,600 | 05 Jan Stock 5,200 | | |
| | 06 Jan Equipment 13,320 | | 06 Jan Equipment 3,000 | | |
| | 09 Jan Creditor 2,600 | | | | |

Using journals, the amounts would appear as follows:

| Date | Account | Statement | Debit | Credit |
|---|---|---|---|---|
| 09 Jan | Creditors | Balance Sheet | 2,600 | |
| | Bank | Balance Sheet | | 2,600 |

## ❑ Receiving Money for a Cash Sale

On 10 January, €2,800 is received by cheque for services provided; an invoice was not prepared for this amount and the customer is not a debtor, therefore the amount is a cash sale and recorded as revenue, which is lodged directly into the bank account. In this case revenue is recognised when the money was received.

Using T accounts, the amounts would appear as follows:

| Bank | | | | | | Revenue | | |
|---|---|---|---|---|---|---|---|---|
| 01 Jan | Capital | 40,000 | 03 Jan | Rent | 3,200 | 10 Jan | Bank | 2,800 |
| 10 Jan | Revenue | 2,800 | 06 Jan | Equipment | 13,320 | | | |
| | | | 09 Jan | Creditors | 2,600 | | | |

Using journals, the amounts would appear as follows:

| Date | Account | Statement | Debit | Credit |
|---|---|---|---|---|
| 10 Jan | Bank | Balance Sheet | 2,800 | |
| | Revenue | Profit & Loss | | 2,800 |

## ❑ Recording a Sales Invoice Issued to a Debtor

On 15 January, a customer is issued with a sale invoice for €9,600. The asset "debtor" is increased with a **debit** and the "revenue" account is increased with a **credit**. Debtors indicate the customer's obligation until it is paid. Revenue is recorded when the invoice is *issued* rather than when the cash is received.

Using T accounts, the amounts would appear as follows:

| Debtors | | | | Revenue | | |
|---|---|---|---|---|---|---|
| 15 Jan | Revenue | 9,600 | | 10 Jan | Bank | 2,800 |
| | | | | 15 Jan | Debtors | 9,600 |

Using journals, the amounts would appear as follows:

| Date | Account | Statement | Debit | Credit |
|---|---|---|---|---|
| 15 Jan | Debtors | Balance Sheet | 9,600 | |
| | Revenue | Profit & Loss | | 9,600 |

## ❑ Revenue Received in Advance

On 19 January, income was received in advance of the work being carried out. Revenue received in advance increases the asset "bank" with a **debit** and increases the liability account "deferred income" with a **credit**. Payment was received before the income is earned; unearned income is a liability in that the company must provide the services in the future. A customer paid €1,400 in advance of work being carried out in February; the money received is not recognised as income until the work is carried out.

Using T accounts, the amounts would appear as follows:

| Bank | | | | | | | Deferred Income | | | |
|---|---|---|---|---|---|---|---|---|---|---|
| 01 Jan | Capital | 40,000 | 03 Jan | Rent | 3,200 | | 19 Jan | Bank | 1,400 |
| 10 Jan | Revenue | 2,800 | 06 Jan | Equipment | 13,320 | | | | |
| **19 Jan** | **Deferred** | **1,400** | 09 Jan | Creditors | 2,600 | | | | |
| | **Income** | | | | | | | | |

Using journals the amounts would appear as follows:

| Date | Account | Statement | Debit | Credit |
|---|---|---|---|---|
| 19 Jan | Bank | Balance Sheet | 1,400 | |
| | Deferred Income | Balance Sheet | | 1,400 |

## ❑ Money Received from a Debtor

On 22 January, a partial payment of €5,000 was received on account from a customer who was billed €9,600 on 15 January. Collection of money from a customer previously billed increases the asset "bank" with a **debit** and decreased the asset account "debtors" with a **credit**.

Using T accounts, the amounts would appear as follows:

| Bank | | | | | | Debtors | | | | |
|---|---|---|---|---|---|---|---|---|---|---|
| 01 Jan | Capital | 40,000 | 03 Jan Rent | 3,200 | | 15 Jan | Revenue 9,600 | **22 Jan** | **Bank 5,000** | |
| 10 Jan | Revenue | 2,800 | 06 Jan Equipment | 13,320 | | | | | | |
| 19 Jan | Deferred | 1,400 | 09 Jan Creditor | 2,600 | | | | | | |
| | Income | | | | | | | | | |
| **22 Jan** | **Debtors** | **5,000** | | | | | | | | |

Using journals the amounts would appear as follows:

| Date | Account | Statement | Debit | Credit |
|---|---|---|---|---|
| 22 Jan | Bank | Balance Sheet | 5,000 | |
| | Debtors | Balance Sheet | | 5,000 |

## ❑ Payment of Expenses by Cheque

On 26 January, employees are paid wages of €4,800. The expense account "wages" will increase with a **debit** and the asset account "bank" will decrease with a **credit**.

Using T accounts the amounts would appear as follows:

| Bank | | | | Wages | | |
|---|---|---|---|---|---|---|
| 01 Jan  Capital | 40,000 | 03 Jan  Rent | 3,200 | 26 Jan  Bank   4,800 | | |
| 10 Jan  Revenue | 2,800 | 06 Jan  Equipment | 13,320 | | | |
| 19 Jan  Deferred Income | 1,400 | 09 Jan  Creditors | 2,600 | | | |
| 22 Jan  Debtors | 5,000 | **26 Jan  Wages** | **4,800** | | | |

Using journals, the amounts would appear as follows:

| Date | Account | Statement | Debit | Credit |
|---|---|---|---|---|
| 26 Jan | Wages | Profit & Loss | 4,800 | |
| | Bank | Balance Sheet | | 4,800 |

## ❑ Expenses Included in Creditors

On 30 January, an invoice in the amount of €680 was received for electricity that will be paid next month. The expense account "light and heat" is increased using a **debit** and the liability account "creditor" is increased using a **credit**. The expense is recorded if the benefit has been received and the amount is owed even if the money is not to be paid until later.

Using T accounts, the amounts would appear as follows:

| Creditors | | | | Light & Heat | | |
|---|---|---|---|---|---|---|
| 09 Jan  Bank   2,600 | | 05 Jan  Stock | 5,200 | 30 Jan  Creditor   680 | | |
| | | 06 Jan  Equipment | 3,000 | | | |
| | | **30 Jan  Light & Heat** | **680** | | | |

Using journals, the amounts would appear as follows:

| Date | Account | Statement | Debit | Credit |
|---|---|---|---|---|
| 30 Jan | Light & Heat | Profit & Loss | 680 | |
| | Creditors | Balance Sheet | | 680 |

## ❑ Dividend Declared and Paid

On 31 January, the company declares and pays a dividend of €2,800. Payment of a dividend will increase the expense "dividend" with a **debit** and decrease the asset account "bank" with a **credit**.

Using T accounts, the amounts would appear as follows:

| Bank | | | | | Dividend | |
|---|---|---|---|---|---|---|
| 01 Jan Capital | 40,000 | 03 Jan Rent | 3,200 | **31 Jan Bank** | **2,800** | |
| 10 Jan Revenue | 2,800 | 06 Jan Equipment | 13,320 | | | |
| 19 Jan Deferred Income | 1,400 | 09 Jan Creditors | 2,600 | | | |
| 22 Jan Debtors | 5,000 | 26 Jan Wages | 4,800 | | | |
| | | **31 Jan Dividend** | **2,800** | | | |

Using journals, the amounts would appear as follows:

| Date | Account | Statement | Debit | Credit |
|---|---|---|---|---|
| 31 Jan | Dividends | Profit & Loss | 2,800 | |
| | Bank | Balance Sheet | | 2,800 |

At the end of January, all the T accounts are closed off (the debits and credits in the accounts are totalled). In each T account, the side with the largest total for debits or credits represents the total on the T account, eg the total on the bank account debit side is €49,200. This amount is included as the total on the credit side and the difference between €49,200 and the total credit side of €26,720 is €22,480, which represents the balance carried down ("balance c/d"). This balance is the balance brought down ("balance b/d") for the next accounting period. See Figure 7.14.

At the end of a trading period all the debits and credits for each account must be added to find the "balance" on each account.

## Steps

1. Total the debit side.
2. Total the credit side.
3. Compare the totals.
4. Put in a figure (on the debit/credit side) to make both sides equal, this will be the "Balance c/d".

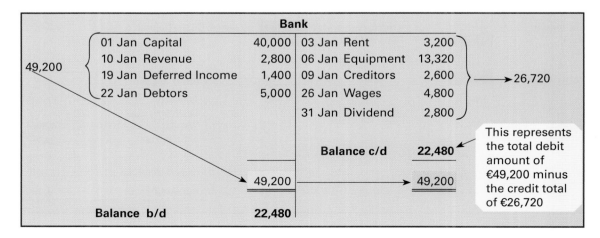

Figure 7.14

Set out in Figure 7.15 is a summary of all the T accounts. Each T account is closed off and the balances analysed into assets, liabilities and shareholders' capital.

| Bank | | | | | | | Creditors | | | | |
|---|---|---|---|---|---|---|---|---|---|---|---|
| 01 Jan | Capital | 40,000 | 03 Jan | Rent | 3,200 | 09 Jan | Bank | 2,600 | 05 Jan | Stock | 5,200 |
| 10 Jan | Revenue | 2,800 | 06 Jan | Equipment | 13,320 | | | | 06 Jan | Equipment | 3,000 |
| 19 Jan | Deferred | 1,400 | 09 Jan | Creditors | 2,600 | | Balance c/d | 6,280 | 30 Jan | Light & | 680 |
| | Income | | 26 Jan | Wages | 4,800 | | | | | Heat | |
| 22 Jan | Debtors | 5,000 | 31 Jan | Dividends | 2,800 | | | 8,880 | | | 8,880 |
| | | | | Balance c/d | 22,480 | | | | | Balance b/d | 6,280 |
| | | 49,200 | | | 49,200 | | | | | | |
| | Balance b/d | 22,480 | | | | | | | | | |

| Ordinary Share Capital | | | | | | Dividend | | | | |
|---|---|---|---|---|---|---|---|---|---|---|
| Balance c/d | 40,000 | 01 Jan | Bank | 40,000 | 31 Jan | Bank | 2,800 | Profit & Loss | 2,800 |
| | 40,000 | | | 40,000 | | | 2,800 | | 2,800 |
| | | | Balance b/d | 40,000 | | | | | |

| Debtors | | | | | | Deferred Income | | | | |
|---|---|---|---|---|---|---|---|---|---|---|
| 15 Jan | Revenue | 9,600 | 22 Jan | Bank | 5,000 | Balance c/d | 1,400 | 19 Jan | Bank | 1,400 |
| | | | | Balance c/d | 4,600 | | 1,400 | | | 1,400 |
| | | 9,600 | | | 9,600 | | | | Balance b/d | 1,400 |
| | Balance b/d | 4,600 | | | | | | | | |

| Revenue | | | | | | Stock | | | | |
|---|---|---|---|---|---|---|---|---|---|---|
| | | | 10 Jan | Bank | 2,800 | 05 Jan | Creditors | 5,200 | Balance c/d | 5,200 |
| Profit & Loss | | 12,400 | 15 Jan | Debtors | 9,600 | | | 5,200 | | 5,200 |
| | | 12,400 | | | 12,400 | | Balance b/d | 5,200 | | |

| Wages | | | | | Prepaid Rent | | | | |
|---|---|---|---|---|---|---|---|---|---|
| 26 Jan | Bank | 4,800 | Profit & Loss | 4,800 | 03 Jan | Bank | 3,200 | Balance c/d | 3,200 |
| | | 4,800 | | 4,800 | | | 3,200 | | 3,200 |
| | | | | | | Balance b/d | 3,200 | | |

| Light & Heat | | | | | Equipment | | | | |
|---|---|---|---|---|---|---|---|---|---|
| 30 Jan | Creditors | 680 | Profit & Loss | 680 | 06 Jan | Creditors | 3,000 | | |
| | | 680 | | 680 | 06 Jan | Bank | 13,320 | Balance c/d | 16,320 |
| | | | | | | | 16,320 | | 16,320 |
| | | | | | | Balance b/d | 16,320 | | |

| Assets | | – | Liabilities | | = | Shareholders' Capital | |
|---|---|---|---|---|---|---|---|
| Equipment | 16,320 | | Creditors | 6,280 | | Share Capital | 40,000 |
| Bank | 22,480 | | Deferred Income | 1,400 | | Retained Profit *(see below)* | 4,120 |
| Debtors | 4,600 | | | | | | 44,120 |
| Stock | 5,200 | | | | | | |
| Prepaid Rent | 3,200 | | | | | | |
| | 51,800 | | | 7,680 | | | |

| Profit & Loss | |
|---|---|
| Revenue | 12,400 |
| **Less Expenses** | |
| Wages | (4,800) |
| Light & Heat | (680) |
| | 6,920 |
| Less Dividends | (2,800) |
| **Retained Profit** | 4,120 |

Figure 7.15

For every amount debited there must be an equal amount credited; this means that the total of debits and credits in all the T accounts must be equal. To test this, the accountant periodically prepares a trial balance. Although a trial balance can be prepared at any time, it is usually prepared on the last day of the accounting period. These are the steps involved in preparing a trial balance:

- List each account that has a balance, with the debit balance in the left column and the credit balance in the right column.
- Total each column.
- Compare the totals of each column.

The trial balance proves whether the ledger is in balance. This means that the total of all the debits recorded equals the total of all the credits recorded. The trial balance does not prove that the transactions were analysed correctly or recorded in the proper accounts. For example, there is no way of determining from the trial balance that a debit should have been made in the stock account rather than the equipment account. The trial balance does not detect whether transactions have been omitted, because equal debits and credits will have been omitted. If an error of the same amount is made to both the debit and credit sides, it will not be evident in the trial balance. The trial balance proves only that the debits and credits in the accounts are in balance, as in Figure 7.16.

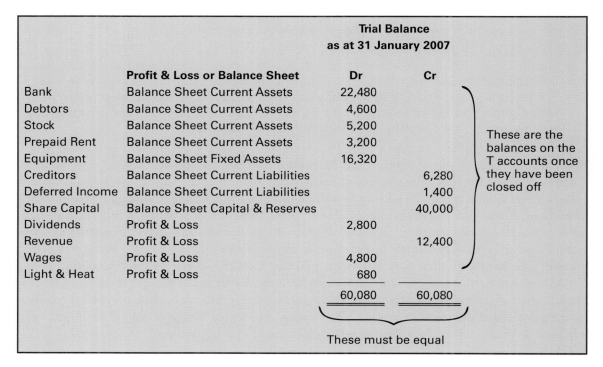

Figure 7.16

## ❏ Finding Trial Balance Errors

If the debit and credit balances in a trial balance are not equal, look for one or more of the following errors:

- Compensating errors—a debit was entered in an account as a credit or vice versa.
- Error of omission—the transaction was completely omitted from the accounting records; the trial balance will still balance.
- An error was made in carrying the account balance to the trial balance.
- Error of commission—the double-entry transaction is recorded, but not in the correct account.
- One-sided entry—this would occur if a debit or credit were recorded without the other side of the transaction being recorded.
- Casting error—the trial balance was totalled incorrectly or the balance on an individual account was totalled incorrectly.
- Error of principle—this is where the transaction is recorded in the wrong type of account; eg motor running costs are recorded as a capital expenditure under the heading of Fixed Asset Motor Vehicle.
- Error of prime entry—the amount recorded in the account does not agree to the amounts recorded in the source documentation.

The two most common mistakes in preparing a trial balance are:

- Recording an account as a credit when it usually carries a debit balance or vice versa. This mistake causes the trial balance to be out of balance by an amount divisible by **2**.
- Transposition error occurs when individual digits making up the number are written in the wrong order, for example writing €23,459 as €23,549. This error causes the trial balance to be out of balance by a number divisible by **9**.

If the trial balance is out of balance and the addition of the columns is correct, determine the amount by which the trial balance is out of balance and divide it by **2** and then by **9**. If the amount is divisible by **2**, look at the trial balance for an amount that is equal to this number. If you find such an amount, chances are it is in the wrong column. If the amount is divisible by **9**, trace each amount back to the T account balance, checking carefully for a transposition error. If neither of these techniques is successful in identifying the error, re-compute the balance on each T account. Then, if you still have not found the errors, retrace each posting from the journal to the T account.

Although transactions can be entered directly into the ledger accounts, this method makes the identification of individual transactions or finding of errors very difficult because the debit is recorded in one account and the credit in another. The solution is to record all transactions chronologically in a journal. Journals include the following information about each transaction:

- The date.
- The name of the accounts debited and credited which appears in the account column.
- The debit amounts, which appear in the debit column opposite the accounts that are debited.

- The credit amounts, which appear in the credit column opposite the accounts credited.
- An explanation should be brief but sufficient to explain and identify the transaction.

| Example of a Journal | | | | |
|---|---|---|---|---|
| Date | Account | Statement | Debit | Credit |
| 03 Jan | Prepaid rent | Balance Sheet | 3,200 | |
| | Bank | Balance Sheet | | 3,200 |
| | Paid 2 months' rent in advance | | | |
| | | Statement | | |
| 05 Jan | Stock | Balance Sheet | 5,200 | |
| | Creditors | Balance Sheet | | 5,200 |
| | Purchase of stock on credit | | | |

## Length of Accounting Periods

Measuring business income requires assigning revenue and expenses to a specific accounting period. However, not all transactions can be easily assigned to specific periods. When a company purchases a building it must estimate the number of years the building will be in use. Financial statements may be prepared for any time period, but generally, to make comparisons easier, the periods are of equal length.

## Matching

The cash basis of accounting is the practice of accounting for revenues in the period in which cash is received and expenses in the period in which cash is paid. Some individuals and businesses use this method. Although the cash basis of accounting works well for some small businesses and many individuals, it does not meet the needs of most businesses. To measure income adequately, revenue and expenses must be assigned to the accounting period in which they occur, regardless of when cash is received or paid. This is the matching rule.

Revenue must be assigned to the accounting period in which the goods are sold or the services performed and expenses must be assigned to the accounting period in which they are used to produce the revenue. A direct cause and effect relationship between expenses and revenue is often difficult to identify.

Applying the matching rule involves making assumptions. Revenue and expenses can be manipulated to achieve specific outcomes. This may be done because:

- There is a previously announced goal, eg increasing sales by 15%.
- The company's share price is dropping.
- A particular employee wants to meet a goal to enable a bonus to be earned.

# ☐ Accrual Accounting

Accrual accounting encompasses all the techniques used to apply the matching rule. In accrual accounting, revenue and expenses are recorded in the periods in which they occur rather than in the periods in which they are received or paid.

Accrual accounting is achieved in the following ways:

- Recording revenue when it is earned—Revenues should only be recognised when a product or service has been delivered, the seller's price to the buyer has been fixed and the collectability is reasonably assured.
- Recording expenses when they are incurred—Expenses are recorded when there is an agreement to purchase goods or services, the goods have been delivered or the services rendered, a price has been established or can be determined and the goods or services have been used to produce revenue.
- Adjusting the accounts.

Accrual accounting also involves adjusting the accounts. Adjustments are necessary because the accounting period, by definition, ends on a particular day, eg 31 December. The balance sheet must list all assets and liabilities as of the end of that particular day and the profit & loss account must contain all income and expenditure applicable to the period ending on that day. Although operating expenditure is a continuous process, there must be a cut-off for the periodic report. Some transactions invariably span the cut-off point and some accounts need adjustment.

Adjusting entries do not affect cash flow in the current period because it never involves the cash account. All adjustments are important because of their effect on profitability and liquidity. Adjusting entries affects the net profit in the profit & loss account and affects profitability comparisons from one accounting period to the next. They also affect assets and liabilities on the balance sheet and thus provide information about a company's future cash inflow and outflows. The potential for abuse arises because considerable accounting judgement underlies the application of adjusting entries.

## The Adjusting Process

Each adjusting entry affects one balance sheet account and one profit & loss account. There are five types of adjusting entries:

### 1. Prepaid Expenses

Allocating costs between two or more accounting periods, eg where rent costs are paid in advance for future accounting periods. Companies often make expenditure that benefits more than one accounting period. These costs are **debited** to an asset account. At the end of an accounting period the amount of the asset that has been used is transferred from the asset account to an expense account. Examples of these types of adjustments are prepaid expenses. The required adjusting entry reduces the asset and increases the expense. If adjusting entries for prepaid expenses are not made at the end of an accounting period the assets will be overstated and the expenses will be understated.

**Example**

Rent of €3,200 is paid on 3 January, for January and February. The prepaid rent account now has a balance of €1,600 (€3,200/2 months), which represents one month's rent that will be expensed in February.

Using T accounts, the amount would appear as follows:

| Prepaid rent | | | | Rent Expense Profit & Loss | | |
|---|---|---|---|---|---|---|
| 3 Jan   Bank   3,200 | 31 Jan    Rent P & L | 1,600 | 31 Jan    Prepaid Rent    1,600 | | | |
| | Balance c/d | 1,600 | | | | |
| 3,200 | | 3,200 | | | | |
| Balance b/d   1,600 | | | | | | |

Using journals, the amount would appear as follows:

| Date | Account | Statement | Debit | Credit |
|---|---|---|---|---|
| 31 Jan | Rent Expense | Profit & Loss | 1,600 | |
| | Prepaid Rent | Balance Sheet | | 1,600 |

## 2. Depreciation

When a business buys a long-term asset such as a building, truck or computer it is prepaying for the usefulness of that asset for as long as it is used by the company. Because a long-term asset is a deferral of an expense, the accountant must allocate the cost of the asset over its estimated useful life. The amount allocated to any one accounting period is called "depreciation". Depreciation refers to the allocation of an asset's cost, not to a decline in the asset's life. It is often impossible to tell how long an asset will last or how much of the asset has been used in any one period. Depreciation is an estimate. A separate account is used to accumulate depreciation on specific long-term assets. The net amount is called the "net book value" of the fixed asset. As the months pass, the amount of the accumulated depreciation increases and the net book value of the asset declines. Depreciation decreases the asset account "equipment" by increasing the contra account "equipment accumulated depreciation" with a **credit** and increasing the expense account "equipment depreciation" with a **debit.**

### Example

An asset is purchased for €16,320 on 6 January. Depreciation is calculated at €300 per month.
    Using T accounts, the amounts would appear as follows:

| Equipment | | | Equipment Depreciation | |
|---|---|---|---|---|
| 6 Jan  Creditor | 3,000 | | 31 Jan   Accumulated Depr    300 | |
| 6 Jan  Bank | 13,320 | | | |
| | 16,320 | | | |

| Equipment Accumulated Depreciation | |
|---|---|
| | 31 Jan Equipment Depr 300 |

Using journals, the amounts would appear as follows:

| Date | Account | Statement | Debit | Credit |
|------|---------|-----------|-------|--------|
| 31 Jan | Equipment Depreciation | Profit & Loss | 300 | |
| | Equipment Accumulated Depreciation | Balance Sheet | | 300 |

### 3. Accrued Expenses

Recognising unrecorded expenses. Examples of these include wages, taxation and interest payable. At the end of an accounting period, it is usual that some expenses incurred during the period have not been recorded in the accounts, eg interest on money borrowed, wages earned but not yet paid.

### Example

Employees were paid €4,800 up to 26 January 2007 but work until 31 January 2007. The employees have earned the wages for those days but will not be paid until the first payday in February 2007. The wages for these five days are rightfully an expense for January and the liabilities should reflect that the company owes the money for those days worked. An adjustment will have to be made to record the wages for 27, 28, 29, 30 and 31 January, which were "earned" but not paid until February. The wages expense will increase by €720 and the company will have a liability at 31 January to pay employees €720, which it pays in the first week of February.

Using T accounts, the amounts would appear as follows:

| Wages Payable Balance Sheet | | Wages Expense Profit & Loss | | |
|---|---|---|---|---|
| | **31 Jan   Wages   720** | 26 Jan  Bank | 4,800 | |
| | | **31 Jan  Wages Payable** | **720** | Profit & Loss   5,520 |
| | | | 5,520 | 5,520 |

Using journals, the amounts would appear as follows:

| Date | Account | Statement | Debit | Credit |
|------|---------|-----------|-------|--------|
| 31 Jan | Wages Expense | Profit & Loss | 720 | |
| | Wages Payable | Balance Sheet | | 720 |

### 4. Deferred Income

Just as expenses can be paid before they are used, revenue can be received before it is earned. When a company receives revenue in advance, it has an obligation to deliver goods or perform services. Unearned revenues are therefore shown in a liability account as deferred income.

Unearned revenue is a liability because there is an obligation to deliver goods or perform a service or to return the payment to the customer. Once the goods have been delivered or the service performed, the liability is converted to revenue. For example, publishing companies usually receive payment in advance for magazine subscriptions. These receipts are recorded in the liability account "deferred income". If the company fails to deliver the magazines, subscribers are entitled to their money back. Once the magazines are delivered, the earned portion must be transferred from the deferred income account to the subscription revenue account.

**Example**

The customer who paid €1,400 in advance on 19 January received €800 worth of the service on 31 January.

Since the service has now been received this will increase the "Revenue" account with a **credit** and decreases the liability account "deferred income" with a **debit**.

Using T accounts the amounts would appear as follows:

| Deferred Income Balance Sheet | | | | Revenue Profit & Loss | | | |
|---|---|---|---|---|---|---|---|
| **31 Jan  Revenue** | **800** | 19 Jan Bank 1,400 | | Profit & Loss | 800 | **31 Jan  Deferred Income** | **800** |
| Balance c/d | 600 | | | | | | |
| | 1,400 | | 1,400 | | 800 | | 800 |
| | | Balance b/d | 600 | | | | |

Using journals, the amounts would appear as follows:

| Date | Account | Statement | Debit | Credit |
|---|---|---|---|---|
| 31 Jan | Deferred Income | Balance Sheet | 800 | |
| | Revenue | Profit & Loss | | 800 |

## 5. Accrued Income

Accrued income recognises income that a company has earned from providing a service but for which it has not issued the invoice at the end of the accounting period. Accrued revenues are revenues that a company has earned by performing a service or delivering goods but for which no entry has been made in the accounting records. Any revenue earned but not recorded during the accounting period requires an adjusting entry that **debits** "debtors" and **credits** a revenue account.

**Example**

Income of €400 was earned but the invoice was not issued at the end of January.

Using T accounts, the amounts would appear as follows:

| Debtors | | | | | | Design Revenue | | | |
|---|---|---|---|---|---|---|---|---|---|
| 15 Jan | Revenue | 9,600 | 22 Jan | Bank | 5,000 | | 31 Jan | Debtors | 400 |
| **31 Jan** | **Revenue** | **400** | Balance c/d | | 5,000 | | | | |
| | | 10,000 | | | 10,000 | | | | |
| Balance b/d | | 5,000 | | | | | | | |

Using journals the amounts would appear as follows:

| Date | Account | Statement | Debit | Credit |
|---|---|---|---|---|
| 31 Jan | Debtors | Balance Sheet | 400 | |
| | Revenue | Profit & Loss | | 400 |

After adjusting entries have been recorded and posted, an adjusted trial balance is prepared by listing all accounts and their balances. If the adjusting entries have been posted to the account correctly, the adjusted trial balance will have equal debits and credits. Notice that some accounts such as "bank" and "stock" have the same balances as in the original trial balance (see Fig 7.15). The balance of other accounts such as "revenue" and "prepaid rent" differ from those in the trial balance because adjusting entries did affect them. The adjusted trial balance also has some new accounts such as "depreciation" and "wages", which did not appear in the original trial balance.

# ❏ Closing Entries

Balance sheet accounts such as "bank" and "creditors" are considered permanent accounts because they carry their end-of-period balance into the next accounting period. In contrast, revenue and expense accounts such as "sales" and "wages" are considered temporary accounts because they begin each accounting period with a zero balance. Closing entries are journal entries made at the end of an accounting period to transfer these balances to the profit and loss account.

The extended trial balance is a special kind of working paper; it is often used as a preliminary step in preparing financial statements. Using an extended trial balance lessens the possibility of leaving out an adjustment and helps the accountant check the arithmetical accuracy of the accounts, as in Figure 7.17.

**Work Sheet for the month ended 31 January 2007**

| Account Name | Column 1 Trial Balance | | Column 2 Adjustments | | Column 3 Adjusted Trial Balance | | Column 4 Profit & Loss | | Column 5 Balance Sheet | |
|---|---|---|---|---|---|---|---|---|---|---|
| | Debit | Credit | Debit | Credit | Debit | Credit | Debit | Credit | Debit | Credit |
| Bank | 22,480 | | | | 22,480 | | | | 22,480 | |
| Debtors | 4,600 | | 400 | | 5,000 | | | | 5,000 | |
| Stock | 5,200 | | | | 5,200 | | | | 5,200 | |
| Prepaid Rent | 3,200 | | | 1,600 | 1,600 | | | | 1,600 | |
| Equipment | 16,320 | | | | 16,320 | | | | 16,320 | |
| Accumulated Depreciation—Equipment | | | | 300 | | 300 | | | | 300 |
| Creditors | | 6,280 | | | | 6,280 | | | | 6,280 |
| Deferred Income | | 1,400 | 800 | | | 600 | | | | 600 |
| Share Capital | | 40,000 | | | | 40,000 | | | | 40,000 |
| Dividends | 2,800 | | | | 2,800 | | 2,800 | | | |
| Revenue | | 12,400 | | 400 | | 13,600 | | 13,600 | | |
| | | | | 800 | | | | | | |
| Wages | 4,800 | | 720 | | 5,520 | | 5,520 | | | |
| Light & Heat | 680 | | | | 680 | | 680 | | | |
| | 60,080 | 60,080 | | | | | | | | |
| Rent Expense | | | 1,600 | | 1,600 | | 1,600 | | | |
| Equipment Depreciation | | | 300 | | 300 | | 300 | | | |
| Wages Payable | | | | 720 | | 720 | | | | 720 |
| | | | 3,820 | 3,820 | 61,500 | 61,500 | 10,900 | 13,600 | 50,600 | 47,900 |
| Net Profit | | | | | Step 5 | | 2,700 | | | 2,700 |
| | | | | | | | 13,600 | 13,600 | 50,600 | 50,600 |
| | See Fig 7.16 | | | | Trial Balance +/– Adjustments | | Adjusted Trial Balance analysed between Profit & Loss and Balance Sheet | | | |
| | Step 1 | | Step 2 | | Step 3 | | Step 4 | | | |

Figure 7.17

**Steps:**

1. Enter the account balances from the trial balance. The debit and credit balances are copied from the T accounts. The total of the debits must equal the total of the credits. See figure 7.16.
2. All of the adjustments are included in the "adjustments" column, eg prepaid expenses, accruals, depreciation. When all of the adjustments have been made, the two adjustment columns must be totalled. This procedure proves that the debits and the credits of the adjustments are equal.
3. Enter and total the account balances in the "adjusted trial balance" column. Combine the amount of each account in the "trial balance" columns (Column 1) with the corresponding amount in the "adjustments" columns (Column 2) and enter each result in the "adjusted trial balance" column (column 3).

4. Analyse the account balance from the "adjusted trial balance" columns (Column 3) to the profit & loss (Column 4) or the balance sheet (Column 5). Every account in the adjusted trial balance should be in the profit & loss or balance sheet.
5. Total the profit & loss and balance sheet columns. Enter the net profit or net loss in both pairs of columns as a balancing figure and re-calculate the column totals.

**Adjusted Trial Balance**
**31st January 2007**

| | | |
|---|---:|---:|
| Bank | 22,480 | |
| Debtors | 5,000 | |
| Stock | 5,200 | |
| Prepaid Rent | 1,600 | |
| Equipment | 16,320 | |
| Accumulated Depreciation | | |
| Equipment | | 300 |
| Creditors | | 6,280 |
| Deferred Income | | 600 |
| Share Capital | | 40,000 |
| Dividends | 2,800 | |
| Revenue | | 13,600 |
| Wages | 5,520 | |
| Light & Heat | 680 | |
| Rent Expense | 1,600 | |
| Equipment Depreciation | 300 | |
| Wages payable | | 720 |
| | 61,500 | 61,500 |

**Balance Sheet**
**as at 31 January 2007**

**Fixed Assets**

| | | | |
|---|---:|---:|---:|
| Equipment | | 16,320 | |
| Less Accumulated Depreciation | | (300) | 16,020 |

**Current Assets**

| | | | |
|---|---:|---:|---:|
| Bank | 22,480 | | |
| Debtors | 5,000 | | |
| Stock | 5,200 | | |
| Prepaid Rent | 1,600 | 34,280 | |

**Liabilities**

| | | | |
|---|---:|---:|---:|
| Creditors | 6,280 | | |
| Deferred Income | 600 | | |
| Wages Payable | 720 | 7,600 | |

| | |
|---|---:|
| **Net Current Assets** | 26,680 |
| **Total Assets Less Current Liabilities** | 42,700 |

**Shareholders Equity**

| | |
|---|---:|
| Share Capital | 40,000 |
| Retained Profit | 2,700 |
| Total Stockholders Equity | 42,700 |

**Profit & Loss**

| | |
|---|---:|
| Revenue | 13,600 |
| **Less expenses** | |
| Wages | (5,520) |
| Light & Heat | (680) |
| Rent Expense | (1,600) |
| Equipment Depreciation | (300) |
| Profit before Dividends | 5,500 |
| Less Dividends | (2,800) |
| Net Profit | 2,700 |

Figure 7.18

## ❑ Ledgers

Each account represents an individual T account. In a manual accounting system used by the smallest of businesses, all T accounts may fit into one book or ledger. In most businesses the volume of transactions and the need for more than one person to have access to make entries means that similar transactions are entered into one particular ledger. This is also true of computerised accounting systems where there are three main ledgers:

- Sales.
- Purchases.
- Nominal.

## ❑ Journals

Double entries are not made directly into the ledgers but are first entered in a book of prime entry from which postings to the relevant ledger account are made later. The books of prime entry are:

- Daybooks—sales and purchases.
- Journals.
- Cashbook—cash payment and cash receipts.

The sales and purchase daybooks act as a kind of diary where all sales and purchases are entered in chronological order. At a later date, each transaction is entered in the named account of the customer or supplier in the sales or purchase ledger respectively, while the total of a batch of similar transactions is entered in the sales account or purchase account in the nominal ledger, so completing the double entry. The amount of VAT is recorded in the relevant side of the VAT account in the nominal ledger. In a similar way, cash transactions are first entered in a cash receipts book or cash payments book. These cash transactions are later posted to the named account of the customer or supplier in the sales ledger or purchase ledger respectively.

   Journals are used to record non-routine transactions that are later posted to the two ledger accounts to complete the double entry. Typical journals would include:

- The correction of errors.
- Adjustment for prepayments or accruals.
- The creation of a provision for bad debts.
- Adjustment for stocks on hand at the end of the accounting period.

## Sales Journal

The sales journal is designed to handle all cash and credit sales.

The debtors account in the general ledger is generally a control account so the company knows how much it is owed by each customer; it keeps a separate account for each customer in the debtors' ledger. See Figure 7.19.

A control account is an account such as debtors that maintains the total of the individual accounts within that ledger; eg the balance on the "debtor control" account is €85. The total of the individual accounts is made up of "Customer B" €35 and "Customer C" €50 giving a total of €85.

A single entry in the debtors control account does not tell how much each customer has bought and how much each customer has paid or still owes. Companies keep an individual account for each customer.

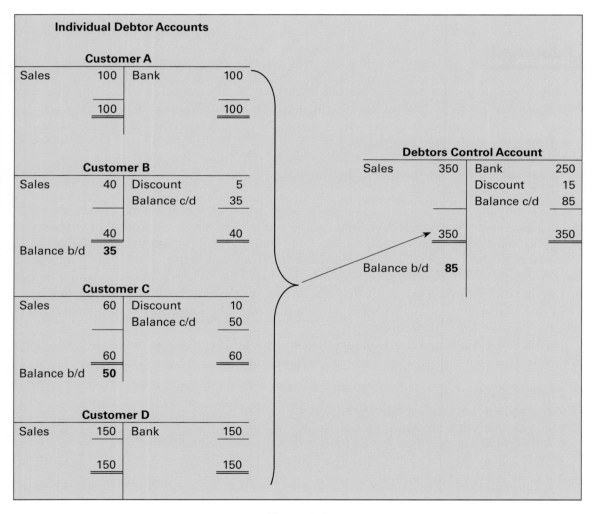

Figure 7.19

## Purchases Journal

The purchase journal is used to record credit purchases. This transaction is recorded with a debit to the purchases account and a credit to the creditors' account. Cash purchases are never recorded in the purchase journal; they are recorded as a cash payment. The creditors' account in the general ledger is generally a control account so the company knows how much it owes all suppliers. It keeps a separate account for each supplier in the creditors' ledger. Similar to the debtors control account set out in Figure 7.19.

## Cash Receipts Journal

All receipts of cash are recorded in the cash receipts journal. Examples of these transactions are cash from cash sales and cash received from credit customers paying their accounts. Although all cash receipts are alike in that they require a debit to bank account, they differ in that the credit can be to debtors/cash sales etc.

The debtor's column in the cash receipts book is used to record the collection of money from debtors. The name of the customer is written in the debtor's column so that the payments can be entered in the corresponding account in the debtor's subsidiary ledger. Posting to the individual debtors account is usually done daily so that each customer's balance is up to date.

The sales column in the cash receipts book is used to record all cash sales. Other accounts are used for receipts that do not relate to cash sales or the receipt of money from debtors. See Figure 7.11.

## Cash Payments Journal

All transactions involving the payment of cheques are recorded in the cash payments journal. A creditors column is used to record payments to suppliers that have extended credit to the company. Each supplier's name is written in the payee column so that payments can be entered in the supplier's account in the creditors' ledger. See Figure 7.10.

## Computerised Accounts

Most businesses use a computerised accounts package. These packages follow the process described in this chapter on bookkeeping.

Keeping good source documents is very important, so that transactions included in the accounts package can be verified.

## Source Documents

Source documentation or written evidence should support each transaction in the accounting system. Source documentation verifies that transactions occurred and provides the details of the transaction, see Figure 7.20.

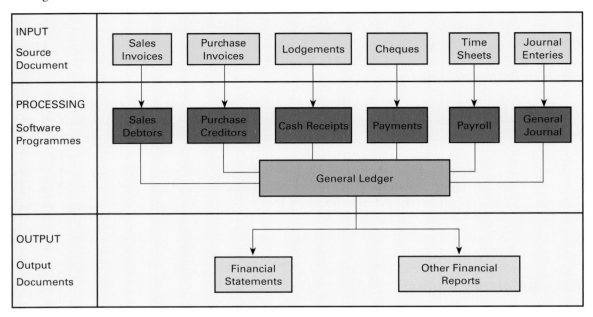

Figure 7.20

**Quick Tip**

At least one source document should support each business transaction entered in the records. The accounting system should provide easy reference to the source documents to facilitate subsequent examination.

The original documentation should be stored so that it can be examined at a later date if a question arises about the accuracy of the accounting records. In a batch processing system, source documents are recorded in the appropriate journal and saved. Posting is done at the end of a day, week or month. In real-time, processing documents are posted as they are recorded in the journal.

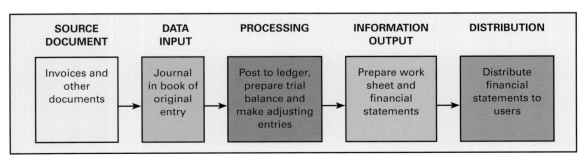

Figure 7.21

# IS IT A DEBIT OR A CREDIT?

## Chapter 8

One of the biggest problem areas in accounting is deciding which account to debit and which account to credit. If the concept of double entry bookkeeping is not understood, mistakes can easily be made. Set out in the next few pages is a list of common journals so that if you are ever stuck and are not quite sure which account to debit and which account to credit, you can check the list.

## ❏ Fixed Assets

| Depreciation | Statement | Debit | Credit | |
|---|---|---|---|---|
| Depreciation Fixtures & Fittings | Profit & Loss | X | | |
| Accumulated Depreciation F&F | Balance Sheet | | X | |

*Depreciation of Fixtures & Fittings for a month/year is recorded as an expense in the profit & loss and as a contra account to the cost of fixtures & fittings in the balance sheet.*

| Disposal of Fixed Assets | Statement | Debit | Credit | |
|---|---|---|---|---|
| Disposal Account | Profit & Loss | X | | |
| Cost—Fixtures & Fittings | Balance Sheet | | X | } Cost of fixtures & fttings |
| Accumulated Depreciation F&F | Balance Sheet | X | | |
| Disposal Account | Profit & Loss | | X | } Balance on the Accumulated Depreciation account |
| Bank | Balance Sheet | X | | |
| VAT (Proceeds × 21%/121%) | Balance Sheet | | X | |
| Disposal Account | Profit & Loss | | X | } Proceeds of sale |

*The cost of the assets is transferred to the disposal account. The accumulated depreciation is transferred to the disposal account. The money received in exchange for the fixed asset is lodged into the bank account and VAT must be charged on the disposal if VAT was claimed on the original purchase of the asset. If the balance on the disposal account is a debit this will be a loss on disposal, if the balance on the disposal account is a credit this will be a gain on disposal.*

## ❏ DEBTORS

| Credit Sale (VAT) | Statement | Debit | Credit |
|---|---|---|---|
| Debtor | Balance Sheet | X | |
| Sales | Profit & Loss | | X |
| VAT | Balance Sheet | | X |

*Recording a sales invoice where VAT is being charged and payment will be made by the customer subsequently.*

| Credit Sale (No VAT) | Statement | Debit | Credit |
|---|---|---|---|
| Debtor | Balance Sheet | X | |
| Sales | Profit & Loss | | X |

*Recording a sales invoice where VAT is NOT being charged and payment will be made by the customer subsequently.*

| Sales Credit Note (VAT) | Statement | Debit | Credit |
|---|---|---|---|
| Sales | Profit & Loss | X | |
| VAT | Balance Sheet | X | |
| Debtor | Balance Sheet | | X |

*Recording a credit note in relation to a sales invoice issued where VAT was previously charged and payment will be made by the customer subsequently.*

| Sales Credit Note (No VAT) | Statement | Debit | Credit |
|---|---|---|---|
| Sales | Profit & Loss | X | |
| Debtor | Balance Sheet | | X |

*Recording a credit note in relation to a sales invoice issued where VAT was NOT previously charged and payment will be made by the customer subsequently.*

## ❑ CREDITORS

| Credit Purchases (VAT) | Statement | Debit | Credit |
|---|---|:---:|:---:|
| Purchases/Stationery etc | Profit & Loss | X | |
| VAT | Balance Sheet | X | |
| Creditors | Balance Sheet | | X |

*Recording a purchase invoice/expense where VAT is being claimed and payment will be made to the supplier subsequently.*

| Credit Purchases (No VAT) | Statement | Debit | Credit |
|---|---|:---:|:---:|
| Purchases/Stationery etc | Profit & Loss | X | |
| Creditor | Balance Sheet | | X |

*Recording a purchase invoice/expense where VAT is NOT being claimed and payment will be made to the supplier subsequently.*

| Purchase Credit Note (VAT) | Statement | Debit | Credit |
|---|---|:---:|:---:|
| Creditor | Balance Sheet | X | |
| VAT | Balance Sheet | | X |
| Purchases/Stationery etc | Profit & Loss | | X |

*Recording a credit note in relation to an invoice/expense where VAT was previously claimed and payment will be made to the supplier subsequently.*

| Purchase Credit Note (No VAT) | Statement | Debit | Credit |
|---|---|:---:|:---:|
| Creditor | Balance Sheet | X | |
| Purchases/Expenses etc | Profit & Loss | | X |

*Recording a credit note in relation to an invoice/expense where VAT was NOT claimed and payment will be made to the supplier subsequently.*

## ❑ Bank

| Bank Lodgement (NOT Debtors) | Statement | Debit | Credit |
|---|---|---|---|
| Current Account | Balance Sheet | X | |
| Rent received/dividend received/cash sale | Profit & Loss | | X |
| *Lodgement of rent/dividend/cash sale into the current account.* | | | |

| Bank Lodgement (Debtors) | Statement | Debit | Credit |
|---|---|---|---|
| Current Account | Balance Sheet | X | |
| Debtors | Balance Sheet | | X |
| *Lodgement of money received where the original invoice was recorded in debtors.* | | | |

| Cheque Payments (NOT Creditors) | Statement | Debit | Credit |
|---|---|---|---|
| Rent/Stationery etc | Profit & Loss | X | |
| Current Account | Balance Sheet | | X |
| *Payment of rent/stationery etc from the current account that is NOT recorded in creditors.* | | | |

| Cheque Payment (Creditors) | Statement | Debit | Credit |
|---|---|---|---|
| Creditor (Courier/Stationery) | Balance Sheet | X | |
| Current Account | Balance Sheet | | X |
| *Payment of courier/stationery etc from the current account where the original invoice was recorded in creditors.* | | | |

| Direct Debit (NOT Creditors) | Statement | Debit | Credit |
|---|---|---|---|
| Bank Charges/Interest | Profit & Loss | X | |
| Current Account | Balance Sheet | | X |
| *Recording bank charges/interest which appear on the bank current account statement.* | | | |

## ❑ Bad Debts

| Bad Debt Provision | Statement | Debits | Credits |
|---|---|---|---|
| Bad Debt | Profit & Loss | X | |
| Bad Debt Provision | Balance Sheet | | X |

*A bad debt is identified and written off to the profit & loss account, the corresponding amount is deducted from debtors. The bad debt remains on the debtors listing.*

| Write-off of Bad Debt (VAT) | Statement | Debits | Credits |
|---|---|---|---|
| Bad Debt Provision | Balance Sheet | X | |
| VAT | Balance Sheet | X | |
| Debtor | Balance Sheet | | X |

*Write-off of bad debt by issuing a credit note. The VAT can be reclaimed as VAT was previously charged on the sales invoice which became a bad debt.*

| Write-off of Bad Debt (No VAT) | Statement | Debits | Credits |
|---|---|---|---|
| Bad Debt Provision | Balance Sheet | X | |
| Debtor | Balance Sheet | | X |

*Write-off of bad debt by issuing a credit note.*

## ❑ Corporation Tax

| Corporation Tax Provision | Statement | Debit | Credit |
|---|---|---|---|
| Corporation Tax Charge | Profit & Loss | X | |
| Corporation Tax Liability | Balance Sheet | | X |

*Provision for corporation tax liability; the amount will be deducted from profit before tax and the liability will remain in creditors due within one year until the amount is paid.*

| Corporation Tax Underprovision | Statement | Debit | Credit |
|---|---|---|---|
| Corporation Tax Charge | Profit & Loss | X | |
| Corporation Tax Liability | Balance Sheet | | X |

*If the actual liability for corporation tax was greater than anticipated, a journal must be included for the underprovision of corporation tax.*

*(Continued)*

| Corporation Tax Overprovision | Statement | Debit | Credit |
|---|---|---|---|
| Corporation Tax Liability | Balance Sheet | X | |
| Corporation Tax Charge | Profit & Loss | | X |

*If the amount of corporation tax liability was less than anticipated, a journal must be done to reduce the liability.*

# ❏ Stock

| Closing Stock | Statement | Debit | Credit |
|---|---|---|---|
| Stock | Balance Sheet | X | |
| Stock (closing) | Profit & Loss | | X |

*Once the stock figure has been agreed, it is included in the balance sheet as an asset and in the profit & loss account as the closing stock figure used to calculate cost of goods sold.*

| Opening Stock | Statement | Debit | Credit |
|---|---|---|---|
| Stock (opening) | Profit & Loss | X | |
| Stock | Balance Sheet | | X |

*The closing stock figure for 2007 in the balance sheet is transferred to the profit & loss account and becomes the opening stock figure for 2008 which is used to calculate cost of goods sold.*

# ❏ Accruals

| Accrual for invoice split between accounting periods | Statement | Debit | Credit |
|---|---|---|---|
| Electricity | Profit & Loss | X | |
| Accrual | Balance Sheet | | X |

*An accrual may be included where the electricity bill covers the current accounting period and the next accounting period.*

| Accrual estimate of invoice | Statement | Debit | Credit |
|---|---|---|---|
| Audit | Profit & Loss | X | |
| Accrual | Balance Sheet | | X |

*An estimate can be included in the accounts as an accrual for expenditure incurred but not yet invoiced eg the audit fee.*

## ❑ Petty Cash

| Petty Cash Analysis | Statement | Debit | Credit |
|---|---|---|---|
| Stationery | Profit & Loss | X | |
| Postage | Profit & Loss | X | |
| Canteen | Profit & Loss | X | |
| VAT | Balance Sheet | X | |
| Petty Cash | Balance Sheet | | X |

*Petty cash expenditure can be recorded as one journal at the end of the month; do not forget that some petty cash expenditure includes deductible VAT.*

## ❑ Prepayment

| Prepaid Expenses | Statement | Debit | Credit |
|---|---|---|---|
| Prepayments | Balance Sheet | X | |
| Rent | Profit & Loss | | X |

*Rent is paid for three months and only one month is included in the financial statements, two months must be taken out of the accounts and moved to the balance sheet until the next accounting periods when it is brought back into the profit & loss account.*

## ❑ Salary

| Salary Analysis | Statement | Debit | Credit |
|---|---|---|---|
| Salaries | Profit & Loss | X | |
| Employer's PRSI | Profit & Loss | X | |
| PAYE/PRSI | Balance Sheet | | X |
| Net Salaries | Balance Sheet | | X |
| Union Subscription | Balance Sheet | | X |
| Pension Deduction | Balance Sheet | | X |

*The gross salary and employer's PRSI are recorded as an expense in the profit & loss account. The PAYE/PRSI needs to be recorded in the balance sheet as a liability until it is paid. The net salary is recorded as a liability until paid. Union subscriptions and pensions deductions are recorded as a liability until the amounts are paid over to third parties.*

## ❏ Accrued Income

| Accrued Income | Statement | Debit | Credit |
|---|---|---|---|
| Accrued Income | Balance Sheet | X | |
| Sales | Profit & Loss | | X |
| *Income has been earned but the invoice has not been issued. The income needs to be recorded in sales and the asset account "accrued income"; which is similar to debtors.* | | | |

## ❏ Deferred Income

| Deferred Income | Statement | Debit | Credit |
|---|---|---|---|
| Sales | Profit & Loss | X | |
| Deferred Income | Balance Sheet | | X |
| *Money has been received in advance of the sale being completed. Sales needs to be reduced and a liability "deferred income" created, which is similar to a creditor.* | | | |

## ❏ Finance Lease

| Lease Set-Up | Statement | Debit | Credit |
|---|---|---|---|
| Fixed Asset | Balance Sheet | X | |
| Lease Creditor Interest | Balance Sheet | X | |
| Lease Creditor | Balance Sheet | | X |
| *This records the purchase of the fixed asset and the liability to the finance lease company, which is made up of capital repayments and lease interest.* | | | |
| **Leased Asset Depreciation** | **Statement** | **Debit** | **Credit** |
| Depreciation | Profit & Loss | X | |
| Accumulated Depreciation | Balance Sheet | | X |
| *The asset needs to be depreciated over its expected life.* | | | |
| **Lease Interest** | **Statement** | **Debit** | **Credit** |
| Lease Interest | Profit & Loss | X | |
| Lease Creditor Interest | Balance Sheet | | X |
| *Interest for the first year is charged to the profit & loss account.* | | | |

(Continued)

| Lease Payment | Statement | Debit | Credit |
|---|---|---|---|
| Lease Creditor | Balance Sheet | X | |
| Bank | Balance Sheet | | X |
| *This records the monthly payment of the lease creditor paid out of the bank account.* | | | |

## ❑ Operating Lease

| Operating Lease (No VAT) | Statement | Debit | Credit |
|---|---|---|---|
| Lease Charge | Profit & Loss | X | |
| Bank Account | Balance Sheet | | X |
| *This records the cost of paying for an operating lease where VAT is NOT charged.* | | | |
| **Operating Lease (VAT)** | **Statement** | **Debit** | **Credit** |
| Lease Charge | Profit & Loss | X | |
| VAT | Balance Sheet | X | |
| Bank Account | Balance Sheet | | X |
| *This records the cost of paying for an operating lease where VAT is being claimed.* | | | |

## ❑ Capital/Drawings

| Sole trader/Partners invests capital | Statement | Debit | Credit |
|---|---|---|---|
| Bank Account | Balance Sheet | X | |
| Capital Account | Balance Sheet | | X |
| *This records the cash invested in the business by the owners.* | | | |
| **Sole trader/Partner takes drawings** | **Statement** | **Debit** | **Credit** |
| Drawings | Balance Sheet | X | |
| Bank Account | Balance Sheet | | X |
| *This records cash being taken out of the business by the owners.* | | | |

Financial statements are a snapshot of a business at a given time. They indicate what the business owns (assets), what it owes (liabilities), the capital and equity in the business, sales, cost of sales, overheads and how much profit or loss the business made. Financial statements are essentially a business management tool because a business will be making decisions based on this information. Financial statements can be prepared monthly, quarterly, half-yearly or annually. Most businesses that only prepare annual financial statements can experience unidentified problems and it is often too late to fix these problems when the financial statements are prepared after the year end.

Why do companies prepare accounts?

- Companies are required by law to prepare a set of accounts comprising of a profit & loss account and balance sheet and to file a set of accounts with the Companies Registration Office.
- Shareholders need to know the financial performance of the company.
- To decide whether to pay a dividend or not.

Where do the figures come from that are included in the financial statements?

- Sources documents—the first rule in accounting is keep a receipt for everything. All transactions are recorded from source documents. If you do not have source documents, the records will be incomplete and transactions will be missing. The accountant will be required to reconstruct the missing information. Examples of source documentation include invoices, bank statements, lodgement books, creditor statements, and credit card statements.
- Source documents are recorded either manually or with the use of computer packages. At the end of the month, all the transactions are totalled (debits must equal credits) and the balance is transferred to the general ledger, which is used to extract the financial statements.

The accounting cycle is set out below.

| |
|---|
| Source documents are recorded into the various journals and balanced at the end of the month. |

| |
|---|
| Monthly balances are transferred into the general ledger, which is then balanced. |

| |
|---|
| The accountant usually prepares other entries called "journal entries" such as depreciation. |

| |
|---|
| A trial balance is prepared; this is the total of debits and credits in the general ledger. |

| |
|---|
| From these figures the financial statements are prepared (annually/quarterly/monthly). |

| |
|---|
| Profit & loss accounts are closed off annually and balance sheet items carried forward to the following year. |

Figure 9.1

## ❑ Financial Statements

Financial statements are the primary means of communicating important accounting information about a business to those who have an interest in the business. The primary statements in the financial statements are the profit & loss account and the balance sheet.

### Profit & Loss Account

The profit & loss account summarises the profit earned and expenses incurred by a business over an accounting period. At the end of the profit & loss account is a statement of the retained profit, which shows the changes in retained profit over an accounting period. See Figure 9.2.

**Rosie Ltd**
**Profit & Loss Account**
**Year ended 31 December 2007**

| | | € |
|---|---|---|
| **Sales** | | |
| Commission | | 70,000 |
| **Expenses** | | |
| Wages | 35,000 | |
| Rent | 4,000 | |
| Office Expenses | 6,500 | |
| Light & Heat | 2,500 | (48,000) |
| Profit before Tax | | 22,000 |
| Corporation Tax | | (2,000) |
| Profit after Tax | | 20,000 |
| Dividends | | (5,000) |
| Profit for the year | | 15,000 |
| Balance at beginning of year | | 20,000 |
| Balance at end of year | | 35,000 |

This figure will be included in the Balance Sheet

Figure 9.2

### *Balance Sheet*

The purpose of a balance sheet is to show the financial position of a business on a certain date, usually the end of the month or year. For this reason it is often called the statement of financial position and is dated as at a specific date, eg **as at 31 December 2007**. The balance sheet presents a view of the business as the holder of resources or assets that are equal to the claims against those assets. The claims consist of the company's liabilities and the shareholders' equity in the company. The date on the balance sheet is a single date whereas the date on the profit & loss account covers a period of time such as a month or year, eg "**Year ended 31 December 2007**".

**Quick Tip**

Financial statements should be reviewed monthly/quarterly so that mistakes can be identified and problem areas reviewed before they get worse. Results of certain strategies and marketing campaigns can be reviewed to identify any changes required.

At the end of the financial statements, the accountant will include notes to the accounts to provide greater details as to how figures were calculated, eg how stock was valued, rates of depreciation used, shareholders loans etc.

## ❑ Trial Balance

The figures included in the financial statements are extracted from the trial balance. Set out in Figure 9.3 is an diagram of a trial balance, which is extracted into a profit & loss account and balance sheet.

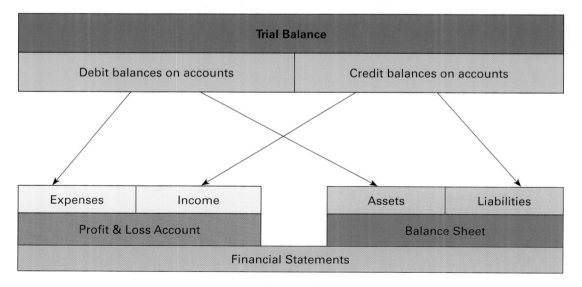

Figure 9.3

Set out in Figure 9.4 is an example of a trial balance that is extracted into a profit & loss account and balance sheet. See Figures 9.5 and 9.6.

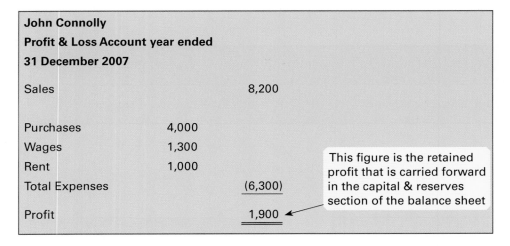

**John Connolly**

**Trial Balance as at 31 December 2007**

| | Debit | Credit | Statement |
|---|---|---|---|
| Bank | 400 | | Balance Sheet |
| Capital | | 500 | Balance Sheet |
| Purchases | 4,000 | | Profit & Loss |
| Creditors | | 200 | Balance Sheet |
| Wages | 1,300 | | Profit & Loss |
| Sales | | 8,200 | Profit & Loss |
| Rent | 1,000 | | Profit & Loss |
| Equipment | 1,500 | | Balance Sheet |
| Debtors | 700 | | Balance Sheet |
| | | | |
| TOTAL | 8,900 | 8,900 | |

These figures must balance

Figure 9.4

**John Connolly**

**Profit & Loss Account year ended**

**31 December 2007**

| | | |
|---|---|---|
| Sales | | 8,200 |
| | | |
| Purchases | 4,000 | |
| Wages | 1,300 | |
| Rent | 1,000 | |
| Total Expenses | | (6,300) |
| | | |
| Profit | | 1,900 |

This figure is the retained profit that is carried forward in the capital & reserves section of the balance sheet

Figure 9.5

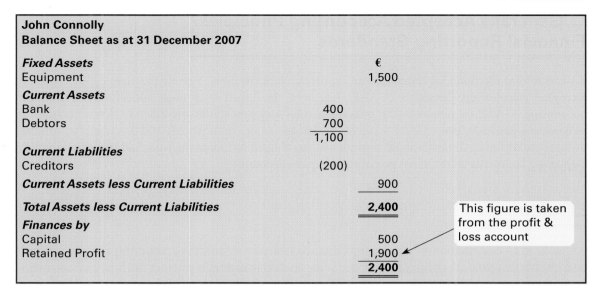

**John Connolly**
**Balance Sheet as at 31 December 2007**

| | | |
|---|---:|---:|
| *Fixed Assets* | | € |
| Equipment | | 1,500 |
| *Current Assets* | | |
| Bank | 400 | |
| Debtors | 700 | |
| | 1,100 | |
| *Current Liabilities* | | |
| Creditors | (200) | |
| *Current Assets less Current Liabilities* | | 900 |
| *Total Assets less Current Liabilities* | | **2,400** |
| *Finances by* | | |
| Capital | | 500 |
| Retained Profit | | 1,900 |
| | | **2,400** |

This figure is taken from the profit & loss account

Figure 9.6

Figure 9.7 sets out graphically how the profit & loss account and Balance Sheet are interlinked to form the Financial Statements.

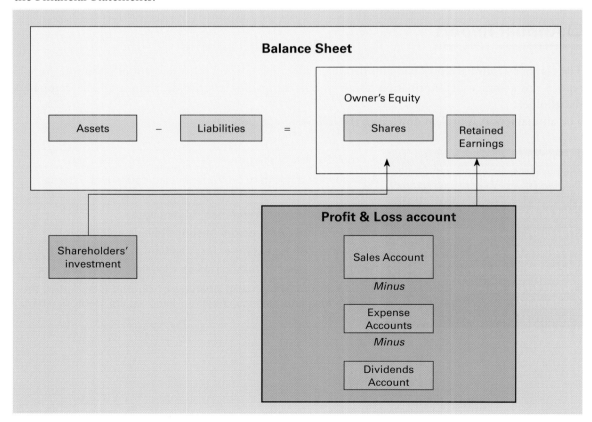

Figure 9.7

## ❑ Generally Accepted Accounting Principles/ Financial Reporting Standards

To ensure that the financial statements are understandable to users, a set of practices called Generally Accepted Accounting Principles (GAAP) has been developed to provide guidelines for financial accounting. GAAP encompasses the principles, rules and procedures necessary to define accounting practice at a particular time. GAAP arises from wide agreement in the theory and practice of accounting at a particular time. All professional accountants are obliged to follow the rules laid down in Financial Reporting Standards (FRS) when preparing company accounts.

## ❑ Audits

An audit is an examination of a company's financial statements and the accounting systems, controls and records that produce them. The purpose of the audit is to ascertain whether the financial statements have been prepared in accordance with GAAP and show a "true and fair" view of the state of affairs of the company. The purpose of an audit is to lend credibility to a set of financial statements. The auditor does not attest to the absolute accuracy of the published information or to the value of the company as an investment. All the auditor gives is an opinion based on appropriate testing of transactions.

## ❑ Annual Report

The company's annual report contains the financial statements and other relevant information. Annual reports are a source of information about public companies and are distributed to the company's shareholders.

The annual report is broken down into the following components:

| Chairman's Statement | A broad review of the progress and changes in strategy. |
|---|---|
| Operating and Financial Review | A detailed commentary on the financial results and external influences. |
| List of Directors | Date of appointment/retirement of directors. |
| Directors' responsibility | A statement of the directors' responsibilities and report. |
| Auditor's report | A statement of the auditors' responsibilities and report. |
| Financial Statements | Profit & loss account, balance sheet, cash flow statements, etc. |
| Notes to the financial statements | Additional breakdown and analysis of figures included in the profit & loss and balance sheet, eg fixed assets, debtors, share capital etc. |

# BALANCE SHEET Chapter 10

A balance sheet is a snapshot at a moment in time. On the one hand, it shows the value of assets owned by the business and on the other it shows who provided the funds with which to finance those assets and to whom the business is ultimately liable.

There are two main types of assets: fixed assets and current assets. Fixed assets are the hardware and the physical assets used by the business itself and are not for sale to customers. Examples of fixed assets include buildings, plant, machinery, vehicles, furniture and fittings.

Current assets include stock, debtors and cash.

Assets can only be bought with funds provided by the owners or borrowed from someone else, eg bank or creditors.

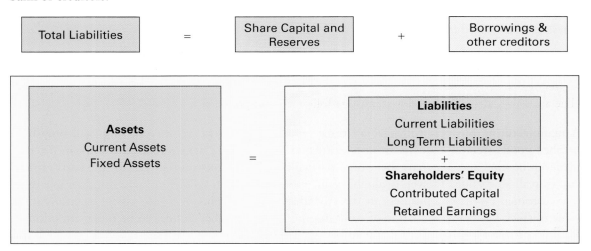

Figure 10.1

## *Assets*

Assets are normally valued at the original cost to the company, which is referred to as historic cost. Sometimes assets are re-valued, eg buildings.

# ❑ Fixed Assets

These assets are held in the business for use rather than for resale and can be regarded as long-term assets to be used for a number of years. They are normally shown in the balance sheet at cost reduced by depreciation, which is written off to the profit & loss account. Depreciation spreads the original cost of the asset over its expected life so that the profit & loss account for any period accounts for a fair share of the original cost of the fixed assets. As a result, the value of fixed assets in the balance sheet may not reflect their saleable vale at the time because of inflation or because of changing technologies. (See Chapter 12 for additional details.)

# ❑ Current Assets

These are the short-term assets which are already cash or which will be turned back into cash in the course of normal trading activity. Current assets include stock, debtors and cash.

## *Stocks*

These can be divided into three groups:

1. Raw materials
2. Work in progress
3. Finished goods

A manufacturing business will have all three types of stock, whereas a retail shop will only have finished goods. Service industry businesses such as an architect's firm would have work in progress made up of time and materials spent on a particular project. Stocks are valued on the basis of their cost or realisable value, if lower. Realisable value means their value to the business, not their sale value to a customer. Profits of a business are directly affected by the value of closing stock, especially if the value of stock has fallen. Valuation of work in progress and finished goods can be more complicated. Work in progress would include direct costs (such as labour and materials) used to make the item and a share of the overheads used to produce the item. (See Chapter 14 for additional details.)

## *Debtors*

Debtors arise when firms sell on credit to customers who do not have to pay immediately for goods and services purchased. Trade debtors are the total value of customer invoices outstanding at the date of the balance sheet. A small adjustment is made to this value to reflect the fact that some customers may not pay their debts. Usually, this is because of a dispute about the goods or services delivered which can arise at a later date. Some customers may go into liquidation. The provision for bad debts is charged as an expense in the profit & loss account and the total value of the debtors is reduced in the balance sheet. (See Chapter 13 for additional details.)

## Cash

Includes cash in tills, petty cash, deposit accounts and the current account, if there is money in the account. If the current account is overdrawn, the figure will appear in current liabilities.

## Balance Sheet Sequence

Fixed assets are listed in the following sequence:

- Land and buildings.
- Plant and equipment.
- Motor vehicles.
- Fixtures and fittings.

The sequence for current assets is as follows:

- Stocks.
- Debtors.
- Cash.

# ❑ Liabilities

Refers to where the business gets the money to fund the business. Categories include the following:

## Shareholders' Equity

This consists of the issued share capital and reserves of various kinds. It represents the amount of money that shareholders have invested directly into the company by buying shares together with retained profits that belong to the shareholders.
Components of equity are:

- Contributed capital—shareholders' investment in the company.
- Retained earnings—the earnings of the company since it commenced trading less any losses and dividends.

## Ordinary Shares

These shares form the bulk of shares issued by most companies. Ordinary shares have no fixed right to dividends. A company does not have to issue all of its authorised shares at once. The total amount of shares that it is authorised to issue must be disclosed in the accounts but only the issued share capital is accounted for in the balance sheet.

## Preference Shares

Preference shareholder usually receives a certain amount of dividends before ordinary shareholders can receive anything. The amount that preference shareholders must be paid before ordinary shareholders can be paid is usually stated as a percentage of the value of the preference share. If the preference share is non-cumulative and the board does not declare a dividend in any given year, the company is under no obligation to make up the missed dividend in future years. If the preference share is cumulative, the dividend amount per share accumulates from year to year and the company must pay the whole amount before it pays any dividend to ordinary shareholders.

## Reserves

Reserves are the profits that have been retained in the company as extra capital. It does not mean money in bank accounts. The main categories of reserves are:

- Retained earnings are the profits earned by the business since it commenced trading, minus any losses or dividends paid to shareholders. The existence of retained earnings means that assets generated by profitable operations have been kept in the company to help it grow or meet other business needs.
- Revaluation reserve is the paper profit that can arise if certain assets are revalued to current price levels without the asset concerned being sold.
- Share premium account will occur if a shareholder pays more than the nominal face value for their shares.

## Creditors

Creditors are normally divided into creditors due within one year and creditors due after one year.

Creditors due within one year would cover the following:

- Bank overdraft. (See Chapter 15)
- Term loan. (See Chapter 15)
- Trade creditors. (See Chapter 17)
- Accruals. (See Chapter 17)
- Finance lease. (See Chapter 20)
- PAYE/PRSI. (See Chapter 23)
- VAT. (See Chapter 18)
- Dividends.

Creditors due after one year would include the amount of the term loan, mortgage or finance lease that is due after one year.

A balance sheet gives information about a firm's financial position in terms of what it owes and what it owns. These facts are relevant to one point in time only: the date shown on the balance sheet. Furthermore, a balance sheet fulfils two important functions in the life of a company: it records the firm's liabilities and assets at the end of a trading period and it forms the starting point for the next trading period in that it shows what is available for use in that period. The link between two successive balance sheets is the profit & loss account. Thus the profit & loss account forms a bridge between two balance sheets and records the operational details of how the firm proceeds from 31/12/07 to 31/12/08, see Figure 10.2.

| Balance Sheet as at 31/12/07 | | Profit & Loss Account for the year ended 31/12/08 | | Balance Sheet as at 31/12/08 | |
|---|---|---|---|---|---|
| Balance Sheet 1 | | Profit & Loss Account | | Balance Sheet 2 | |
| Assets | Liabilities | Income | Expenditure | Assets | Liabilities |
| Land & Buildings | Shares | Sales | Overheads | Land & Buildings | Shares |
| Equipment | Reserves | Rent income | Goods purchased | Equipment | Reserves |
| Debtors | Loans | Interest received | Interest paid | Debtors | Loans |
| Cash | Creditors | Dividend received | | Cash | Creditors |
| Stock | Bank overdraft | Retained profit | | Stock | Bank overdraft |
| Shows the assets and liabilities available for use at the start of the financial year. | | Shows how the profit arose from the firm's trading operations during the year. | | Shows how the assets at the start of the year have changed as a result of the trading activities included in the profit & loss account. | |

Figure 10.2

# PROFIT & LOSS ACCOUNT   Chapter 11

A profit & loss account is a summary of the firm's trading income from its customers, offset by the cost of goods or services sold and other running expenses for the same period of time.

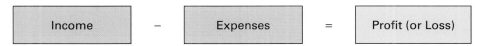

Not-for-profit organisations call a profit & loss account an "income and expenditure" account. Both are prepared on the same principles. Non-profit-seeking organisations use the term "surplus or deficit" in place of "profit or loss".

Income is mainly as sales to customers but also includes rent or investment income received. The realisation principle states that income is recorded when delivery of goods or services takes place and not at the time cash is actually received in settlement of sales made on credit.

Expenses are the cost of wages, materials and overheads used up during the same period. Accountants refer to running or operating costs as "revenue expenditure" to distinguish them from the cost of new physical assets, such as buildings, equipment and vehicles. The acquisition cost of these assets is referred to as "capital expenditure".

There are two tests as to whether an expense is recognised in the profit & loss account:

1. The expense must relate to the time period covered by the profit & loss account irrespective of whether payment has been made.
2. The expenses must match the sales income in the same statement; for example, rent for January 2008 would not be included in the profit & loss account for the year ended 31 December 2007.

It is a common misconception to think of the profit & loss account as a summary of all **cash** flowing into and out of the business and that the excess of cash receipts over payments represent the profit. A loan is a cash receipt but it cannot be counted as income in the profit & loss account as it must be repaid at some future time. When the loan is repaid, that repayment is not an expense in the profit & loss account but a reduction in the "cash" asset and the loan account.

Set out in Figure 11.1 is an example of the layout for the profit & loss account for a service company and a manufacturing company.

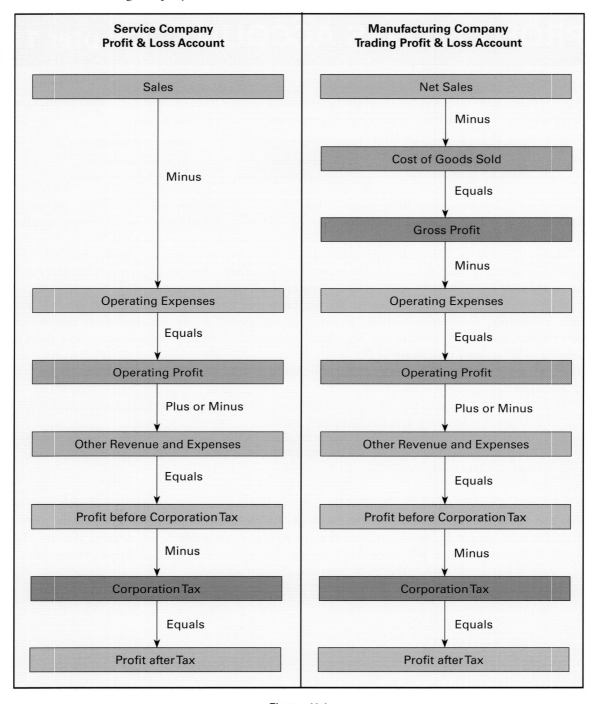

Figure 11.1

Set out in Figure 11.2 is an example of a manufacturing trading profit & loss account.

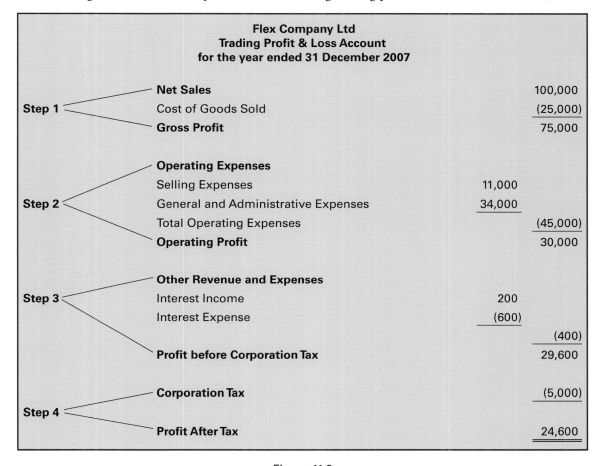

**Flex Company Ltd**
**Trading Profit & Loss Account**
**for the year ended 31 December 2007**

| | | | |
|---|---|---|---|
| | **Net Sales** | | 100,000 |
| Step 1 | Cost of Goods Sold | | (25,000) |
| | **Gross Profit** | | 75,000 |
| | | | |
| | **Operating Expenses** | | |
| | Selling Expenses | 11,000 | |
| Step 2 | General and Administrative Expenses | 34,000 | |
| | Total Operating Expenses | | (45,000) |
| | **Operating Profit** | | 30,000 |
| | | | |
| | **Other Revenue and Expenses** | | |
| Step 3 | Interest Income | 200 | |
| | Interest Expense | (600) | |
| | | | (400) |
| | **Profit before Corporation Tax** | | 29,600 |
| | | | |
| | **Corporation Tax** | | (5,000) |
| Step 4 | | | |
| | **Profit After Tax** | | 24,600 |

Figure 11.2

- **Step 1** involves calculating the gross profit, which is the difference between net sales and the cost of goods sold. To be successful, companies must achieve a gross profit sufficient to cover operating expenses and provide an adequate after-tax profit.
- **Step 2** involves deducting all the operating expenses, which are expenses incurred in running a business, other than the cost of goods sold. Operating expenses are often grouped into categories of "selling expenses" and "general and administrative expenses". Selling expenses include the cost of storing goods and preparing them for sale, eg advertising. General and administrative expenses include expenses for accounting, personnel, etc.
- **Step 3** involves identifying interest due and interest received.
- **Step 4** involves the calculation of corporation tax. Corporation tax is shown as a separate item on the profit & loss account.

This chapter sets out the accounting treatment for fixed assets, depreciation, profit or loss on disposal and an example of a fixed asset register and controls required for fixed assets.

## ❏ Accounting Treatment for Fixed Assets

The term fixed asset describes the firm's investment in long-lived assets: physical assets that the firm still possesses and which are expected to continue contributing to its profit in future years. Fixed assets are capital expenditure; capital expenditure is identified if at the time of the purchase it was the intention to use it for a period longer than one year. Capital expenditure is recorded in a fixed asset account because it benefits future accounting periods. Revenue expenditure is an expenditure made for the ordinary repair and maintenance needed to keep a fixed asset in good operating condition. Expenditure of this type is recorded in an expense account because the benefits are realised in the current period.

### Types of Assets

Fixed assets consist of assets that are used to create the setting (eg land and buildings), facilitate production processes (eg plant & machinery) or support the administration of a business (eg computers).

Land—The purchase price of land should be **debited** to the "land" account. Other expenditure that should be debited to this account includes auctioneering and legal fees connected with the purchase of land.

Buildings—when a company buys a building, the cost includes the purchase price and other expenditure required to put the building in a usable condition. The costs should be **debited** to the "building" account.

Leasehold improvements—if a tenant installs light fittings, carpets or partitions these would be considered a leasehold improvement. These improvements are usually classified as fixed assets in the leasehold improvement account in the balance sheet. The cost should be **debited** to the "leasehold improvement" account.

Plant & Machinery/Computers—includes all expenditure connected with purchasing the equipment and preparing it for use and should be **debited** to the "plant & machinery/computer" account.

### Matching Rule

When a company records expenditure as a long-term asset, it is deferring the expense until a later period. The current period's profitability looks better than it would if the expenditure had been expended immediately.

The following questions should be asked in relation to fixed assets:

1. How is the cost of the fixed asset determined?
2. How should the cost of the fixed asset be allocated over time?
3. How should subsequent expenditure such as repairs and additions be treated?
4. How should disposals of the long-term asset be recorded?

The distinction between capital and revenue expenditure is important in applying the matching rule. If the purchase of a machine that will benefit a business for several years is mistakenly recorded as revenue expenditure and included as an expense in the profit & loss account, this will result in net profits being lower in the current accounting period and in future accounting periods being higher. If, on the other hand, revenue expenditure such as the repair of a machine is mistakenly included in fixed assets, expenses in the current period will be understated. Many companies establish policies to define when expenditure should be recorded as an expense or as an asset. For example, small expenses for items which qualify as fixed assets may be treated as expenses because the amounts involved are not material in relation to net profit.

Fixed assets last for a number of years and it would be unfair to charge the whole purchase cost against one month's or one year's profit. This problem is overcome by simply charging a portion of the cost in each profit & loss account over the whole life of the asset. Set out in Figure 12.1 is an example of how the profit figure would be distorted if the fixed asset were written off as an expense in Year 1 (Option 1) rather than depreciating the asset over three years (Option 2).

| Option 1 | | Option 2 | | |
|---|---|---|---|---|
| Fixed asset charged to Profit & Loss Account | | Fixed Asset depreciated over 3 years | | |
| | € | € | € | € |
| Sales | 10,000 | 10,000 | 10,000 | 10,000 |
| Less: Cost of sales | (3,000) | (3,000) | (3,000) | (3,000) |
| Gross Profit | 7,000 | 7,000 | 7,000 | 7,000 |
| *Less Expenses* | | | | |
| **Fixed Asset Cost** | **(3,000)** | – | – | – |
| **Depreciation** | – | **(1,000)** | **(1,000)** | **(1,000)** |
| Salary | (3,000) | (3,000) | (3,000) | (3,000) |
| Light & Heat | (500) | (500) | (500) | (500) |
| Insurance | (600) | (600) | (600) | (600) |
| Printing, Postage & Stationery | (400) | (400) | (400) | (400) |
| Rent | (500) | (500) | (500) | (500) |
| Advertising | (500) | (500) | (500) | (500) |
| Expenses | (8,500) | (6,500) | (6,500) | (6,500) |
| Profit/(Loss) | **(1,500)** | **500** | **500** | **500** |

Figure 12.1

The term "fixed assets at valuation" recognises that some businesses revise the book values of their fixed assets so as to bring them more into line with their current prices. This process is termed "revaluing" the fixed assets. Where assets are revalued, the annual depreciation charge will be based upon the revalued figures and will therefore increase. Following the recording of more realistic fixed asset values in the balance sheet, the company's power to borrow may be enhanced, resulting from greater asset values being available to act as security for additional borrowings.

# ❏ What is Depreciation?

Depreciation is the periodic allocation of the cost of a fixed asset over the asset's estimated useful life. All fixed assets except land, have a useful life and the cost of these assets must be distributed over the years that benefit. Assets physically deteriorate but periodic repairs and a good maintenance policy may keep buildings and equipment in good operating order. Certain fixed assets, such as computers, can go out of date. Depreciation refers to the allocation of the cost of fixed assets to the periods that benefit from the asset, not to the asset's physical deterioration or decrease in value. The term depreciation describes the gradual conversion of the cost of the asset into an expense.

## *Factors in Computing Depreciation*

- Cost—this is the purchase price of an asset plus all reasonable and necessary expenditure to get it in place and ready for use.
- Residual value—this is an asset's estimated scrap, salvage or trade-in value on the estimated date of disposal. Residual value is the portion of an asset's acquisition cost that a company expects to recover when it trades-in the asset.
- Depreciable cost—this is an asset's cost less its residual value.
- Estimated useful life—this is the total number of years of use expected from a fixed asset.

The accumulated depreciation included in the balance sheet is a proportion of the original asset's costs or valuation consumed to date. Included in the profit & loss account will be the depreciation relating to each of the years during which the firm owned the fixed assets. The addition of these separate yearly depreciation charges produces the accumulated depreciation amount.

If a fixed asset is capitalised and depreciated there will be two accounts for each type of asset that go into the balance sheet.

- Fixed Asset Cost Account (Dr).
- Fixed Asset Accumulated Depreciation (Cr).

There will also be a depreciation expense account that feeds into the profit & loss account. An asset cannot be depreciated beyond nil value.

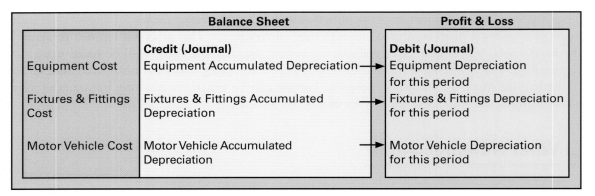

Figure 12.2

Set out in Figure 12.3 is a graphical presentation of how a depreciation charge of €2,000 is portrayed in the profit & loss account and how that the amount accumulated in the balance sheet increases by €2,000 each year.

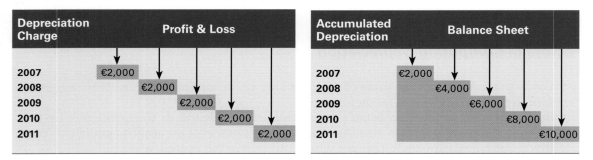

Figure 12.3

## ❑ Methods for Calculating Depreciation

There are three main methods for calculating depreciation:

### Straight-Line Method

- The straight-line method charges the same amount of depreciation in Year 1 as in Year 3; it assumes that the asset depreciates at the same rate each year.
- When the straight-line method is used to calculate depreciation, the asset's depreciable cost is spread evenly over the estimated useful life of the asset. The straight-line method is based on the assumption that depreciation depends only on the passage of time. The depreciation expense for each period is computed by dividing the depreciable cost by the number of accounting periods in the asset's estimated useful life. The rate of depreciation is the same each year.

## *The Production Method*

- The production method allocates depreciation for machinery based on annual usage of the machine.
- The production method is based on the assumption that depreciation is solely the result of use and that the passage of time plays no role in the process. The amount of depreciation each year is directly related to the units used.

## *Reducing Balance Method*

- The reducing balance method charges a larger amount of depreciation in the earlier years and reduces this amount in later years. The asset will never get to zero until it is scrapped.
- The reducing balance method of depreciation results in relatively large amounts of depreciation in the early years of an asset's life and smaller amounts in later years. This type of method, which is based on the passage of time, assumes that fixed assets are most efficient when new and so provide the greatest benefits in their early years. An argument in favour of using the reducing balance method is that repair expenses are likely to increase as an asset ages. The reducing balance method is appropriate for assets that provide the greatest benefits in their earlier years. Under the reducing balance method depreciation charges will be highest in years when revenue generation from the asset is highest.

## *Capital Allowances*

If a fixed asset is depreciated at a high rate, this will not result in a lower tax liability, as the Revenue ignores the amount of depreciation included in the financial statements and instead will allow capital allowances in the business's tax computation. Capital allowances are determined by tax law.

| Capital Allowance rates | |
|---|---|
| Industrial Building | 4% |
| Plant & Machinery | 12.5% |
| Motor Vehicles | 12.5% |

### Example—Straight-Line Method
A computer server costs €12,500 and is expected to last three years with a residual cost of €500.
Cost – residual value = €12,500 – €500 = €12,000
Estimated useful life: three years, annual depreciation €12,000/3 = €4,000.

|         | Cost € | Straight-line Depreciation € | Accumulated Depreciation € | Net Book Value € |
|---------|--------|------------------------------|----------------------------|------------------|
|         | 12,500 |                              |                            | 12,500           |
| Year 1  | 12,500 | 4,000                        | 4,000                      | 8,500            |
| Year 2  | 12,500 | 4,000                        | 8,000                      | 4,500            |
| Year 3  | 12,500 | 4,000                        | 12,000                     | 500              |

Residual Cost

## Example—Production Method

If a truck is capable of driving 100,000km, cost €100,000 and has a residual value of nil, then it will be depreciated at €1 per km.

$$\frac{\text{Cost} - \text{Residual Value}}{\text{Estimated Units of Useful life}} \qquad \frac{€100,000 - 0}{100,000\text{km}} = €1 \text{ euro per km}$$

|         | Cost € | Kilometres | Production Method Depreciation € | Accumulated Depreciation € | Net Book Value € |
|---------|--------|------------|----------------------------------|----------------------------|------------------|
|         | 100,000 |           |                                  |                            | 100,000          |
| Year 1  | 100,000 | 40,000    | 40,000                           | 40,000                     | 60,000           |
| Year 2  | 100,000 | 30,000    | 30,000                           | 70,000                     | 30,000           |
| Year 3  | 100,000 | 30,000    | 30,000                           | 100,000                    | –                |

## Example—Reducing Balance Method

An asset costs €10,000 and is depreciated at 20% reducing balance.

|         | Cost € | Reducing Balance Calculation | Reducing Balance Depreciation € | Accumulated Depreciation € | Net Book Value € |
|---------|--------|------------------------------|----------------------------------|----------------------------|------------------|
|         | 10,000 |                              |                                  |                            | 10,000           |
| Year 1  | 10,000 | (20% × €10,000)              | 2,000                            | 2,000                      | 8,000            |
| Year 2  | 10,000 | (20% × €8,000)               | 1,600                            | 3,600                      | 6,400            |
| Year 3  | 10,000 | (20% × €6,400)               | 1,280                            | 4,880                      | 5,120            |
| Year 4  | 10,000 | (20% × €5,120)               | 1,024                            | 5,904                      | 4,096            |
| Year 5  | 10,000 | (20% × €4,096)               | 819                              | 6,723                      | 3,277            |

**Note:** the calculation of depreciation will continue until the asset's net book value approaches zero.

Assume an asset costing €10,000 is purchased in Year 1. Set out below is a comparison of how the depreciation will be different depending on whether depreciation is calculated using the straight-line or reducing balance method. Under the reducing balance method, the depreciation charge is the same for the first year as the straight-line method. After the first year, the straight-line depreciation is greater than the reducing balance method. See Figure 12.4.

| | Straight line depreciation method 20% | Accumulated Depreciation | Net Book Value | | Reducing balance method 20% | Accumulated Depreciation | Net Book Value |
|---|---|---|---|---|---|---|---|
| | € | € | € | | € | € | € |
| Cost | 10,000 | | | | 10,000 | | |
| Year 1 | 2,000 | 2,000 | 8,000 | | 2,000 | 2,000 | 8,000 |
| Year 2 | 2,000 | 4,000 | 6,000 | | 1,600 | 3,600 | 6,400 |
| Year 3 | 2,000 | 6,000 | 4,000 | | 1,280 | 4,880 | 5,120 |
| Year 4 | 2,000 | 8,000 | 2,000 | | 1,024 | 5,904 | 4,096 |
| Year 5 | 2,000 | 10,000 | – | | 819 | 6,723 | 3,277 |
| Year 6 | – | – | – | | 655 | 7,378 | 2,622 |
| Year 7 | – | – | – | | 524 | 7,902 | 2,098 |
| Year 8 | – | – | – | | 420 | 8,322 | 1,678 |

Figure 12.4

# ❑ Profit or Loss on Disposal

If a fixed asset is disposed of, how is the cost of the asset and the accumulated depreciation removed from the books?

1. Identify the asset being sold.
2. How much did it cost?
3. When was it purchased? Can you identify it in the financial statements as an addition?
4. How much was it sold for? Was it scrapped?

**Example—Loss or disposal**
An asset cost €10,000 on 1 January 2005 and is depreciated at 20% straight line in 2005 and 2006. The asset is sold on 30 June 2007 for €1,000.

| Date | | € | |
|---|---|---|---|
| 01/01/2005 | Cost | 10,000 | |
| 31/12/2006 | Accumulated Depreciation | (4,000) | (10,000 × 20% × 2 years) |
| 31/12/2006 | Net Book Value | 6,000 | (Cost – Accumulated Depreciation) |
| 30/06/2007 | Proceeds | 1,000 | |
| | Loss on disposal | (5,000) | |

The asset is worth €6,000 (net book value) but sold for only €1,000. Therefore there is a loss on disposal of €5,000.

The steps necessary are set out below. The figures in black are the balances before the disposal, and the figures in red are the journals necessary to record the disposal.

| Fixed Asset | | | | | Fixed Asset Accumulated Depreciation | | | | |
|---|---|---|---|---|---|---|---|---|---|
| 1 Jan 05 | Bank | 10,000 | 30 Jun 07 Disposal | 10,000 | 30 Jun 07 Disposal | 4,000 | 31 Dec 05 Depreciation | 2,000 | |
| | | | | | | | 31 Dec 06 Depreciation | 2,000 | |
| | | 10,000 | | 10,000 | | 4,000 | | 4,000 | |

| Bank | | | | | Disposal Account | | | | |
|---|---|---|---|---|---|---|---|---|---|
| 30 Jun 07 Disposal | 1,000 | 1 Jan 05 Fixed Asset | 10,000 | | 30 Jun 07 Fixed Asset | 10,000 | 30 Jun 07 Accumulated Depreciation | 4,000 | |
| | | | | | | | 30 Jun 07 Bank | 1,000 | |
| | | | | | | | 30 Jun 07 Loss | 5,000 | |
| | | | | | | 10,000 | | 10,000 | |

| Loss on Disposal (P&L) | | | Fixed Asset Depreciation | | |
|---|---|---|---|---|---|
| 30 Jun 07 Disposal | 5,000 | | 31 Dec 05 Accumulated Depreciation | 2,000 | |
| | | | 31 Dec 06 Accumulated Depreciation | 2,000 | |

## Example of Fixed Asset Disposals

When an asset is disposed of, the business must bring the depreciation up to date and remove all evidence of ownership of the asset, including the accumulated depreciation.

An asset cost €10,000 having accumulated depreciation of €4,000. When an asset is sold for cash, a gain or loss equals the cash received minus the carrying value of the asset.

### Example—No profit or loss on disposal

Assume the asset is sold for €6,000 (ie the carrying value) on 4 February 2007, the accounting treatment is as follows:

| 4 Feb | Account | Statement | Debit | Credit |
|---|---|---|---|---|
| | Fixed Asset | Balance Sheet | | 10,000 |
| | Disposal A/c | Profit & Loss | 10,000 | |
| | Accumulated Depreciation | Balance Sheet | 4,000 | |
| | Disposal A/c | Profit & Loss | | 4,000 |
| | Bank A/c | Balance Sheet | 6,000 | |
| | Disposal A/c | Profit & Loss | | 6,000 |

## Example—Loss on Disposal

Assume that the asset is sold for €2,000 on 4 February 2007, which is less than the carrying value (€6,000); this will result in a loss, the accounting treatment is as follows:

| 4 Feb | Account | Statement | Debit | Credit |
|---|---|---|---|---|
| | Fixed Asset | Balance Sheet | | 10,000 |
| | Disposal A/c | Profit & Loss | 10,000 | |
| | Accumulated Depreciation | Balance Sheet | 4,000 | |
| | Disposal A/c | Profit & Loss | | 4,000 |
| | Bank A/c | Balance Sheet | 2,000 | |
| | Disposal A/c | Profit & Loss | | 2,000 |
| | Loss on Disposal | Profit & Loss | 4,000 | |
| | Disposal A/c | Profit & Loss | | 4,000 |

## Example—Gain on Disposal

Assume that the asset is sold for €8,000 on 4 February 2007, which is more than the carrying value (€6,000); this will result in a gain on disposal of €2,000.

| 4 Feb | Account | Statement | Debit | Credit |
|---|---|---|---|---|
| | Fixed Asset | Balance Sheet | | 10,000 |
| | Disposal A/c | Profit & Loss | 10,000 | |
| | Accumulated Depreciation | Balance Sheet | 4,000 | |
| | Disposal A/c | Profit & Loss | | 4,000 |
| | Bank A/c | Balance Sheet | 8,000 | |
| | Disposal A/c | Profit & Loss | | 8,000 |
| | Gain on Disposal | Profit & Loss | | 2,000 |
| | Disposal A/c | Profit & Loss | 2,000 | |

In order to determine whether a disposal of a fixed asset will result in a profit or loss on disposal, the net book value must be compared to the sales proceeds. If the proceeds are greater than the net book value, this will result in a profit on disposal whereas if the proceeds are less than the net book value then this will result in a loss on disposal, see Figure 12.5.

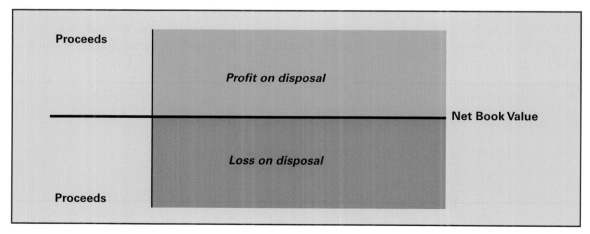

Figure 12.5

## Disclosure of Fixed Assets in Financial Statements

A note will be included in the financial statements to show the breakdown of the opening cost and accumulated depreciation for each category of fixed assets together with any additions and disposals of assets during the year. Set out in Figure 12.6 is an example of a fixed asset note that would appear in the financial statements.

| | Computer Equipment | Fixtures & Fittings | Office Equipment | Motor Vehicles | Total | |
|---|---|---|---|---|---|---|
| | € | € | € | € | € | |
| **Cost** | | | | | | |
| At 1 January 2007 | 6,000 | 16,000 | 22,000 | 20,000 | 64,000 | These values come from the financial statements of the previous year. |
| Additions | 1,500 | – | – | – | 1,500 | |
| Disposals | – | – | – | – | – | |
| At 31 December 2007 | 7,500 | 16,000 | 22,000 | 20,000 | 65,500 | These values come from the financial statements of the previous year. |
| **Depreciation** | | | | | | |
| At 1 January 2007 | 4,000 | 6,400 | 8,800 | 8,000 | 27,200 | |
| Charge | 2,500 | 3,200 | 4,400 | 4,000 | 14,100 | |
| Disposals | – | – | – | – | – | |
| At 31 December 2007 | 6,500 | 9,600 | 13,200 | 12,000 | 41,300 | |
| **Net Book Value** | | | | | | These values come from the financial statements of the previous year. |
| At 31 December 2007 | 1,000 | 6,400 | 8,800 | 8,000 | 24,200 | |
| At 31 December 2006 | 2,000 | 9,600 | 13,200 | 12,000 | 36,800 | |

Figure 12.6

Also included in the financial statements will be a fixed asset accounting policy which includes the rate of depreciation used for each group of fixed assets. Set out below is an example of an accounting policy note.

| Fixed assets are stated at cost less accumulated depreciation. Depreciation is calculated in order to write off fixed assets on a straight-line basis at the following annual rates: | |
|---|---|
| Fixtures and Fittings | 20% |
| Office Equipment | 20% |
| Computer Equipment | $33\frac{1}{3}\%$ |
| Motor Vehicles | 20% |

## ❑ Fixed Asset Register

Most businesses own some form of fixed assets. Good practice requires that a fixed asset register is set up and maintained regularly. The fixed asset register is a record of all of the fixed assets of the business, their value and location (this usually only includes fixed assets over a certain threshold, eg €250). This information is important for keeping control of the assets, providing figures for the annual financial statements and recording depreciation or a deduction in value of an asset. All assets should be tagged with a fixed asset number. A spot check should be carried out every six months to ensure that the assets included on the fixed asset register matches the physical assets held by the business. If an item is destroyed or stolen, it will have to be removed from the register.

A fixed asset register can help keep track of:

- The supplier of the asset.
- The estimated life of the asset.
- The method of depreciation and the rate that is applied.
- The original cost, annual depreciation and accumulated depreciation.
- Insurance details.
- Major repairs and maintenance.
- The method and proceeds of disposal or sale of the asset.

Set out in Figure 12.7 is an example of a fixed asset register:

## Fixed Asset Register

| Date of Purchase | Supplier | Location | Person Responsible | Tag Number | Model | Description | Cost | Computer Equipment 20% Straight Line Depreciation | Fixtures & Fittings 12.5% Straight Line Depreciation | Office Equipment 20% Straight Line Depreciation | Depreciation 2006 |
|---|---|---|---|---|---|---|---|---|---|---|---|
| *Mar 06* | Computers Ltd | Finance Dept | T.Clarke | 1 | 1000SX | Optiplex Laptop | 3,000 | 3,000 | | | 600 |
| *Aug 06* | Topfurn Ltd | Reception | M.Burke | 2 | 5009A | Office Desk | 1,000 | | 1,000 | | 125 |
| *Sep 06* | Easyprint Ltd | Admin Dept | M.Burke | 3 | 126660 | Printer/ Photocopier | 5,600 | | | 5,600 | 1,120 |
| *Oct 07* | FileCabs PLC | CEO Office | S.Smyth | 4 | 700LFC | Filing Cabinet | 750 | | 750 | | – |
| *Oct 07* | Fastprint Ltd | Reception | M.Burke | 5 | 720F | Laser Printer | 450 | 450 | | | – |
| *Total* | | | | | | € | 10,800 | 3,450 | 1,750 | 5,600 | 1,845 |

Figure 12.7

Calculation of depreciation:

- Optiplex laptop cost €3,000 in 2006; depreciation rate 20% straight-line
  €3,000 × 20% = €600

- Office equipment cost €1,000 in 2006; depreciation rate 12.5% straight-line
  €1,000 × 12.5% = €125

- Printer/photocopier cost €5,600 in 2006; depreciation rate 20% straight-line
  €5,600 × 20% = €1,120

**Note:** *depreciation of assets purchased in 2007 will be calculated at the end of 2007.*

Each asset is listed separately so that depreciation can be recorded for each individual asset, eg asset Number 002, rather than categories of assets, eg fixtures & fittings.

**Quick Tip**

All fixed assets should be tagged with a number for identification purposes; this number should correspond to the number included on the fixed assets register.

## ❏ Fixed Asset Controls

- Capital expenditure should be properly planned, budgeted, approved and authorised by management.
- Expenditure is correctly identified as capital expenditure.
- Every year, a charge is included in the profit & loss account for depreciation. The charging of depreciation is a book entry and does not involve cash.
- An annual review of assets for disposals should be carried out.
- The disposal proceeds received for an asset should be properly recorded as a sale of asset.
- A fixed asset register should be maintained and reconciled to the annual accounts.
- The fixed assets must be adequately protected on site and, at least once a year, a spot check/verification of fixed assets should be carried out.
- All the assets listed on the balance sheet should be adequately insured.

This chapter sets out the accounting treatment for debtors, the calculation of bad debts and the identification of prepayments. Debtors are included as part of current assets in the balance sheet.

## ❏ Trade Debtors

"Trade debtors" is the amount of money the company expects to receive from those who have purchased its goods or services on credit. Where the settlement of any of these debts appears to be in doubt, or where some reduction in the amounts is expected, the value of those debtors should be reduced in the balance sheet.

If a business sells to its customer on credit, ie the customer does not pay for the goods/services immediately, the balance is included in the balance sheet to show that the business is owed money. Debtors are analysed based on how long the debt is outstanding. Set out in Figure 13.1 is an example of an aged debtor listing. Aged debtor analysis shows the age of all outstanding debts and how much is owed. This information is valuable for monitoring potential bad debts and for collection purposes.

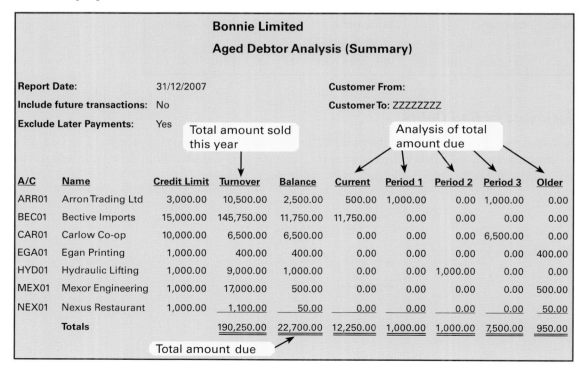

**Bonnie Limited**

**Aged Debtor Analysis (Summary)**

| Report Date: | 31/12/2007 | Customer From: | |
| Include future transactions: | No | Customer To: ZZZZZZZZ | |
| Exclude Later Payments: | Yes | | |

Total amount sold this year

Analysis of total amount due

| A/C | Name | Credit Limit | Turnover | Balance | Current | Period 1 | Period 2 | Period 3 | Older |
|---|---|---|---|---|---|---|---|---|---|
| ARR01 | Arron Trading Ltd | 3,000.00 | 10,500.00 | 2,500.00 | 500.00 | 1,000.00 | 0.00 | 1,000.00 | 0.00 |
| BEC01 | Bective Imports | 15,000.00 | 145,750.00 | 11,750.00 | 11,750.00 | 0.00 | 0.00 | 0.00 | 0.00 |
| CAR01 | Carlow Co-op | 10,000.00 | 6,500.00 | 6,500.00 | 0.00 | 0.00 | 0.00 | 6,500.00 | 0.00 |
| EGA01 | Egan Printing | 1,000.00 | 400.00 | 400.00 | 0.00 | 0.00 | 0.00 | 0.00 | 400.00 |
| HYD01 | Hydraulic Lifting | 1,000.00 | 9,000.00 | 1,000.00 | 0.00 | 0.00 | 1,000.00 | 0.00 | 0.00 |
| MEX01 | Mexor Engineering | 1,000.00 | 17,000.00 | 500.00 | 0.00 | 0.00 | 0.00 | 0.00 | 500.00 |
| NEX01 | Nexus Restaurant | 1,000.00 | 1,100.00 | 50.00 | 0.00 | 0.00 | 0.00 | 0.00 | 50.00 |
| | **Totals** | | 190,250.00 | 22,700.00 | 12,250.00 | 1,000.00 | 1,000.00 | 7,500.00 | 950.00 |

Total amount due

Figure 13.1

## Interpretation of Aged Debtor Analysis

A credit limit is set for each debtor showing the amount of credit the business is prepared to extend to the debtor. The credit limit is based on their credit history. Limits are set so that too much credit is not given to businesses that may be unable to pay. The "Turnover" figure is the amount that the individual debtor has purchased from Bonnie Limited since the start of the financial year. The "Balance" is the total amount outstanding that is analysed into categories such as "Current" (less than 30 days), "Period 1" (30–60 days), "Period 2" (60–90 days), "Period 3" (90–120 days) and then "Older". This analysis can be useful in identifying potential bad debts; eg Egan Printing has gone into liquidation and it is unlikely that the €400 owed will be received; therefore this will be written off as a bad debt in the profit & loss account.

> **Quick Tip**
>
> Consider including your bank details on sales invoices so that customer can pay the money owed directly into your bank account, in order to improve your cash flow.

## ❑ Bad Debts

Losses from credit sales should be recognised at the time the sales are made so that they are matched to the revenue they generate. Set out below is an example of how the bad debt from Egan Printing of €400 is being written off against the profit & loss account.

| Date | Account | Statement | Debit | Credit |
|------|---------|-----------|-------|--------|
| 31 Dec | Bad Debt Expense | Profit & Loss | 400 | |
| | Bad Debt Provision | Balance Sheet | | 400 |

### Disclosure of Bad Debts

The bad debt expense appears in the profit & loss account as an operating expense. The bad debt provision appears in the balance sheet as a contra account that is deducted from debtors. It reduces the amount expected to be collected in cash from the debtor as follows:

|  | € |
|---|---|
| Debtors per report | 22,700 (see Figure 13.1) |
| Less: Provision for bad debts | (400) |
| | 22,300 |

## Calculation of Bad Debts

There are two methods for calculating bad debts:

1. Percentage of sales method.
2. Aged debtor analysis.

## Percentage of Sales Method

This method looks at the net sales and estimates how much will not be collected. If the business estimates that 2% will be un-collectible, a provision is made for bad debts of that amount, as set out in Figure 13.2.

| | € |
|---|---|
| Sales | 150,000 |
| Less: sales returns | (5,000) |
| Less: sales discount | (5,000) |
| Net sales | 140,000 |
| Bad debts          2% | 2,800 |

Figure 13.2

## Aged Debtor Analysis

The aged debtors analysis looks at the debtors' balance to estimate how much will not be collected. With this method, the bad debt provision is determined directly through an analysis of debtors. In this process each debtor account is listed according to the due date for payment. If the customer's account is past due, there is a possibility that the account will not be paid. That possibility increases as the account extends further beyond the due date. The ageing of debtors helps evaluate the credit and collection policies and alerts the business to possible problems. Once the target balance for bad debt provision has been found it is necessary to determine the amount of the adjustment to the bad debt provision (see Figure 13.3). The amount depends on the current balance of the bad debt provision account. When the write-off in the current accounting period exceeds the amount of the provision, this will result in the bad debt expense being debited and bad debt provision being credited.

| Customer | Balance | Current | Period 1 | Period 2 | Period 3 | Older |
|----------|---------|---------|----------|----------|----------|-------|
| A | 150 | | 150 | | | |
| B | 400 | | | 400 | | |
| C | 1,000 | 900 | 100 | | | |
| D | 250 | | | | 250 | |
| Others | 45,350 | 30,000 | 6,000 | 4,500 | 3,000 | 1,850 |
| Total | 47,150 | 30,900 | 6,250 | 4,900 | 3,250 | 1,850 |
| Estimated percentage uncollectible | | 1% | 2% | 10% | 30% | 50% |
| Allowance for uncollectible accounts | **2,824** | 309 | 125 | 490 | 975 | 925 |

Figure 13.3

| | |
|---|---|
| Current provision for bad debts | 400 |
| New provision for bad debts | 2,824 |
| Increase in bad debt required | 2,424 |

| Date | Account | Statement | Debit | Credit |
|------|---------|-----------|-------|--------|
| 31 Dec | Bad Debt | Profit & Loss | 2,424 | |
| | Bad Debt Provision | Balance Sheet | | 2,424 |

## Comparison of the Two Methods

Both the percentage of net sales and the aged analysis of debtors estimate the uncollectible amount in accordance with the matching rule but it is done in different ways. The percentage of net sales method is a profit & loss account approach; the aged debtor analysis method is a balance sheet approach. See Figure 13.4.

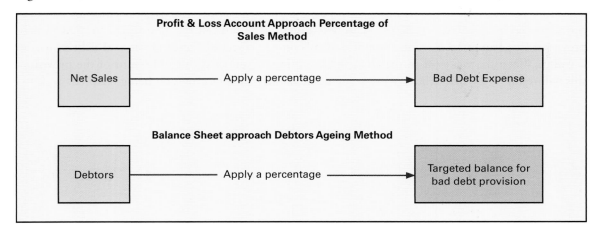

Figure 13.4

## *Writing Off Bad Debts*

Regardless of the method used to estimate bad debts, the total debtors written off in an accounting period will rarely equal the estimated bad debt provision. When it becomes clear that specific debtors will not be collected the amount should be written off.

The journal to record a provision for a bad debt of €1,000 in 2007 is set out below.

| Date | Account | Statement | Debit | Credit |
|------|---------|-----------|-------|--------|
| 31 Dec 07 | Bad Debt | Profit & Loss | 1,000 | |
| 31 Dec 07 | Bad Debt Provision | Balance Sheet | | 1,000 |

The un-collectable debt has already been accounted for as an expense in the profit & loss at the time the provision was created. When writing off an individual account, **debit** "bad debt provision" and not the "bad debt" expense account. The bad debt provision was made in 2007 but the actual removal of the debt from debtors does not occur until 2008.

The actual bad debt written off in 2008 is €1,000, and therefore the journal will appear as follows:

| Date | Account | Statement | Debit | Credit |
|------|---------|-----------|-------|--------|
| 31 Dec 08 | Bad Debt Provision | Balance Sheet | 1,000 | |
| 31 Dec 08 | Debtors | Balance Sheet | | 1,000 |

## ❑ Prepayments

Prepayments occur when an invoice is paid that covers a timeframe different to the year end, eg insurance or rent. Prepayments are used in monthly management accounts when certain expenses are paid for in the year but only one month needs to be included in the management accounts.

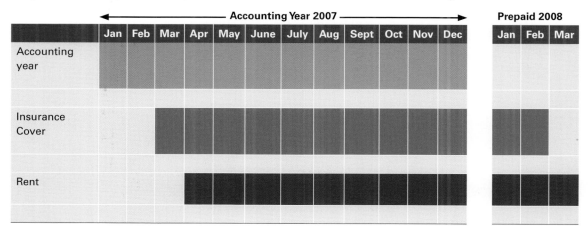

Figure 13.5

**Example**

As set out in Figure 13.5, the accounting year runs from January to December 2007. The business has issued a cheque for €1,200 for insurance covering March 2007–February 2008; therefore, the business has paid in advance for two months of 2008; the prepaid amount is €1,200/12 months × 2 months = €200.

Similarly, a cheque was issued for €60,000 for rent from April 2007–March 2008; therefore money was paid in advance for three months of 2008; the prepaid amount is €60,000/12 months × 3 months = €15,000.

# STOCK Chapter 14

Stock is included as an asset in the balance sheet of the financial statements. It includes raw materials, work-in-progress and finished goods. This chapter covers stock-processing systems, stock-costing methods, valuation methods, stock levels, stock takes and stock controls.

In most businesses, goods purchased or manufactured are rarely all sold in the same accounting period of purchase or manufacture. Stocks will be held at the month or year end. A basic principle of the profit & loss account is that sales must be matched with the **cost of goods sold** and not with the **cost of goods purchased.**

In an ongoing business there are two stock figures: the opening stock at the beginning of the period and the closing stock at the end of the same period. Opening stock is an expense brought forward from the previous period to the present one, while closing stock is an expense to carry forward to the next accounting period.

If a company sold all the goods available for sale during an accounting period, the cost of goods sold would equal the cost of goods purchased. In most businesses some stock remains unsold and on hand at the end of the period. This closing stock must be deducted from the cost of goods purchased to determine the cost of goods sold.

The primary objective of stock accounting is to determine income properly by matching costs of the period against revenues for the period. Management must choose from different processing systems, costing methods and valuation methods. These different systems and methods usually result in different amounts of reported profit. Management's choice affects investors' and creditors' evaluation of a company as well as internal evaluations such as performance reviews and bonuses. The figures for closing stock and cost of goods sold are related; a misstatement in the stock figure at the end of the year will cause an equal misstatement in the gross profit. The effect of a misstatement in Year 1 will be cleared by Year 2 since the closing stock in one period becomes the opening stock in the following period.

The consistency convention requires that once a business has decided on a system and method in accounting for stock, it must use it from one accounting period to another unless management can justify the change. When a change is justifiable the full disclosure convention requires that the company clearly describes the change and its effect in the notes to the financial statements.

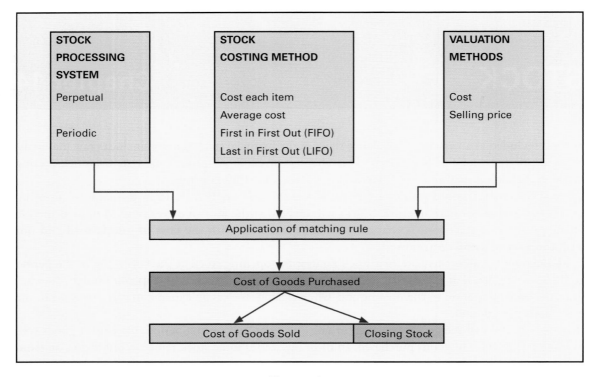

Figure 14.1

## ❑ Stock Processing System

There are two methods of recording stock in an accounts system:

- Perpetual stock system—the stock account and the cost of goods sold are updated with every sale. This system continuously records the quantity and the cost of individual items as they are bought and sold. At all times the balance on the stock account equals the cost of goods on hand and the balances in cost of goods sold equals the cost of stock sold to customers. The perpetual stock system does not eliminate the need for a physical stock count. A stock count should be taken periodically to ensure that the actual quantity of goods on hand matches the quantity indicated by the computer records.
- Periodic stock system—the value of closing stock on the balance sheet is determined by multiplying the quantity of each stock item by its unit cost. Under the periodic stock system, the stock not yet sold is counted periodically. The physical count is usually taken at the end of the accounting period. The figure for stock on hand is accurate only on the balance sheet date. Some retail and wholesale businesses use the periodic stock system because it reduces the amount of clerical work.

## *Perpetual Stock System Example*

On 3 October Frederick Ltd received goods purchased on credit at a cost of €9,780, invoice dated 1 October, payment due within 10 days. Under the perpetual stock system, the cost of stock is recorded in the stock account at the time of purchase. In the transaction described here, payment is due 10 days from the invoice date. On 6 October, Frederick Ltd returned part of the merchandise received on 3 October for a credit note of €960. Under the perpetual stock system, when a buyer is allowed to return all or part of a purchase or is given an allowance, or a reduction in the amount to be paid, stock is reduced. On 10 October, Frederick Ltd paid €8,820 in full, due for the purchases received on 3 October, part of which was returned on 6 October.

| Bank | | | | Creditors | | | | | |
|---|---|---|---|---|---|---|---|---|---|
| | 10 Oct | Creditor | 8,820 | 6 Oct | Stock | 960 | 1 Oct | Stock | 9,780 |
| | | | | 10 Oct | Bank | 8,820 | | | |
| | | | | | | 9,780 | | | 9,780 |

| Stock | | | | | | |
|---|---|---|---|---|---|---|
| 1 Oct | Creditor | 9,780 | 6 Oct | Creditor | | 960 |

## *Periodic Stock System Example*

On 3 October, Leeson Ltd received stock on credit at a cost of €9,780, invoice dated 1 October and payment due within 10 days. Under the periodic stock system, the cost of purchases is recorded in the purchase account at the time of purchase. This account is a temporary one used only with the periodic stock system. Its sole purpose is to accumulate the total cost of purchases for resale during an accounting period. On 6 October, Leeson Ltd returned part of the goods received on 3 October for a credit note of €960. The amount of the return or allowance is recorded in the purchase return account; this account is a contra purchase account with a normal credit balance and it is deducted from purchases in the profit & loss account. Creditors are also reduced, by €960.

| Bank | | | | Purchases | | |
|---|---|---|---|---|---|---|
| | 10 Oct  Creditor | 8,820 | | 1 Oct  Creditors  9,780 | | |

| Creditors | | | | Purchases Returned | | |
|---|---|---|---|---|---|---|
| 6 Oct  Purchases Returned | 960 | 1 Oct  Purchases | 9,780 | | 6 Oct  Creditors  960 | |
| 10 Oct  Bank | 8,820 | | | | | |
| | 9,780 | | 9,780 | | | |

The primary difference between the perpetual and the periodic stock system is that in the perpetual stock system the stock account is adjusted each time a purchase, sale or other stock transaction occurs, whereas in the periodic stock system the stock account stays at its opening balance until the physical stock is recorded at the end of the period. In the periodic system, a purchase account is used to accumulate the purchases of stock during the accounting period, and a purchase return and allowances account is used to accumulate returns and allowance.

## ❑ Stock-Costing Method

Cost is usually the most appropriate basis for valuation of stock. Stock may at times be shown in the financial statements at less than historic cost if the market value of the stock falls below the historic cost due to deterioration, obsolescence or decline in price. The rule for stock valuation is that it must be valued at the lower of cost and net realisable value. Any loss arising is recognised immediately.

The process of valuing stocks of raw materials starts with the cost of acquisition. The term "cost" includes such expenses as were necessary to bring stock to its present state, where it is available for use. Once the cost of the raw material stock has been determined, the value at which such stock is shown in the balance sheet should not exceed the cost figure. In certain situations it may be necessary to record a lower value than cost for stock shown in the balance sheet. This would result from the need to recognise that a fall in value (below cost) had taken place and the need to ensure that such a fall in value was properly written off to the profit and loss account.

## ❑ Identifying Stock Items

When a company deals in stock items, it is often impossible to identify the cost of items sold and which are still in stock. When that is the case, it is necessary to make an assumption about the order in which items have been sold. The assumed sequence of sale may or may not be the same as the actual sequence of sale.

There are several rules that can be used to determine the flow of goods:

- First In First Out (FIFO)—assumes that goods bought first are sold first. This rule assumes that the cost of the first items acquired should be assigned to the first items sold. The cost of the goods on hand at the end of the period is assumed to be from the most recent purchases. The effect of the FIFO method is to value the closing stock at the most recent costs.
- Last In First Out (LIFO) method—assumes goods bought last are sold last. The LIFO method of costing stock is based on the assumption that the cost of closing stock reflects the cost of goods purchased earliest.

## ❏ Valuation Methods

Stock needs to be valued at the lower of cost and net realisable value (the amount the stock items could be sold for). Although cost is usually the most appropriate basis for the valuation of stock, there are times when stock may be properly shown in the financial statements at less than its cost: for example, if the market value of stock falls because of physical deterioration or obsolescence. This loss must be recognised by writing the stock down to net realisable value. The cost must be determined by using FIFO, LIFO or average cost before the market value is compared with it. The term "net realisable value" means the amount that could be obtained from selling stock, in normal trading operations. Furthermore, any expenditure that would appear to be necessary for the disposal of the stock would be deducted in arriving at the net realisable value, see Figure 14.2.

| Description | Quantity | Cost ex VAT | Net Realisable Value | Lower of Cost and Net Realisable Value |
|---|---|---|---|---|
| Black & White Jerseys | 4 | 15.50 | 19.00 | 62.00 |
| Purple & Green Jerseys (including Logo) | 11 | 16.00 | 14.00 | 154.00 |
| Yellow & Green Tee Shirts | 4 | 5.00 | 9.00 | 20.00 |
| Black Rugby Shorts | 26 | 10.00 | 11.00 | 260.00 |
| Yellow Shorts (can not be sold) OBSOLETE | 4 | 5.00 | – | – |
| Navy Rugby Shorts | 5 | 10.00 | 12.00 | 50.00 |
| Green & Black Jerseys | 1 | 15.50 | 18.00 | 15.50 |
| Black Tee Shirts | 14 | 5.00 | 6.50 | 70.00 |
| White Tee Shirts | 4 | 5.00 | 6.50 | 20.00 |
| White Shorts with Logo | 10 | 7.75 | 9.00 | 77.50 |
| | | | | **729.00** |

Figure 14.2

It is usually difficult to count every stock item and assign a cost to each item. There are two methods that may be used to count stock.

- Retail method—The retail method estimates the cost of closing stock by using the ratio of cost to retail price. Retail businesses use this method for two reasons:
  1. To prepare financial statements for each accounting period. The retail method can be used to estimate the cost without taking the time to determine the cost of each item of stock.
  2. Items in the retail shop have a price tag: it is common practice to take a physical stock-take using the retail price from these price tags and to reduce the total value to cost by using the profit ratio. When the retail method is used to estimate closing stock, the records must show the opening stock at cost and at retail price. It must also show the amount of goods purchased during the period at cost and at retail price. The net sales at retail price are the balance of the sales account less the returns and allowances. When estimating stock by the retail method it is not necessary to count the stock. The retail method may be difficult to implement in practice due to changes in retail prices and different mark-ups.

- Gross profit method—The gross profit margin assumes that the ratio of gross profit margin for the business remains relatively static from year to year. The gross profit method is used in place of the retail method when records of the retail price of opening stock and purchases are not available. It is a way of estimating stock when stock is destroyed by fire etc. The cost of goods sold is estimated by deducting the estimated gross margin from sales. Finally the estimated cost of goods sold is deducted from the goods purchased for sale in order to arrive at the estimated cost of stock.

## ❑ Stock Levels

Some of the costs of carrying quantities of stock are insurance, storage and administration. These costs are usually substantial. If a business can maintain low stock levels, it will increase profitability. On the other hand low levels of stock can result in disgruntled customers and lost sales. A small retail shop can carry a large amount of stock, equating to large amounts of cash sitting on the shelves. Poor stock control means that slow-moving products will eventually have to be sold at a lower price.

One measure that managers commonly use to evaluate stock levels is stock turnover, which is the average number of times a company sells its stock during accounting periods.

$$\text{Stock turnover} = \frac{\text{Cost of goods sold}}{\text{Average stock (Opening Stock – Closing Stock) / 2}}$$

Another measure of stock levels is days' stock on hand, which is the average number of days it takes a company to sell its stock.

$$\text{Days' stock on hand} = \frac{\text{number of days in the accounting period}}{\text{Stock turnover (See above)}}$$

Stock is particularly susceptible to fraudulent financial reporting as it is easy to overstate or understate stock by including end of year purchases and sales transactions in the wrong financial year or simply by misstating stocks.

## ❑ Stock Takes

A stock take is a physical count of the stock on hand. It involves comparing the stock records with the physical stock. It is done at least once a year when preparing the financial statements. In order to make the process as painless as possible, the following should be considered.

- Have two people count each item together as this will minimise errors.
- Do not count fixed assets as fixed assets are not part of the stock for resale.
- Obsolete items should be identified and valued at their estimated sale price.
- Use pre-numbered stock sheets so that at the end of the count there are no missing sheets.
- Use a template such as the one below (in Excel) so that as soon as the physical stock-take has been carried out the stock description and quantities can be transferred and prices allocated. Simply use Excel to calculate the cost of each stock item (not the selling price) and then calculate the total stock value. Using Excel rather than paper will save time and will be easier for the accountant to use.
- Costs can be obtained from purchase invoices. Remember to take into account any discounts received. If the stock was purchased from abroad, use the exchange rate that was used to record the purchase of the stock.

Set out in Figure 14.3 is an example of a stock sheet before the prices are allocated to each stock item.

| Stock Sheet 1 of 15 | | | | | |
| --- | --- | --- | --- | --- | --- |
| **Description** | **Location** | **Quantity** | **Cost** | **Net Realisable Value** | **Value** |
| Black & White Jerseys | Storeroom 1 | 4 | | | |
| Purple & Green Jerseys (including Logo) | Storeroom 1 | 11 | | | |
| Yellow & Green Tee Shirts | Storeroom 1 | 4 | | | |
| Black Rugby Shorts | Storeroom 1 | 26 | | | |
| Yellow Shorts (can not be sold) OBSOLETE | Storeroom 1 | 4 | | | |
| Navy Rugby Shorts | Storeroom 1 | 5 | | | |
| Green & Black Jerseys | Storeroom 1 | 1 | | | |
| Black Tee Shirts | Storeroom 1 | 14 | | | |
| White Tee Shirts | Storeroom 1 | 4 | | | |
| White Shorts with Logo | Storeroom 1 | 10 | | | |

Figure 14.3

## ❏ Control Over Stock

Management is responsible for establishing control procedures to protect the company's assets. These systems and procedures are called internal controls. Taking a physical stock count is an example of a control over retail stock. A company's retail stock includes all goods intended for sales regardless of where they are located, eg shelves, storehouse, in transit. Other stock control includes electronic tagging and physical security features such as security guards and alarm systems.

## ❏ Retail v Service Businesses

Retail businesses that buy and sell stock require a more complex profit & loss account than service businesses. The main difference between a retailer's profit & loss account and the profit & loss account of a service business is that the retailer must compute gross profit before operating expenses are deducted. The computation of gross profit means that opening and closing stock figures must be calculated, as in Figure 14.4.

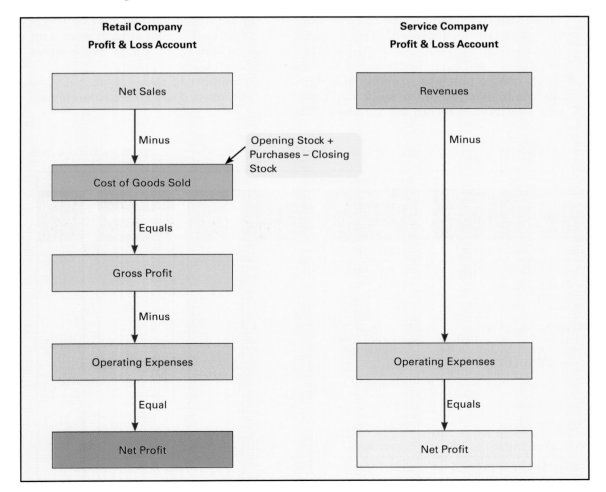

Figure 14.4

## Net Sales

Net sales are proceeds from sales less sales returns and discounts. Gross sales are the total cash sales and total credit sales during an accounting period. Sales returns and allowances are contra revenue accounts used to record cash refunds and reductions in selling prices made to customers who have received defective or otherwise unsatisfactory products.

## Cost of Goods Sold

Cost of goods sold is the amount a retailer paid for the stock sold during an accounting period or the cost to a manufacturer of making the goods that were sold. The method of computing cost of goods sold must take into account opening and closing stock. The closing stock appears in the balance sheet at the end of one accounting period and becomes the opening stock for the next accounting period. An important component of the cost of goods sold section is purchases, which consists of net purchases plus freight charges less deductions such as purchases returns and a discount allowed by suppliers.

### Example

Closing stock at 31 December 2007 is €52,800. This is transferred using a journal to the profit & loss account and becomes the opening stock of the following year (2008). Stock is physically counted at 31 December 2008 and is valued at €48,300. This is included in the balance sheet as a **debit** and **credited** to the profit & loss account as the closing stock figure as set out in Figure 14.5.

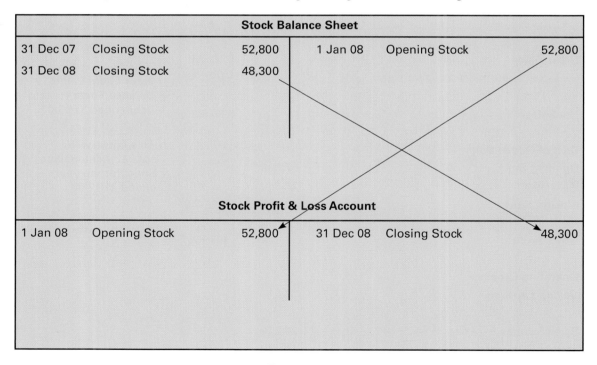

Figure 14.5

## Gross Profit

Gross profit is the difference between net sales and cost of goods sold. The percentage of gross margin is computed by dividing the amount of gross profit by net sales.

## Operating Expenses

Operating expenses are the expenses incurred in running a business other than cost of goods sold. It is customary to group operating expenses into categories such as "selling expenses" and "general and administrative expenses". Selling expenses include the cost of storing goods, preparing them for sale, displaying, advertising and other promotional costs.

## Net Profit

Net profit is what remains after operating expenses are deducted from gross profit. It is the amount that is transferred to owner's equity from all the income-generating activities during the period.
Set out in Figure 14.6 is an example of how the stock figures would appear in the profit & loss account.

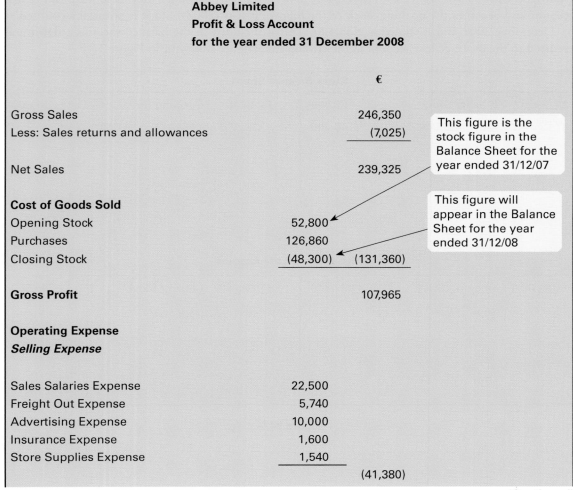

|  | | € |
|---|---|---|
| **Abbey Limited** | | |
| **Profit & Loss Account** | | |
| **for the year ended 31 December 2008** | | |
| Gross Sales | | 246,350 |
| Less: Sales returns and allowances | | (7,025) |
| Net Sales | | 239,325 |
| **Cost of Goods Sold** | | |
| Opening Stock | 52,800 | |
| Purchases | 126,860 | |
| Closing Stock | (48,300) | (131,360) |
| **Gross Profit** | | 107,965 |
| **Operating Expense** | | |
| **Selling Expense** | | |
| Sales Salaries Expense | 22,500 | |
| Freight Out Expense | 5,740 | |
| Advertising Expense | 10,000 | |
| Insurance Expense | 1,600 | |
| Store Supplies Expense | 1,540 | |
| | | (41,380) |

This figure is the stock figure in the Balance Sheet for the year ended 31/12/07

This figure will appear in the Balance Sheet for the year ended 31/12/08

(Continued)

*General and Administrative Expenses*

| | | |
|---|---:|---:|
| Office Salaries Expense | 26,900 | |
| Insurance Expense General | 4,200 | |
| Office Supplies Expense | 1,204 | |
| Depreciation Building | 2,600 | |
| Depreciation Office | 2,200 | |
| | | (37,104) |
| | | |
| Total Operating Expenses | | (78,484) |
| | | |
| **Net Profit** | | 29,481 |

Figure 14.6

# BANK/LOANS/ OVERDRAFTS

## Chapter 15

This chapter deals with the reconciliation of a bank account, recording invoices in foreign currencies, the repayment of a loan and procedures to control the operation of a bank account.

## ❑ Bank Reconciliation

Bank accounts provide improved control by minimising the amount of cash a business needs to keep on hand and by supplying a permanent record of payments and receipts. Carrying out the monthly bank reconciliation is one of the most important accounting controls and should be seen as a priority. It is rare that the balance of a business's bank account in the nominal ledger will exactly equal the balance shown on the bank statement. The bank may not have recorded certain transactions shown in the business's records and certain transactions made by the bank may not appear in the business's records.

The bank reconciliation is a process of accounting for the differences between the balance appearing on the bank statements and the balance of the bank account in the business records. A reconciliation is carried out in order to test the accuracy of the business records and the bank's records in relation to receipts and payments. When the bank sends a statement, it shows a copy of the bank's financial record, not the customer's. When the bank receives €100 it **debits** the bank's own cash account and **credits** the customer's account. A bank statement should mirror the bank account maintained by the business but this may not happen and outlined in Figure 15.1 are some of the reasons why.

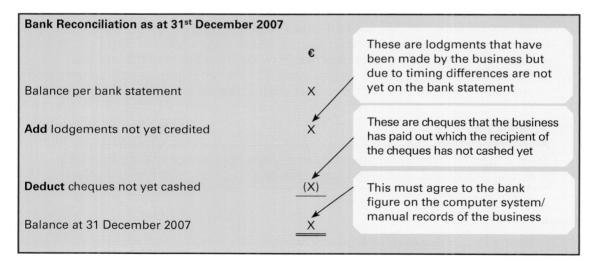

Figure 15.1

## *Categories of Reconciling Items*

1. Outstanding cheques: Items shown as payments in the books, but not yet shown on the bank statements.
2. Outstanding lodgements: Items shown as receipts in the books, but not yet shown as a credit on the bank statements.
3. Additional direct debits: payments for bank charges and other debits made by the bank against the bank account and recorded on the bank statement, but not yet recorded in the business's books. These items should be entered into the business's books after receiving the bank statements. Examples are: bank charges, interest and standing orders/direct debits.
4. Additional credits: amounts credited to the account but not yet entered as receipts in the business's books. These items should be entered in the books after receiving the bank statements. Examples are: bank interest received and money transferred into the account directly by customers.
5. Errors: Items incorrectly charged or credited to the bank account by the bank, that do not relate to the business. In this case the business should contact the bank to get the errors corrected and deleted from the bank account.

The following steps should be followed when carrying out a bank reconciliation:

1. Compare all entries on the bank statement with the entries in the cash receipts and cheque payments book, marking off each item in the business records and the bank statements where the items correspond exactly.
2. Locate all items, both in the business's books and on the bank statements that have not been marked off.
3. Decide into which of the above five categories of reconciling items the differences fall.
4. Commence the bank reconciliation, starting with the balance as per the bank statement. If the balance per the bank statement is an overdrawn balance rather than a credit balance, be especially careful as to how any adjustments may affect the balance.
5. Taking the balance per the bank statement, add any outstanding lodgements and deduct any outstanding cheques and adjust for any errors.
6. Taking the balance per the business's books, adjust it for additional direct debits and credits. It is essential that correcting entries be made in the books of the business.
7. The figure arrived at the end of stages 5 and 6 of the procedure should be the same in both cases if the reconciliation has been done correctly.

Do not close off the bank account in your books until additional direct debits, standing orders and errors have been included.

## Example

Set out in Figures 15.2–15.6 is an example of bank reconciliation: lodgement will appear in the business receipts and payments book as a **debit**; however, it will be recorded on the bank statement as a **credit**, and vice versa for payments.

**Irish Bank**

145 Lower Main Street Dublin 3     Tel 01 555 6786

Fax 01 555 6787

Branch Code 80-67-76

John Lynch Ltd

11 Smythfield Road     **Account name**     John Lynch Ltd

Blackrock

Co Dublin     **Account Number**     99996574

The IBAN is made up of the branch code and account number. This is required to make a bank transfer outside Ireland

**IBAN**     IE56 IB 8067 7699 9965 74

**Statement Date**     01-Jan-08     Number 12

| Date | Transaction Details | Payments - out | Payments - in | Balance €  |
|------|--------------------|----------------|---------------|-----------|
| 01/12/2007 | Balance b/f |  |  | 2,000.00 |
| 02/12/2007 | Lodgement 16 |  | 412.00 | 2,412.00 |
| 06/12/2007 | Cheque 46 | 813.00 |  | 1,599.00 |
| 09/12/2007 | Lodgement 17 |  | 615.00 | 2,214.00 |
| 12/12/2007 | Cheque 48 | 96.00 |  | 2,118.00 |
| 12/12/2007 | S/O Term Loan | 100.00 |  | 2,018.00 |
| 15/12/2007 | Lodgement 18 |  | 735.00 | 2,753.00 |
| 22/12/2007 | Cheque 51 | 231.00 |  | 2,522.00 |
| 22/12/2007 | Lodgement 19 |  | 185.00 | 2,707.00 |
| 24/12/2007 | Bank Charges | 25.00 |  | **2,682.00** |

This is a credit on the Bank Statement but it will appear in the business's books as a debit

Figure 15.2

**John Lynch Ltd Receipts and Payments Book**

| | | DR € | | | CR € |
|------|------------|-------|------------|----------------|-----|
| 01/12/2007 | Balance b/d | 2,000 | 05/12/2007 | Cheque no. 46 | 813 |
| 02/12/2007 | Lodgement 16 | 412 | 10/12/2007 | Cheque no. 47 | 407 |
| 09/12/2007 | Lodgement 17 | 509 | 11/12/2007 | Cheque no. 48 | 96 |
| 09/12/2007 | Lodgement 17 | 106 | 19/12/2007 | Cheque no. 49 | 421 |
| 15/12/2007 | Lodgement 18 | 735 | 20/12/2007 | Cheque no. 50 | 549 |
| 22/12/2007 | Lodgement 19 | 175 | 21/12/2007 | Cheque no. 51 | 123 |
| 28/12/2007 | Lodgement 20 | 404 | 28/12/2007 | Cheque no. 52 | 42 |
| 28/12/2007 | Lodgement 21 | 276 | | | |

Figure 15.3

**Note:** All cheques should be written in numerical order and lodgements should be recorded in date order.

## Solution

**Irish Bank**  145 Lower Main Street Dublin 3  Tel 01 555 6786

Fax 01 555 6787

Branch Code 80-67-76

John Lynch Ltd
11 Smythfield Road     **Account name**     John Lynch Ltd
Blackrock
Co Dublin               **Account Number**   99996574

**IBAN**            IE56 IB 8067 7699 9965 74

**Statement Date**     01-Jan-08     Number 12

| Date | Transaction Details | Payments - **out** | Payments - in | Balance € |
|------|---------------------|--------------------|---------------|-----------|
| 01/12/2007 | Balance b/f |  |  | 2,000.00 |
| 02/12/2007 | Lodgement 16 |  | *412.00 | 2,412.00 |
| 06/12/2007 | Cheque 46 | *813.00 |  | 1,599.00 |
| 09/12/2007 | Lodgement 17 |  | *615.00 | 2,214.00 |
| 12/12/2007 | Cheque 48 | *96.00 |  | 2,118.00 |
| 12/12/2007 | S/O Term Loan | 100.00 |  | 2,018.00 |
| 15/12/2007 | Lodgement 18 |  | *735.00 | 2,753.00 |
| 22/12/2007 | Cheque 51 | 231.00 |  | 2,522.00 |
| 22/12/2007 | Lodgement 19 |  | 185.00 | 2,707.00 |
| 24/12/2007 | Bank Charges | 25.00 |  | **2,682.00** |

Note 1. S/O Term Loan not recorded in the business's books. Has to be recorded as a direct debit.

Note 2. Cheque error in the business's cheque payments book should be €231, and therefore €108 to be adjusted in the cheque payments book.

Note 4. Bank Charges not recorded in the business's receipts and payments book, so the amount has to be recorded as a direct debit.

Note 3. Lodgement in the business's receipts and payments book states €175; €10 difference to be added to the lodgement book.

Figure 15.4

**John Lynch Ltd Receipts and Payment Book**

| | | | DR €| | | | CR €|
|---|---|---|---|---|---|---|---|
| 01/12/2007 | Balance b/d | | 2,000 | 05/12/2007 | Cheque no. 46 | * | 813 |
| 02/12/2007 | Lodgement 16 | * | 412 | 10/12/2007 | Cheque no. 47 | O/S | 407 |
| 09/12/2007 | Lodgement 17 | * | 509 | 11/12/2007 | Cheque no. 48 | * | 96 |
| 09/12/2007 | Lodgement 17 | * | 106 | 19/12/2007 | Cheque no. 49 | O/S | 421 |
| 15/12/2007 | Lodgement 18 | * | 735 | 20/12/2007 | Cheque no. 50 | O/S | 549 |
| 22/12/2007 | Lodgement 19 | (note 3) | 175 | 21/12/2007 | Cheque no. 51 | (note 2) | 123 |
| 28/12/2007 | Lodgement 20 | O/S | 404 | 28/12/2007 | Cheque no. 52 | O/S | 42 |
| 28/12/2007 | Lodgement 21 | O/S | 276 | | | | |
| | | | | 12/12/2007 | Standing Order Term Loan | (note 1) | 100 |
| 22/12/2007 | Error re Lodgement | (note 3) | 10 | 24/12/2007 | Bank Charges | (note 4) | 25 |
| | | | | 21/12/2007 | Error re cheque no. 52 | (note 2) | 108 |
| | | | | | Balance c/d | | 1,943 |
| | | | 4,627 | | | | 4,627 |
| Balance b/d | | | **1,943** | | | | |

Figure 15.5

**Note:** Items marked with * are transactions matched from the receipts and payments book to the bank statement. Items marked with O/S are transactions that have not yet appeared on the bank statements and are outstanding cheques or lodgements.

Bringing all the figures together, the balance per the bank statement is the closing balance at the end of the monthly bank statement, adding outstanding lodgements and deducting outstanding cheques.

---

**John Lynch Ltd**

**Bank Reconciliation as at 31 December 2007**

|  |  |  | € |
|---|---|---|---|
| Balance per bank statement 31/12/07 |  |  | 2,682 |
| Add: | Outstanding Lodgements |  |  |
|  | 28/12/2007 | Lodgement 20 | €404 |  |
|  | 28/12/2007 | Lodgement 21 | €276 | 680 |
| Less: | Outstanding Cheques |  |  |
|  | 10/12/2007 | Cheque no. 47 | €407 |
|  | 19/12/2007 | Cheque no. 49 | €421 |
|  | 20/12/2007 | Cheque no. 50 | €549 |
|  | 28/12/2007 | Cheque no. 52 | €42 | (1,419) |
| Balance per Accounts 31/12/07 |  |  | **1,943** |

---

Figure 15.6

**Quick Tip**

Reconcile your bank on a daily, or at least weekly basis. This will ensure that any errors made by the business or the bank or any fraudulent interceptions of cheques can be identified immediately and action taken to rectify the error.

**Quick Tip**

When writing a cheque always write on the cheque stub who the cheque was paid to and for what, eg office repairs €105 12/1/07.

**Quick Tip**

If cheques are not cashed for six months, they will become out of date and will not be accepted by the bank.

The purpose of the bank reconciliation is to:

- Pick up bank errors.
- Make sure all the money paid in has actually been credited to the account.
- Identify cheques not yet presented. If a supplier does not cash a cheque within two months establish whether they have received the cheque. If a cheque is not cashed during the month then it is included in the list of outstanding cheques at the end of the month.
- Make sure to pick up mistakes early.

## Checklist If the Bank Reconciliation Does Not Balance:

1. Look at the last bank reconciliation statement. Have all the outstanding cheques been cleared? Are they included as outstanding this month?
2. Scan the cheque payments book and cash receipts book for any unticked items.
3. Make sure there are not any missing pages in the bank statements.
4. If the difference is divisible by 9 then it may be a transposition error, eg a cheque for €423 is recorded as €432.
5. Look at the cheque book stubs. Have **all** the cheques been entered?
6. Let someone else have a look at it. Often you cannot see a mistake that is obvious to someone else.

Once the bank is reconciled you should sign and date the reconciliation. Review the bank reconciliation if lodgements are outstanding; contact the bank as the money may have been incorrectly credited to another bank account. If the cheque has been lost, contact the bank to cancel the cheque and issue a replacement cheque. Each bank reconciliation should be kept on file.

To cancel a cheque in the books it needs to be recorded as a debit; you can record the amount as a negative amount in the cheque payments book. Void cheques should be marked "void" in the cheque payments book and cancelled with the bank.

### Example

Assume that cheque number 49 for €421 needs to be cancelled, as it has been lost, as in Figure 15.7.

**John Lynch Ltd cheque payments book**

|            |                          | CR    |
|------------|--------------------------|-------|
|            |                          | €     |
| 05/12/2007 | Cheque no. 46            | 813   |
| 10/12/2007 | Cheque no. 47            | 407   |
| 11/12/2007 | Cheque no. 48            | 96    |
| 19/12/2007 | Cheque no. 49            | 421   |
| 20/12/2007 | Cheque no. 50            | 549   |
| 21/12/2007 | Cheque no. 51            | 123   |
| 28/12/2007 | Cheque no. 52            | 42    |
| 12/12/2007 | Standing Order Term Loan | 100   |
| 24/12/2007 | Bank Charges             | 25    |
| 21/12/2007 | Error re cheque no. 52   | 108   |
|            |                          |       |
| 31/12/2007 | Cancelled Cheque no. 49  | (421) |
|            |                          |       |
|            |                          | 2,263 |

Figure 15.7

**Quick Tip**

Never sign a blank cheque; if it falls into the wrong hands it can be filled out for any amount.

**Quick Tip**

All cheques should be crossed and "Account payee only, not negotiable" written between the lines. A stamp can be purchased with these words contained on it.

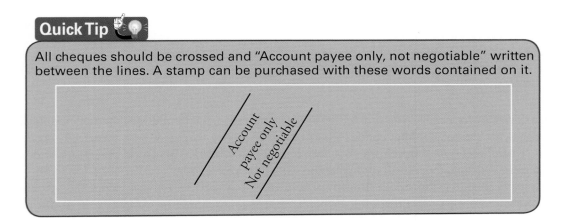

## Electronic Funds Transfer

Electronic Funds Transfer (EFT) is a method of conducting business transactions that does not involve the actual transfer of cash or writing of cheques. With EFT, a company electronically transfers cash from its bank account to another company's bank account; this method is often used for the payment of salaries so that employees do not have to go to the bank to lodge their wages.

## Cheque Requisition Form

When paying suppliers, a cheque requisition form should be attached to the invoice(s) so that all the details relating to the transaction and cheque signatories are on one page. When invoices are being paid or items are being paid on delivery by cheque, it is good practice to put in place a process to record the authorisation of the cheque. This process records who authorises the invoice being paid and who approves the issuing of the cheque.

Set out in Figure 15.8  is an example of a cheque requisition form.

**Cheque Requisition Form — Purchase Invoices**

| Nominal Code: | 7400 | Cheque Number: | 10641 |
|---|---|---|---|
| Purchase Order Number: (Delivery Docket should be attached where appropriate) | 146 | Date paid: | 20/12/07 |
| Purchase Invoice Numbers and Date: | Invoice 41036 28/11/07 Invoice 41039 30/11/07 | | |
| Payee: | Sports Supplies | | |
| Amount in Euros: | €2,500.00 | Date Received Invoice: | 5/12/07 |
| Additional Comments (if none insert N/A): | | | |
| Purchase Invoice Authorised by: | Don Reynolds | | |
| Cheque Signatories: | 1. *John Murphy* | | |
| | 2. Mary Smyth | | |

Figure 15.8

# ❑ Foreign Exchange Conversion

When a business purchases or  sells in a foreign currency, one currency has to be translated into another using an exchange rate. An exchange rate is the value of one currency stated in terms of another. For example, if an Irish company purchases goods from the United States and pays in US dollars, they must exchange euros for US dollars before making payment. The value of other currencies in relation to the euro rise and fall daily. Thus if there is a delay between the date of sale or purchase and the date of receipt of payment, the amount of cash involved may differ from the amount originally agreed; this will result in a foreign exchange gain or loss.

When a business quotes a price to a foreign customer it has to decide whether to quote in euros or in the importer's currency or in some other nominated currency, eg US dollars. When quoting in euro the exporter will know with certainty the value receivable and be able to calculate the profit on the transaction. However, if the exporter quotes in a foreign currency then the profit is subject to the uncertainty of fluctuations in the rate of exchange between the euro and that currency up to the time of payment. Pricing in a foreign currency makes the deal more attractive to the foreign purchaser who knows their exact commitment because it is expressed in their own currency.

**Example**

An Irish company invoiced a customer for the sale of goods for €160,000 at £100,000 stg, reflecting the exchange rate of €1.60 ~ £1 sterling on 1 January 2007. Assume on the date of payment that the exchange rate has fallen to €1.50 ~ £1 sterling. When the Irish company receives its £100,000 stg it will only be worth €150,000; it will have incurred an exchange loss of €10,000. See Figure 15.9.

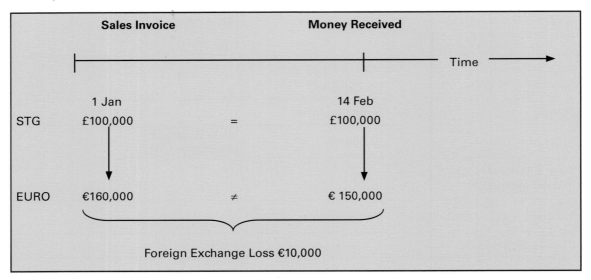

Figure 15.9

**Example**

Assume that the Irish company purchased goods from the UK for €80,000, reflecting the exchange rate of €1.60 ~£1 stg on 1 January 2007. However, as the UK company expects to be paid in sterling, the Irish company will have an exchange gain because it agreed to pay £50,000 stg on 14 February; between the date of purchase and payment the exchange value of the pound decreased from €1.60 to €1.50. See Figure 15.10.

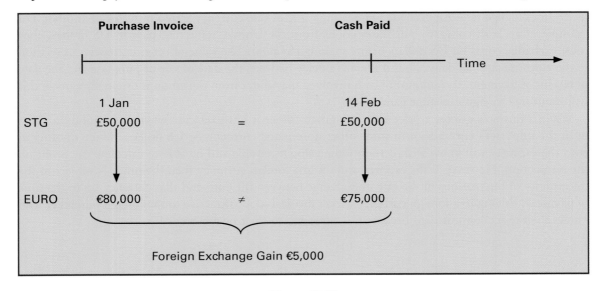

Figure 15.10

The preceding examples dealt with transactions that were completed during the accounting year. In each case the exchange gain or loss was recognised on the date of receipt or payment. If the financial statements are prepared before the transactions are finalised then the invoice in the foreign currency must be converted at the exchange rate applicable at the year end. This will result in an unrealised foreign exchange gain or loss.

**Example**

In Figure 15.11 the creditors invoices were recorded in the books at the rate of exchange applicable at the invoice date. The exchange rate at the year end is lower than the previous rates and this results in a foreign exchange gain when the invoices are reconverted at the closing exchange rate.

| Creditor invoices | Sterling | Rate | Euro |
|---|---|---|---|
| | £ | | € |
| 01/12/2007 | 1,000 | 1.6 | 1,600 |
| 10/12/2007 | 800 | 1.55 | 1,240 |
| 20/12/2007 | 500 | 1.5 | 750 |
| | 2,300 | | 3,590 |
| Closing rate 31/12/07 | 2,300 | 1.4 | 3,220 |
| Exchange Gain | | € | 370 |

Figure 15.11

The invoices were converted at the exchange rate using the date of the purchase invoice. Between the date of each invoice and the year end the rate has fallen to €1.40~£1 stg. Therefore, there is a foreign exchange gain of €370, all the sterling invoices are converted using the closing rate of €1.40~£1 stg and compared against the actual exchange rate used.

## ❑ Loan Account

When a company takes out a loan, interest and capital loan repayments will have to be made. The interest will be recorded in the profit & loss account as an expense and the capital repayment will be deducted from the total outstanding loan. Set out in Figure 15.12 is an example where the company is repaying a fixed amount of €1,000 per month. The repayment reduces the loan account by €1,000 per month. Interest is added on to the amount outstanding. The amount of interest charged decreases over time as the amount of the loan outstanding decreases.

| **Loan Account** | | | | | | **Interest Profit & Loss** | | | | |
|---|---|---|---|---|---|---|---|---|---|---|
| | | | Loan Advanced | 20,000 | | | | | | |
| 5 Jan | Current A/c | 1,000 | 5 Jan | Interest | 83 | 5 Jan | Loan A/c | 83 | | |
| 5 Feb | Current A/c | 1,000 | 5 Feb | Interest | 80 | 5 Feb | Loan A/c | 80 | | |
| 5 Mar | Current A/c | 1,000 | 5 Mar | Interest | 76 | 5 Mar | Loan A/c | 76 | | |
| 5 Apr | Current A/c | 1,000 | 5 Apr | Interest | 72 | 5 Apr | Loan A/c | 72 | | |
| 5 May | Current A/c | 1,000 | 5 May | Interest | 68 | 5 May | Loan A/c | 68 | | |
| 5 Jun | Current A/c | 1,000 | 5 Jun | Interest | 64 | 5 Jun | Loan A/c | 64 | Profit & Loss | 743 |
| 5 Jul | Current A/c | 1,000 | 5 Jul | Interest | 60 | 5 Jul | Loan A/c | 60 | | |
| 5 Aug | Current A/c | 1,000 | 5 Aug | Interest | 56 | 5 Aug | Loan A/c | 56 | | |
| 5 Sep | Current A/c | 1,000 | 5 Sep | Interest | 52 | 5 Sep | Loan A/c | 52 | | |
| 5 Oct | Current A/c | 1,000 | 5 Oct | Interest | 48 | 5 Oct | Loan A/c | 48 | | |
| 5 Nov | Current A/c | 1,000 | 5 Nov | Interest | 44 | 5 Nov | Loan A/c | 44 | | |
| 5 Dec | Current A/c | 1,000 | 5 Dec | Interest | 40 | 5 Dec | Loan A/c | 40 | | |
| Balance c/d | | 8,743 | | | | | | | | |
| | | 20,743 | | | 20,743 | | | 743 | | 743 |
| | | | Balance b/d | | 8,743 | | | | | |

| **Extract from Current Account** | | | | |
|---|---|---|---|---|
| | | 5 Jan | Loan A/c | 1,000 |
| | | 5 Feb | Loan A/c | 1,000 |
| | | 5 Mar | Loan A/c | 1,000 |
| | | 5 Apr | Loan A/c | 1,000 |
| | | 5 May | Loan A/c | 1,000 |
| | | 5 Jun | Loan A/c | 1,000 |
| | | 5 Jul | Loan A/c | 1,000 |
| | | 5 Aug | Loan A/c | 1,000 |
| | | 5 Sep | Loan A/c | 1,000 |
| | | 5 Oct | Loan A/c | 1,000 |
| | | 5 Nov | Loan A/c | 1,000 |
| | | 5 Dec | Loan A/c | 1,000 |

**SUMMARY**

| Loan | Interest @ 5% | Repayment | Balance |
|---|---|---|---|
| 20,000 | 83 | 1,000 | 19,083 |
| 19,083 | 80 | 1,000 | 18,163 |
| 18,163 | 76 | 1,000 | 17,239 |
| 17,239 | 72 | 1,000 | 16,311 |
| 16,311 | 68 | 1,000 | 15,379 |
| 15,379 | 64 | 1,000 | 14,443 |
| 14,443 | 60 | 1,000 | 13,503 |
| 13,503 | 56 | 1,000 | 12,559 |
| 12,559 | 52 | 1,000 | 11,611 |
| 11,611 | 48 | 1,000 | 10,659 |
| 10,659 | 44 | 1,000 | 9,703 |
| 9,703 | 40 | 1,000 | 8,743 |
| | 743 | | |

Figure 15.12

## ❑ Controls for Operating a Bank Account

A business's banking procedures should ensure that all bank and cash transactions are authorised and accurately accounted for.

- A signatory who authorises and approves the purchase of goods and services cannot also be the cheque signatory certifying payment for these purchases. There must be segregation of duties.
- Maintain an up-to-date list of all direct debits for each bank account detailing the beneficiary, amount, frequency and account to be debited.
- All direct debit mandates and amendments should be authorised by two bank signatories and copies retained on file.
- Safeguard all unused cheque books, cancelled cheques, cheque book stubs, lodgement books and lodgement stubs.
- Maintain a register of used and cancelled cheques for audit trail purposes.
- Bank statements should be reconciled to the bank account every month and all unreconciled items resolved. The bank reconciliation should be signed off and any adjusting entries authorised.

This chapter sets out how the petty cash system operates and the controls that should be exercised over petty cash. Nearly every business will have some petty cash expenses. The petty cash book is similar to the cheque payments book and it is used to record minor cash payments made for goods and services. Most organisations draw one cheque made out to cash, which is entered as a payment in the cheque payments book and analysed under the heading "petty cash". This cheque is cashed and the cash is kept in a safe place. When small payments are to be made and cash is used, a petty cash voucher will be written up and the details recorded in the petty cash book.

Petty cash vouchers should be supported by attaching receipts in respect of any payments made. The vouchers are then recorded in the petty cash book in the same manner as cheques are entered in the cheque payments book. The petty cash book should be totalled on a regular basis, ensuring that the total column is equal to the sum of the analysis columns. Set out in Figure 16.1 is an example of a petty cash book:

## Petty Cash Book—December 2007

| Date | Details | Voucher No. | Total Cr− | VAT @ 21 % Dr+ | VAT @13.5% Dr+ | Stationery Dr+ | Canteen Dr+ | Courier/ Taxi Dr+ | Postage Dr+ | Newspaper Dr+ |
|------|---------|-------------|-----------|----------------|----------------|----------------|-------------|-------------------|-------------|---------------|
| 1 Dec | Pens and Envelopes | 1 | 13.31 | 2.31 | | 11.00 | | | | |
| 5 Dec | Milk and Coffee | 2 | 7.80 | | | | 7.80 | | | |
| 8 Dec | Courier | 3 | 18.15 | 3.15 | | | | 15.00 | | |
| 11 Dec | Stamps | 4 | 9.60 | | | | | | 9.60 | |
| 19 Dec | Newspapers | 5 | 10.00 | | 1.19 | | | | | 8.81 |
| 22 Dec | Taxi | 6 | 10.50 | | | | | 10.50 | | |
| | Total at 31/12/07 € | | 69.36 | 5.46 | 1.19 | 11.00 | 7.80 | 25.50 | 9.60 | 8.81 |
| | | | = | + | + | + | + | + | + | + |

| Record in Petty Cash Nominal in Balance Sheet | Record in VAT Nominal in Balance Sheet | Record in VAT Nominal in Balance Sheet | Record in Stationery Nominal in Profit & Loss | Record in Canteen Nominal in Profit & Loss | Record in Courier/ Taxi Nominal in Profit & Loss | Record in Postage Nominal in Profit & Loss | Record in Sundry Nominal in Profit & Loss |
|---|---|---|---|---|---|---|---|

Figure 16.1

**Quick Tip**

Always keep receipts for petty cash: Do not forget about VAT in relation to petty cash expenses as you maybe able to claim back the VAT on certain purchases such as stationery, couriers, etc.

## ❏ Control Over Petty Cash

It is essential that the petty cash system is only used for purchasing incidental items and also that a limit is put on the total of each petty cash claim, eg €100.

Petty cash must be safeguarded and accurately recorded:

- Set a lower and upper limit on the amount of cash to be held at any one time.
- Ensure the petty cash box is secure at all times.
- Set limits for petty cash advances and ensure there is only one petty cash float.
- Petty cash transactions should be authorised.
- The petty cash book should be reconciled to cash held and petty cash vouchers every month.
- The petty cash balance should be reconciled to the general ledger every month.

# CREDITORS

## Chapter 17

Creditors are included in the balance sheet, they include trade creditors, bank loans, finance leases, accruals, taxes and social welfare, VAT and corporation tax liabilities. This chapter includes a description of some of the creditors included in the balance sheet. Additional information in relation to specific types of creditors are set out in separate chapters.

Recognition—timing is important in the recognition of liabilities. Failure to report a liability in an accounting period very often goes hand in hand with failure to record an expense. The two errors lead to an understatement of expenses and an overstatement of profit. One of the key reasons for making adjusting entries at the end of an accounting period is to recognise unrecorded liabilities that accrue during the period. Accrued liabilities include salaries payable and interest payable. Tax liabilities must also be recognised.

Valuation—on the balance sheet, a liability is generally valued at the amount of money needed to pay the debt or at the fair market value of the good or service to be delivered.

Classification—current liabilities are debts and obligations that a company expects to satisfy within one year. Long-term liabilities are liabilities due beyond one year. The purpose of incurring long-term liabilities is to finance long-term assets.

Disclosure—a business may have to include additional explanations of some liabilities in the notes to its financial statements.

## ❏ Trade Creditors

These are short-term obligations to suppliers for goods and services. The amount included in creditors is generally supported by a creditors' ledger, which contains an individual account for each person or company to whom money is owed.

### Aged Creditor Analysis

An analysis of the length of time that the creditor is owed money is called an aged creditor analysis. Aged creditor analysis shows the age of all outstanding amounts owed and how much is owed. This information is valuable for monitoring settlement of supplier invoices. The aged creditor analysis will also include "Turnover" to-date—this is the amount that the business has bought from the supplier in the current year. A credit limit will be set by each supplier. This will be based on the business credit history. Limits are set so that too much credit is not given to businesses that will be unable to pay. The "balance" is the total amount outstanding, analysed into categories such as "Current" (less than 30 days), "Period 1" (30–60 days), "Period 2" (60–90 days), "Period 3" (90–120 days) and then "Older". See Figure 17.1. This analysis can be useful to identify when invoices have to be paid and to pinpoint disputed debts. In the example Carr/Van Ltd is owed €11,000 for over 90 days; this is as a result of the goods having been damaged during transportation.

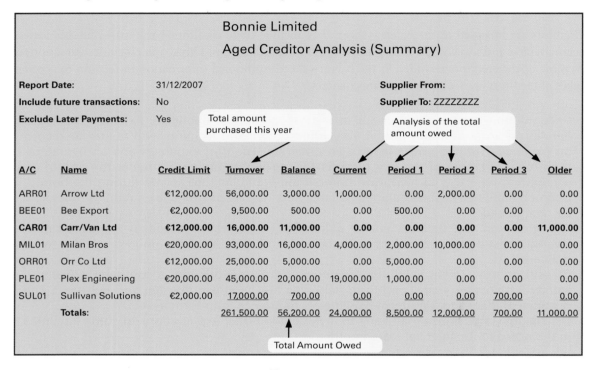

| A/C | Name | Credit Limit | Turnover | Balance | Current | Period 1 | Period 2 | Period 3 | Older |
|---|---|---|---|---|---|---|---|---|---|
| ARR01 | Arrow Ltd | €12,000.00 | 56,000.00 | 3,000.00 | 1,000.00 | 0.00 | 2,000.00 | 0.00 | 0.00 |
| BEE01 | Bee Export | €2,000.00 | 9,500.00 | 500.00 | 0.00 | 500.00 | 0.00 | 0.00 | 0.00 |
| CAR01 | Carr/Van Ltd | €12,000.00 | 16,000.00 | 11,000.00 | 0.00 | 0.00 | 0.00 | 0.00 | 11,000.00 |
| MIL01 | Milan Bros | €20,000.00 | 93,000.00 | 16,000.00 | 4,000.00 | 2,000.00 | 10,000.00 | 0.00 | 0.00 |
| ORR01 | Orr Co Ltd | €12,000.00 | 25,000.00 | 5,000.00 | 0.00 | 5,000.00 | 0.00 | 0.00 | 0.00 |
| PLE01 | Plex Engineering | €20,000.00 | 45,000.00 | 20,000.00 | 19,000.00 | 1,000.00 | 0.00 | 0.00 | 0.00 |
| SUL01 | Sullivan Solutions | €2,000.00 | 17,000.00 | 700.00 | 0.00 | 0.00 | 0.00 | 700.00 | 0.00 |
| | Totals: | | 261,500.00 | 56,200.00 | 24,000.00 | 8,500.00 | 12,000.00 | 700.00 | 11,000.00 |

Figure 17.1

## Creditor Reconciliation

Every month, the aged creditor analysis should be reconciled to creditor statements. This will ensure that the balance account agrees to the third party claim.

Advantages of carrying out these reconciliation:

- Any missing invoices/credit notes issued by the supplier and not recorded can be identified.
- Ensure payments made to the supplier appear on the statement.
- Posting errors can be identified, eg incorrect amounts or amounts recorded in the wrong supplier account.

Set out in Figure 17.2 is an example of a creditor statement. Phone Distributors has received a creditor statement from City Wide Couriers indicating that €114.95 is owed. A printout of a supplier activity report from Phone Distributors' account system (Figure 17.3), indicates that there is a balance owed of €173.64. Each of the figures must be checked in the records of City Wide Couriers (creditor statement) and Phone Distributors (supplier activity report) in order to carry out the reconciliation.

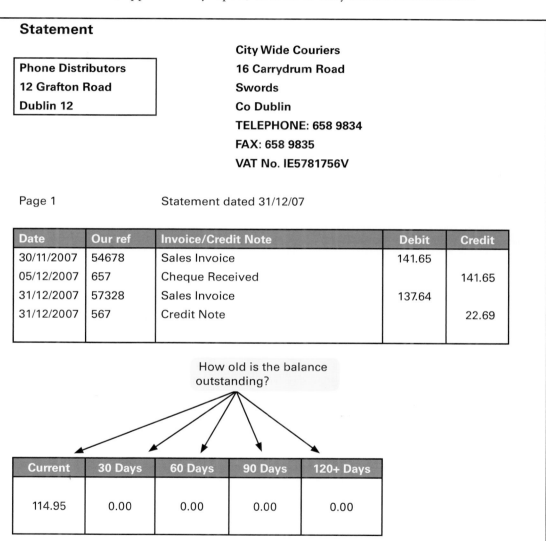

**Statement**

| Phone Distributors | City Wide Couriers |
| 12 Grafton Road | 16 Carrydrum Road |
| Dublin 12 | Swords |
| | Co Dublin |
| | TELEPHONE: 658 9834 |
| | FAX: 658 9835 |
| | VAT No. IE5781756V |

Page 1                    Statement dated 31/12/07

| Date | Our ref | Invoice/Credit Note | Debit | Credit |
| --- | --- | --- | --- | --- |
| 30/11/2007 | 54678 | Sales Invoice | 141.65 | |
| 05/12/2007 | 657 | Cheque Received | | 141.65 |
| 31/12/2007 | 57328 | Sales Invoice | 137.64 | |
| 31/12/2007 | 567 | Credit Note | | 22.69 |

How old is the balance outstanding?

| Current | 30 Days | 60 Days | 90 Days | 120+ Days |
| --- | --- | --- | --- | --- |
| 114.95 | 0.00 | 0.00 | 0.00 | 0.00 |

Figure 17.2

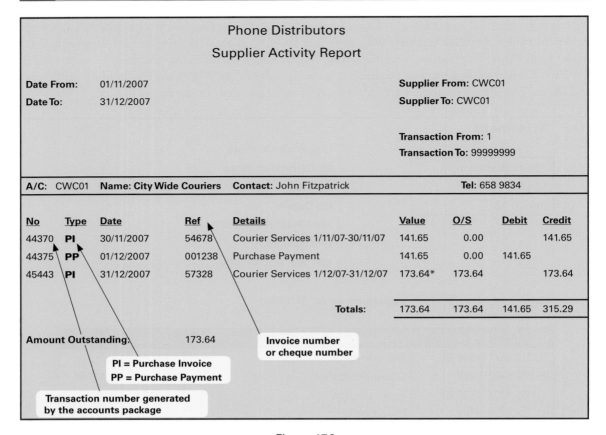

Figure 17.3

On reconciling the City Wide Courier statement to the supplier activity report, a difference of €58.69 emerges (114.95 − 173.64). The supplier activity report is compared to each invoice/credit note and payment on the creditor statement. Credit note number 567 for €22.69 has not been recorded by Phone Distributors and invoice number 57328 in the amount of €137.64 has been incorrectly recorded in the books of Phone Distributors, as being for €173.64. The company's records need to be corrected to the right amount, as in Figure 17.4.

|  | € |
|---|---|
| **Per Supplier Activity Report, City Wide Couriers** | 173.64 |
| Less: Credit Note 567 not recorded | (22.69) |
| Less: Invoice 57328 incorrectly recorded | (173.64) |
| Plus: Invoice 57328 correct amount | 137.64 |
|  |  |
| Total | **114.95** |
|  |  |
| **Per Creditor Statement** | **114.95** |

Figure 17.4

## ❑ Bank Loan

A company often establishes a line of credit with its bank. This arrangement allows the company to borrow funds as needed to finance current operations. The amount borrowed can be increased up to the limit when cash is needed and reduced when the company has enough cash of its own. The bank may require the company to reach certain financial goals to maintain its line of credit.

## ❑ Finance Lease

Leases are classified as operating leases and finance leases. Operating leases are like a rental agreements in that all the costs are included in the profit & loss account. Finance leases involve capitalising the fixed asset and setting up a lease creditor to record the liability owed to the lease company. (See Chapter 20 for more details.)

## ❑ Accruals

A key reason for making adjusting entries at the end of an accounting period is to recognise liabilities that are not already in the accounting records. In accordance with the matching rule, an adjusting entry is made at the end of each accounting period to record liabilities such as loan interest.

Accruals take into account what has been used rather than what has been invoiced for. Accruals are adjustments made to accounts.

- Bills not paid which relate to the period.
- Estimates of amounts owing for work done or services received which have not yet been invoiced.

**Example**

A business receives an invoice in February 2008 for legal fees relating to work carried out in October 2007. An adjustment will have to be made to include the costs in 2007 (assuming the year end is 31 December 2007) as the costs relate to 2007 rather than 2008. Alternatively, an invoice may be received covering two accounting periods, eg electricity may cover December 2007 and January 2008. An adjustment will have to be made to include half of the invoice in 2007 and half in 2008. See Figure 17.5.

| | Jan | Feb | Mar | Apr | May | Jun | Jul | Aug | Sep | Oct | Nov | Dec | Jan | Feb |
|---|---|---|---|---|---|---|---|---|---|---|---|---|---|---|
| Accounting year | | | | | | | | | | | | | | |
| Legal fees for work in October 2007 | | | | | | | | | | Work Carried out | | | | Date on Invoice |
| Electricity bill Dec/Jan 08 | | | | | | | | | | | | Apportion Electricity Bill | Invoice Dec/ Jan 08 | |

2007 Accounting Year          2008 Accrual

Figure 17.5

## ❑ Taxes and Social Welfare

Employers are liable to pay employees (wages and salaries) and also various other agencies, eg pension companies for amounts withheld from wages.

The amount paid to employees for salaries is less than the amount of their gross earnings. This occurs because employers are required by law or are requested by employees to withhold certain amounts from wages and send them directly to government agencies, eg Revenue and other organisations, eg trade union. Each deduction must be shown to have been paid to the proper agency and the employee must receive a report of the deductions made every month. This is shown on their payslip.

Income tax is deducted every time an employee is paid, if their salary is above a minimum amount. PRSI is also deducted. Many organisations also make pension contributions which provide for future benefits for employees when they retire. A portion of the pension contribution is withheld from the employee's salary and the organisation pays the deduction plus an employer's contribution into the pension fund. (See Chapter 23 for additional information.)

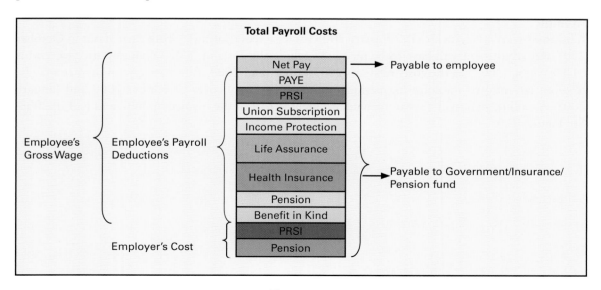

Figure 17.6

# ❏ VAT

A retailer who sells goods and services subject to VAT must collect the VAT from the customer, deduct any VAT they are entitled to reclaim and forward the balance periodically to the Revenue. Until the retailer remits the tax to the Revenue it represents a current liability in the balance sheet. (See Chapter 18 VAT for additional details.)

# ❏ Corporation Tax Liability

The amount of corporation tax payable depends on the results of a company's operations, which are often not known until after the end of the year. An adjusting entry is necessary to record the estimated tax liability. Currently, corporation tax is levied at 12.5% for trading profits and 25% for rental income, deposit interest and certain other non-trading income. If a business is trading as a company it must submit a "corporation tax return, CT1" within nine months of the end of the accounting period. The corporation tax system operates on a self-assessment basis; it is the responsibility of the company to submit and file its tax return. For 2007 the dates on which preliminary tax must be paid are as follows for year ended 31 December 2007:

| | |
|---|---|
| 21 November 2007 | Preliminary tax. |
| 21 September 2008 | Submit tax return and pay balance of tax due. |

Corporation tax is the system of taxation that applies to the profits of all limited companies. Income tax applies to the profits of sole traders and partnerships. The main differences between the two systems relate to the tax rates and the timing of the tax payments.

## *Corporation Tax Assessment*

The profit on which corporation tax is assessed is not identical to the profit as disclosed in the company's profit & loss account, but is an adjusted profit figure after some costs have been disallowed and some other allowances included. (See Chapter 19 for additional details.)

## *Income Tax*

Profits for sole traders and partnerships are taxed under the income tax system. Unlike limited companies, the self-employed do not pay dividends and any drawings or salary they pay themselves are not allowed when computing the taxable profit. Profits earned by the business are deemed to be the income of the individual or partner. Collection of income tax from employees takes place weekly or monthly under the PAYE system. The Revenue cannot operate the same system for the self-employed because its income or profits are not known until the accounting year end.

## ❑ Dividends Payable

Companies sometimes declare dividends. The company has no liability for dividends until the date of declaration. The time between the date the dividend is declared and the date of payment of the dividend is usually short. During this brief interval, the dividends declared are treated as current liabilities of the company.

## ❑ Current Portion of Long-Term Debt

If a company has a term loan or a finance lease that represents a liability for more than one year, it is split in the balance sheet between "creditors due within one year" and "creditors due after more than one year". If a portion of long-term debt is due within the next year and is to be paid from current assets, that portion is classified as a current liability.

## ❑ Deferred Income

Deferred income is advance payment received for providing goods and services which a company must provide in future accounting periods.

## ❑ Contingent Liabilities

A contingent liability is not an existing liability; rather it is a potential liability because it depends on a future event arising out of a past transaction, eg a lawsuit. Two conditions must be satisfied for determining whether a contingency should be entered in the accounting records:

- The liability must be probable.
- The liability can be reasonably estimated.

# VAT

## Chapter 18

This chapter gives a brief overview of Value Added Tax and how it is operated, together with an example of how to complete a VAT return.

VAT is an indirect tax that arises in the case of purchases and sales of taxable goods and services. Different goods and services attract different VAT rates. VAT is often referred to as a chain reaction tax in that all the manufacturers, distributors and retailers of goods and services are involved in collecting the VAT but it is ultimately the consumer who pays it. VAT is paid all along the supply chain to ensure that the Revenue receives the amount of VAT equal to the growth in value of the particular product at that point in the chain. The VAT system operates in such a way that the retailer acts as a VAT collector for the Revenue. The retailer takes money from customers on behalf of the Revenue. At the end of a two-month VAT period businesses must calculate how much VAT it has collected and pay this to the Revenue, less the amount the business is claiming on purchases that it has made.

If the VAT claimed by the business is greater than the VAT charged by the business, the business will be entitled to a refund.

VAT is a high-risk tax, as a mistake in accounting for VAT can result in significant liabilities, due to interest and penalties.

Set out in Figure 18.1 is an example of the chain reaction effect of VAT:

| | Purchases | Sells | A VAT claimed | B VAT charged | A – B Net VAT Liability |
|---|---|---|---|---|---|
| Producer | 50.00 | 60.00 | 50 × 21% = 10.50 | 60 × 21% = 12.60 | 2.10 |
| Manufacturer | 60.00 | 75.00 | 60 × 21% = 12.60 | 75 × 21% = 15.75 | 3.15 |
| Wholesaler | 75.00 | 100.00 | 75 × 21% = 15.75 | 100 × 21% = 21.00 | 5.25 |
| Retailer | 100.00 | 150.00 | 100 × 21% = 21.00 | 150 × 21% = 31.50 | 10.50 |
| Customer | 181.50 | | 59.85 | 80.85 | 21.00 |

Figure 18.1

**Note:** the value of the goods has increased from when the producer purchased the goods for €50 to when the goods are sold to the customer for €150 plus VAT @ 21%. There is an increase of €100 × 21% VAT = €21, the €21 is collect at various stages along the supply chain.

## ❏ Registration for VAT

A business must register and charge VAT if the expected turnover in the business exceeds, or is likely to exceed, €35,000 in a continuous 12-month period if the business is supplying **services**. If the business is supplying **goods** it must register if the expected turnover exceed, or is likely to exceed, €70,000 in a continuous 12-month period. A business can also elect to register for VAT if its turnover threshold is lower than the above limits. If a business registers for VAT it must complete Form TR2 (Company) or Form TR1 (Sole Trader/Partnership). VAT returns must be completed every two months, eg January/February, March/April, etc. The return must be filed and paid by the 19th day of the month following the end of the taxable period, ie the VAT return for January/February 2007 must be paid by 19 March 2007.

## ❑ Net and Gross Price

When businesses refer to the net and gross price of a good or service, the net price is the amount excluding VAT. When VAT is added on, this results in the gross price. Set out below is an example of net and gross prices.

|  | € |  |
|---|---|---|
| Goods | 1,500 | Net price exclusive of VAT |
| VAT @ 21% | 315 | VAT |
| Gross Price | 1,815 | Price inclusive of VAT |

## ❑ VAT Rates

The VAT acts list which goods and services are exempt from VAT or which are liable to VAT at 0% and 13.5%. All other goods and services are liable to VAT at the standard rate of 21%. The 13.5% rate covers electricity, building services, newspapers, etc. The 0% rate covers exports, books, certain food and drinks.

> **Quick Tip**
>
> The Revenue Commissioners lists over 2,500 goods and services with the relevant VAT rates on their website at www.revenue.ie
>    Click on "for Businesses".
>    Click on "VAT".
>    Click on "VAT rates".

### VAT on Sales

When a sale is made, the supplier provides the customer with an invoice that sets out the net price, the rate of VAT, the calculation of VAT and the gross price. The seller is responsible for using the correct VAT rate and for calculating VAT. Certain suppliers are prohibited from charging VAT on sales as its goods or services are regarded as exempt. Insurance companies, for example, cannot charge VAT on an insurance policy.

## VAT on Purchases

VAT can be claimed on most purchases. This is called an **input credit** and in effect it reduces the VAT liability. The goods and services must be used for business purposes. There are certain expenses on which the Revenue does not allow businesses to claim VAT such as food, drink, accommodation, petrol, entertainment and personal expenses. If the owner takes goods out of a business and an input credit was claimed in relation to the goods then this is deemed a self-supply and gives rise to a VAT liability. Businesses need to analyse their records for purchases distinguishing between "purchases for resale" and "purchases not for resale", as this information will be required for the annual VAT Return of Trading Details.

**Quick Tip**

There is a very useful Revenue guide called "VAT for small businesses", available at www.revenue.ie

## Special VAT Rules

- Cocktail rule—If a business supplies two items as a package where one item is liable to VAT @ 0% and another item is liable to VAT @ 21%, then both items are liable to VAT @ 21%.
- The two-thirds rule—if the supply of services also requires the supply of goods, the overall consideration is deemed to apply to the goods. If the cost of the goods exceeds two-thirds of the total contract price.

### Example of two-thirds rule

Installation of bathroom: Cost excluding VAT is €3,000. The cost of the bathroom suite is €2,400 excluding VAT. The VAT rate applicable to the sale of a bathroom suite is 21%. VAT is normally charged at 13.5% on labour. Since the cost of the bathroom suite is 80% of the contract price and therefore more than two-thirds of the contract price then the entire contract is liable to VAT at 21%.

## Cash Receipts Basis

Businesses whose sales are under €1m or where 90% of sales are to non-VAT registered persons, they may be able to account for VAT on a cash receipts basis. This results in a cash flow benefit for small businesses since they are only liable to pay VAT on sales when the customer has actually paid for the goods or services, rather than when the invoice was issued. If this basis is used, the cash receipts book needs to be analysed according to the amount paid by debtors, broken down into net sales and VAT, as this will be used in the VAT return rather than the VAT figure taken from the sales daybook.

## VAT Return

VAT figures included in the purchases daybook, sales daybook and petty cash book are posted to the VAT nominal. Set out in Figure 18.2 is an example of the VAT nominal using the figures taken from the purchases daybook, purchases return book, sales daybook, sales return book, cheque payments book and petty cash book as set out in the chapter on bookkeeping (Chapter 7) and petty cash

(Chapter 16). The figures are analysed into purchases and sales and included on the VAT return (the cash receipts basis was not used in this example).

| VAT | | | | VAT Return Figures |
|---|---|---|---|---|
| Sales Return | 142.80 | Balance b/d | 1,535.00 | **Sales** |
| Purchases not for resale | 195.30 | Sales | 3,540.60 | 3,397.80 |
| Purchases not for resale | 27.00 | Purchases not for resale Return | 10.50 | |
| Purchases for resale | 1,060.71 | Purchases for resale Return | 158.55 | **Purchases** |
| Petty cash | 5.46 | | | 1,120.61 |
| Petty cash | 1.19 | | | |
| Bank | 1,535.00 | | | |
| Balance c/d | 2,277.19 | | | |
| | | | | **Payable** |
| | 5,244.65 | | 5,244.65 | 2,277.19 |
| | | Balance b/d | 2,277.19 | |

Figure 18.2

**Note:** where accounting software is used, these amounts will be posted automatically when purchase invoices and sales invoices are entered on the system.

Set out in Figure 18.3 are the VAT return figures as calculated in Figure 18.2.

In all correspondence please quote:

Registration No:   IE 1452471T
Notice No:         06350802-28108E

Collector-General
Sarsfield House
Francis Street
Limerick
District: 002     Unit: 013

**VAT Period:**
01 Nov 2007
to
31 Dec 2007

V408    92640 215350 92360 214799 070504VAT3EE    DIST.002

SPORTS LIMITED
11 GRAFTON STREET
DUBLIN 2

Enquiries: 1890 203070

**Payment due by:**
19 Jan 2008

**VAT 3 RETURN**

Please complete and sign the return below. The return should then be detached and forwarded (with payment or debit instructions, if liability arises) in the prepaid envelope enclosed, to arrive no later than the due date as shown above. **Guidelines on the correct completion of the return are shown overleaf.**

**IMPORTANCE OF PROMPT PAYMENTS**
- Make sure that you allow sufficient time - at least three working days - for your payment to reach the Collector-General.
- Late payment of tax may incur an interest charge.
- Failure to pay a tax liability, or to pay on time, can result in enforced collection through the Sheriff, Court proceedings or Attachment.

**Enforcement carries additional costs to any interest charged.**

**METHOD OF PAYMENT**
**Single Debit Authority:** If you want your payment to be debited directly from your bank account, complete the bank details on the left of the return below, ensuring that the amount of the payment you wish to make is entered in the Debit Amount box.
Please note that the account must be in a bank within the Republic of Ireland and must be a current account.
- Simply provide your bank details and the amount you wish to have debited from your account.
- Forward the completed return to the Collector-General at the address above.
- A once-off deduction will be taken from your account and credited against your tax liability as specified on the return below.
- The once-off deduction will not be taken from your account in advance of the due date for the taxable period in question.
**Cheque:** All cheques should be made payable to the Collector-General and forwarded to the address above. Do not enclose cash.
**Revenue On-Line Service (ROS):** You can make this return and pay your VAT on-line using ROS. For details visit the Revenue website at www.revenue.ie or Phone 1890 20 11 06.
**Direct Debit:** For information on how to pay VAT by monthly Direct Debit, please contact the Helpline at 1890 20 30 70.

**METHOD OF REPAYMENT**
Any repayment due will be credited to your bank/building society account. Account details are only required **if** this return is a repayment (T4 line completed) **and** you have not previously advised Revenue of the account details **or** you wish to amend the account details to which previous repayments were credited.

Please print one figure only in each space using a black ball-point pen.
Do not write NIL on any line.

€: Enter whole Euro only - do not enter cent.
Photocopies of this form are not acceptable.

**Revenue**

| ↓ **VAT3 RETURN (and PAYSLIP)** | Please complete below, detach and return ↓ |
|---|---|

**Bank Details** - to be supplied if :

⇒ Payment is being made by Single Debit Authority
   *(do not complete this authority if you are paying by cheque)*, or
⇒ A repayment is being sought (*see Method of Repayment above*).

Office Use
AMD
O/S

T1 [           3 , 3 9 8 .00]

| Branch Sort Code | 9 9  1 6  5 2 | T2 [           1 , 1 2 1 .00] |
| Account Number | 4 0 6 5 4 3 2 1 | T3 [           2 , 2 7 7 .00] |
| Debit Amount | 2 , 2 7 7 .00 | T4 [                 .00] |

[                 .00]

*Please debit my account with the amount specified.*

I declare that this is a correct return of Value Added Tax for the period specified.

VAT3 B

E1 [         , , .00]

Signed:- *John Murphy* _____    Date:- 14/1/08

E2 [         , , .00]

**Name:** SPORTS LIMITED
**Reg No:** 1452471T  **VAT Period:** 01 Nov 2007 to 31 Dec 2007

VAT3 B

<063508022810811422     x

Figure 18.3

T1 = VAT on Sales
T2 = VAT on Purchases
T3 = VAT payable
T4 = VAT repayable
E1 = Value of goods dispatched to EU Member states
E2 = Value of goods acquired from EU Member states

## ❏ New Payment Arrangement for VAT

The Revenue has introduced a new arrangement for businesses whose VAT liability in a year is less than €3,000 or between €3,000 and €14,000. If a business's VAT liability is less than €3,000 in a year it is only required to submit and pay VAT every six months. If a business's VAT liability is between €3,000 and €14,000 in a year then it is required to submit three VAT returns. The table below summarises the new arrangement.

### Businesses whose VAT liability is less than €3,000 per annum:

| VAT Period | Frequency | File & Pay |
| --- | --- | --- |
| July–December 2007 | Bi-annual | VAT 3 return and payment by 19 January 2008 |
| January–June 2008 | Bi-annual | VAT 3 return and payment by 19 July 2008 |

### Business whose VAT liability is between €3,000 and €14,000 per annum:

| VAT Period | Frequency | File & Pay |
| --- | --- | --- |
| September–December 2007 | Four-monthly | VAT 3 return and payment by 19 January 2008 |
| January–April 2008 | Four-monthly | VAT 3 return and payment by 19 May 2008 |
| May–August 2008 | Four-monthly | VAT 3 return and payment by 19 September 2008 |
| September–December 2008 | Four-monthly | VAT 3 return and payment by 19 January 2009 |

### VAT Return of Trading Details

Once a year, businesses need to complete a "VAT Return of trading details". This analyses sales between exports, exempt and domestic sales at the various VAT rates. Purchases are analysed between goods purchased for resale and goods not purchased for resale.

# TAXATION  Chapter 19

This chapter sets out a list of expenses that are disallowed when calculating taxable profit for a sole trader/partnership or a company. Taxation liabilities in respect of VAT and PAYE/PRSI are set out in Chapter 18 and 23. This chapter also includes the requirements that need to be followed in order to pay travel and subsistence expenses to employees, tax-free.

## ❏ Expenses Disallowed by the Revenue

Regardless of whether you are operating as a sole trader or a company there are certain expenses or income that are allowed for the purposes of preparing financial statements but are not allowed by the Revenue in the calculation of taxable profits. When calculating taxable profits for a business, you must start with the profit per the accounts and then "add back" expenses that are disallowed—this will increase the profits liable to tax.

- Depreciation is the write-off against profits for accounting purposes of the cost of the capital assets over their useful economic life. It must be **added back**. Capital allowances (which are like depreciation) are based on the cost of qualifying assets which may be claimed.
- Interest incurred must be wholly and exclusively for the purposes of the trade.
- Owners' salaries are a deductible expense for a company, but not for a sole trader/ partner as it is treated as drawings by the sole trader/partner.
- Interest on late payment of taxes is **not** allowed as a deductible expense.
- Personal expenses, eg home electricity bill, home phone bill (unless you run the office from home) groceries, etc are **not** deductible against trading profits.
- Write-off of bad debts which are specific to a certain customer are **allowable** but general provisions to provide for the write-off of say 5% of debtors as potential bad debts is **not an allowable** deduction for tax.
- The interest paid for finance leases is **added back**. The total repayment to the lease company is **allowed** as a deduction. In effect, the cost of the asset is allowed for tax purposes over a number of years.
- Political subscriptions/donations are **not allowable**.
- General provisions such as provision for repair of a building, which the business may incur in the next year, are **not allowable**.
- Parking fines are **not allowable**.
- Capital expenditure, such as the purchase of fixed assets, can **not be included** as an expense, nor can legal fees and stamp duty paid in relation to the purchase of a fixed asset. Capital expenditure may qualify for capital allowances.
- Legal fees incurred for revenue/trading purposes such as contracts with customers are **allowable**.

- Entertainment of clients **can not** be included as part of the calculation of taxable profit. This includes food, drink, accommodation, rugby tickets, etc. Staff entertainment such as the office Christmas party is an entertainment expense that is allowable.
- Travel and subsistence expenses using civil service rates or lower rates can be included as an expense when calculating the taxable profits.
- Certain motor expenses will be **disallowed**, especially if the car is above a certain value.
- Profit or loss on the sale of fixed assets is not treated as part of a business's trading profit for taxation purposes.

## ❏ Allowable Expenses

Employees working for a business are not allowed deductions for expenses unless it can be shown that the expenses are incurred "wholly, exclusively and necessarily" in the performance of the employment, for example an employee can not claim for the cost of getting to work every day. There are certain expenses that the Revenue will allow. These are "flat rate expenses" that are included in the employee's tax credit certificate, eg special clothing, tools, allowance, etc.

There are certain expenses that an employee can claim from his/her employer:

- Reimbursement of expenses incurred on behalf of the employer.
- Travel and subsistence expenses.

## ❏ Travel

If an employee uses his/her own car for the purposes of the employer's business (the employee must pay for all costs of running the car), civil service motor travel rates as published by the Department of Finance[8] can be paid. (These rates are updated and are available on the Department of Finance website.) The rate claimed depends on:

- The engine size of the car.
- Annual number of business kilometres.

Revenue has allowed employees in private companies to be paid motor travel rates in accordance with the agreed civil service rates. Revenue guidelines are set out in Revenue booklet IT51.[9] Employers can pay a lower kilometre rate than those set out in the civil service motor travel rate; if they pay higher rates, the excess amount is regarded as a benefit in kind and is subject to income tax, unless agreed with Revenue. Guidelines to be operated when using civil service motor travel rates:

- A business journey is one in which the employee travels from one place of work to another place of work in the performance of the duties of employment.
- The distance in kilometres is the lower of the distance between the employee's home to the customer and the office to the customer.

---

[8]  www.finance.gov.ie
[9]  www.revenue.ie/leaflets/it51.htm

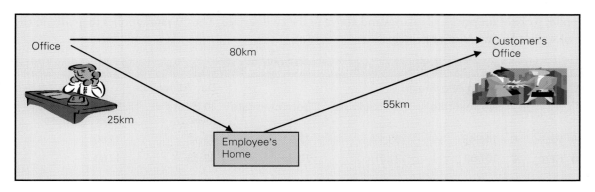

Figure 19.1

In Figure 19.1 the employee can claim 55km since this is the lower of the distance between the employee's home to the customer's office as compared to travelling from the employee's office to the customer's office.

- Expenses that are incurred by employees travelling to and from their place of employment are not allowable.
- Prior Revenue approval is not necessary in order to operate this scheme.
- The employer must operate a satisfactory recording and internal control system.
- Employers should keep records of each business journey, including the following:
    - The date of journey.
    - The reason for the journey.
    - The distance (km).
    - Records must be kept for six years.

The current rates are as follows:

| Motor Cars | | | |
|---|---|---|---|
| Official motor travel in a calendar year | Engine Capacity | | |
| | Up to 1,200cc | 1,201cc to 1,500cc | 1,501cc and over |
| Up to 6,437km | 52.16 cent | 61.66 cent | 78.32 cent |
| 6,437km and over | 26.97 cent | 30.96 cent | 36.65 cent |

## ❑ Subsistence

If an employee is required to work away from the employer's premises he/she will be entitled to a subsistence payment, or the employer may decide to pay actual expenses, such as meals and accommodation. The advantage of using subsistence rates is that it cuts down on the amount of paperwork required. The Department of Finance issues subsistence rates; which are updated. The Revenue has a leaflet[10] that set out the rules to be followed when paying subsistence. The "A rate"

---

[10]  www.revenue.ie/leaflets/it54.htm

applies to assistant principal salaries and above in the civil service. The "B rate" applies to grades in the civil service below assistant principal.

| Subsistence Rates | | | | | |
| --- | --- | --- | --- | --- | --- |
| Class of Allowance | Night Allowance | | | Day Allowance | |
| | Normal rate | Reduced rate | Detention rate | 10 Hours or more | 5 hours but less than 10 hours |
| A- Rate   € | 144.45 | 133.17 | 72.21 | 43.13 | 17.60 |
| B- Rate   € | 101.60 | 121.11 | 70.83 | 43.13 | 17.60 |

## Guidelines to Be Operated When Using Civil Service Subsistence Rates:

- Day allowances are payable if the employee is continuously absent for five hours or more provided the absence is not at a place within five kilometres of the employee's home or normal place of work. There are two rates applicable: one for 5–10 hours and the other for 10 hours or more.
- The normal rate for night allowances applies to absences for up to 14 nights.
- The reduced rate for night allowances applies for the next 14 nights.
- The detention rate for night allowances applies for the next 28 days.
- Records must be kept of:
  - The date(s) and duration of the absence.
  - The reason for the absence.
  - The location(s) involved.
- Records must be kept for six years.

Set out in Figure 19.2 is an example of a travel and subsistence claim form that can be used by employees to make a claim for expenses.

## Leeson Limited Monthly Travel, Subsistence and Miscellaneous Expense Claim Form

Name: John Lynch          Month Ending: Dec-07

| Date and Time of Departure | | Date and Time of Return | | Details of Journey (From/To) | | Reason for Trip AND/OR Details of Expense (eg Attending Conference etc.) | Mode of Travel | Kilo-metres (one line per trip) | Kilometre Rates € | Travel € | Hotel & Food Claim/Subsistence Claim € | Other Expenses € | TOTAL € |
|---|---|---|---|---|---|---|---|---|---|---|---|---|---|
| Date | Time | Date | Time | From (eg Office) | To | | | | | | | | |
| 01-Dec-07 | 9am | 1-Dec-07 | 6pm | Home | Cork & return | Meeting with supplier | Car | 250 | 0.7832 | 195.80 | 17.60 | Toll 3.80 | 217.29 |
| 16-Dec-07 | 9am | 16-Dec-07 | 9pm | Office | Galway & return | Meeting with supplier | Car | 430 | 0.7832 | 336.78 | 43.13 | | 379.91 |
| 19-Dec-07 | 11am | 19-Dec-07 | 3pm | Office | Wicklow & return | Meeting with supplier | Car | 50 | 0.7832 | 39.16 | Hotel Receipt 40.16 | Toll 3.80 | 83.12 |
| | | | | | | | | | | | | | |
| | | | | | | | | | | | | | |
| | | | | | | | | | | | | | |
| | | | | | | | | | | | | | |
| | | | | | | | | | | | | | |
| | | | | | | | | | | | | | |
| | | | | | | | | | | | | | |
| | | | | | | | | TOTAL | 730 | 571.74 | 100.89 | 7.60 | 680.23 |

I certify that:

(a) the expenses claimed were necessarily incurred by me in respect of **Leeson Limited.**

(b) the particulars furnished herein are in all respects true.

(c) no claim in respect of the same trip has been made or will be made against any other organisation.

(d) expense receipts and relevant documentation are attached.

| Date | 20/12/2007 | Signed | John Lynch |
|---|---|---|---|
| Date | 21/12/2007 | Authorised | Mary Smyth |

Figure 19.2

# LEASES

This chapter sets out how to account for a lease. A distinction has to be made between an operating lease and a finance lease. The former would describe the short-term hire of an asset, eg renting a motor vehicle or a piece of equipment for a few weeks or months. Operating leases are charged to the profit & loss account when incurred and no entry is made in the balance sheet.

A finance lease is often used to buy plant and machinery and motor vehicles. It is, in effect, a loan in that there is an interest element included in the amount that is repaid to the lease company as well as a capital repayment element. The interest is charged to the profit & loss account and the repayment of capital is deducted from the amount owed to the lease company. Finance leases are, seen as conferring all the benefits of outright ownership and the asset is depreciated each year.

## ❑ Types of Leases

1. An operating lease—payments on operating leases are treated as a rent expense. The owner (lease company) retains all the risk and rewards of ownership.
2. Finance lease—a finance lease is, in substance, an instalment purchase. The leased asset and related liability must be recognised. The characteristics of a finance lease are that it cannot be cancelled and its duration is about the same as the useful life of the asset. The business leasing the asset (the lessee) must record the asset and the liability in the balance sheet. The amount recorded as the fixed asset will be the cost and the amount of the liability will be the capital repayments. The difference between the two amounts will be the interest to be paid over the duration of the lease. The monthly repayments made by the lessee will be made up of a capital repayment and interest. The amount of interest can be allocated using several methods:
   - The level spread method—if the interest is €3,260 over the duration of the lease (say six years) then the interest allocated each year would be €543 (€3,260/6 years).
   - The actuarial method—this method uses a rate of interest which is calculated on the remaining liability so that the interest charged in the earlier years will be higher than at the end of the lease.
   - Sum of digit method—this is an approximation method that will yield similar results to the actuarial method. Set out in Figure 20.1 is an example using the sum of digit method.

**Example: Sum of digits method**

On 1 January a company signs a lease agreement for a fixed asset which will require repayments of €3,000 for six years. The asset cost €14,740. The useful life of the asset is six years with a nil residual value. Straight-line depreciation is charged. Interest of €3,260 (€3,000 × 6 years = €18,000 − €14,740) will have to be allocated over the six years. In order to carry out this allocation, the sum of digits method is used. The total of the number of years is the denominator and the total number of years to be allocated is the numerator, eg in Year 1 the allocation is 6/21 (The 21 is calculated as follows 1 + 2 + 3 + 4 + 5 + 6 = 21, being the sum of the number of years). Using this method results in higher interest being charged in the early years of the lease and lower interest being charged when the lease is coming towards the end of its term.

1. The asset will need to be recorded in the books of the lessee.

| Date | Account | Statement | Debit | Credit |
|------|---------|-----------|-------|--------|
| 1 Jan | Fixed Asset | Balance Sheet | 14,740 | |
| 1 Jan | Finance Lease Creditor | Balance Sheet | | 14,740 |

2. Depreciation must be recorded each year for six years.
   Cost €14,740/6 years = €2,457

| Date | Account | Statement | Debit | Credit |
|------|---------|-----------|-------|--------|
| 31 Dec | Fixed Asset Depreciation | Profit & Loss | 2,457 | |
| 31 Dec | Fixed Asset Accumulated Depreciation | Balance Sheet | | 2,457 |

3. The interest must be recorded as an expense in the profit & loss account and an increase in the finance lease creditor.

| Date | Account | Statement | Debit | Credit |
|------|---------|-----------|-------|--------|
| 31 Dec | Finance Lease Interest | Profit & Loss | 931 | |
| 31 Dec | Finance Lease Creditor | Balance Sheet | | 931 |

The calculation of interest using the sum of digits method is set out below:

| Year | Lease Payments | Interest | Reduction in lease obligation | Finance Lease Creditor |
|------|----------------|----------|-------------------------------|------------------------|
| | € | € | € | € |
| Cost | | | | 14,740 |
| 1 | 3,000 | 931 | 2,069 | 12,671 |
| 2 | 3,000 | 776 | 2,224 | 10,447 |
| 3 | 3,000 | 621 | 2,379 | 8,068 |
| 4 | 3,000 | 466 | 2,534 | 5,534 |
| 5 | 3,000 | 311 | 2,689 | 2,845 |
| 6 | 3,000 | 155 | 2,845 | – |
| | 18,000 | 3,260 | 14,740 | |

(*Continued*)

Sum of digits method total number
of Years 1 + 2 + 3 + 4 + 5 + 6 = 21 (denominator)

|  | € |
|---|---|
| Total Repayments | 18,000 |
| Less Cost | (14,740) |
| Total Interest | 3,260 |

| Year | Allocation basis | Interest | Allocation |
|---|---|---|---|
|  |  | € | € |
| 1 | 6/21 | 3,260 | 931.43 |
| 2 | 5/21 | 3,260 | 776.19 |
| 3 | 4/21 | 3,260 | 620.95 |
| 4 | 3/21 | 3,260 | 465.71 |
| 5 | 2/21 | 3,260 | 310.48 |
| 6 | 1/21 | 3,260 | 155.24 |
|  |  |  | 3,260.00 |

Figure 20.1

Set out in Figure 20.2 is an extended Trial Balance showing the journals necessary and whether the figures are in the profit & loss account or balance sheet.

| Account Name | Adjustments | | Adjustments | | Adjusted Trial Balance | | Profit & Loss | | Balance Sheet | |
|---|---|---|---|---|---|---|---|---|---|---|
|  | Dr | Cr | Dr | Cr | Dr | Cr | Dr | Cr | Dr | Cr |
| Fixed Asset | 14,740 |  |  |  | 14,740 |  |  |  | 14,740 |  |
| Finance Lease Creditor |  | 14,740 | 3,000 | 931 |  | 12,671 |  |  |  | 12,671 |
| Fixed Asset Depreciation | 2,457 |  |  |  | 2,457 |  | 2,457 |  |  |  |
| Fixed Asset Accumulated Depreciation |  | 2,457 |  |  |  | 2,457 |  |  |  | 2,457 |
| Finance Lease Interest |  |  | 931 |  | 931 |  | 931 |  |  |  |
| Bank |  |  |  | 3,000 |  | 3,000 |  |  |  | 3,000 |
|  | 17,197 | 17,197 | 3,931 | 3,931 | 18,128 | 18,128 | 3,388 |  | 14,740 | 18,128 |

Figure 20.2

This chapter sets out what should be included on a sales invoice and a credit note, the rules are governed by VAT regulations. A sales invoice must be issued by the 15th working day of the month following the month in which the goods/services were supplied or when payment is received, whichever is the earlier.

## ❏ What Should Be on a Sales Invoice?

- Date of issue.
- An invoice number in sequential order.
- Name, address and VAT number.
- The customer's name, billing address and delivery address.
- The quantity and description of the goods supplied.
- Date on which the goods/service were supplied.
- Unit price excluding VAT and discounts.
- Consideration excluding VAT and the rate of VAT charged.
- VAT payable.
- If the supply of goods is to a VAT-registered business in another member state include on the invoice the customer's VAT number and an indication that it is an intra-community acquisition of goods.
- Instructions as to the method of payment required.

**Example**

If City Wide Couriers Ltd provides services to Phone Distributors Ltd, City Wide Couriers will issue a sales invoice that will be recorded in their sales daybook. Phone Distributors, as the purchaser of the service, will record this invoice as a purchase invoice in their purchases daybook. The same invoice will be recorded as a sales invoice in one company and as a purchase invoice in the other company.

Set out in Figure 21.1 is an example of an invoice issued by City Wide Couriers to Phone Distributors for services provided.

| INVOICE | | City Wide Couriers | | | |
|---|---|---|---|---|---|

Phone Distributors
12 Grafton Road
Dublin 12

**City Wide Couriers**

**16 Carrydrum Road
Swords
Co Dublin
TELEPHONE: 658 9834
FAX: 658 9835
VAT No. IE 5781756V**

Page: 1          Invoice No: 57328          Date 31/12/07

| OUR REF | DATE | YOUR REF | FROM | TO | VALUE |
|---|---|---|---|---|---|
| A7639 | 01/12/2007 | Kate | Office | Vodafone, Grafton Street | 15.00 |
| A4637 | 06/12/2007 | Mary | Office | O2, Dundrum | 16.50 |
| A5729 | 11/12/2007 | Stephen | Office | Metor, Lucan | 18.75 |
| A7895 | 15/12/2007 | Kate | Office | Vodafone, Swords | 11.00 |
| A9684 | 18/12/2007 | Mary | Office | O2, St Stephen's Green | 15.00 |
| A5294 | 22/12/2007 | Stephen | Office | Meteor, Ringsend | 18.75 |
| **A5398** | **29/12/2007** | **Stephen** | **Office** | **Dublin Port** | **18.75** |

| Net Amount | 113.75 |
|---|---|
| VAT @ 21% | 23.89 |
| TOTAL | 137.64 |

**Net payment 30 days**

Figure 21.1

## ☐ What Should be on a Credit Note?

- Date of issue.
- Sequential number.
- Name, address and VAT number of the seller.
- The customer's name and address.
- Reason why the credit note is being issued.
- Total value excluding VAT.
- Rate of VAT and the amount of VAT at each rate.

City Wide Couriers incorrectly invoiced Phone Distributors for a job (reference no A5398 dated 29/12/07). To correct this error they issued a credit note for €18.75 plus VAT. Set out in Figure 21.2 is an example of a credit note issued by City Wide Couriers.

| CREDIT NOTE | City Wide Couriers |
|---|---|

**CREDIT NOTE**

Phone Distributors
12 Grafton Road
Dublin 12

**City Wide Couriers**

**16 Carrydrum Road**
**Swords**
**Co Dublin**
**TELEPHONE: 658 9834**
**FAX: 658 9835**
**VAT No. IE 5781756V**

| Page: 1 | Credit Note No: 567 | Date 31/12/07 |
|---|---|---|

| OUR REF | DATE | YOUR REF | FROM | TO | VALUE |
|---|---|---|---|---|---|
| A5398 | 29/12/2007 | Stephen | Office | Dublin Port | 18.75 |
| Invoice issued to customer in error | | | | | |

| | |
|---|---|
| Net Amount | 18.75 |
| VAT @ 21% | 3.94 |
| TOTAL | 22.69 |

Figure 21.2

## ❑ Sales Terms

When goods are sold on credit, both parties should understand the amount and timing of payments as well as other terms of the purchase, for example who will pay for delivery charges and whether warranties and right of return apply. The terms of sale are usually printed on the sales invoice and they constitute part of the sales agreement. Terms differ from industry to industry. Sometimes a supplier will offer a discount for early payment of an invoice.

### Example of a Sales/Purchases Discount

Alltrade sells concrete blocks to Builders Ltd on 10 August for €500. If Builders Ltd pays within 10 days they may claim a discount of 2%. The invoice must be paid within 30 days.

Alltrade records the sale as €500 as they do not know if Builders Ltd will pay early and avail of the discount; if Builders Ltd pays on 15 August they are entitled to a 2% discount, so they will pay Alltrade €490. Alltrade will record the receipt of €490. There will be a debit balance left in debtors of €10, which represents the discount of €10. Debtors will need to be credited and sales discount debited. Sales discount is a contra account to sales and is netted against sales when presented in the profit & loss account.

Using journals, the amounts appear as follows:

| Date | Account | Statement | Debit | Credit |
|---|---|---|---|---|
| 15 Aug | Sales Discount | Profit & Loss | 10 | |
| 15 Aug | Debtors | Balance Sheet | | 10 |
| Discount allowed for early settlement of invoice. | | | | |

If Builders Ltd pays on 15 August they will record the original invoice of €500 as a purchase of goods. They will offset the €490 paid against creditors outstanding and the credit balance of €10 as a purchase discount. Creditors must be debited and purchase discount credited. Purchase discount is a contra account to purchases and is netted against purchases when presented in the profit & loss account.

Using journals, the amounts appear as follows:

| Date | Account | Statement | Debit | Credit |
|------|---------|-----------|-------|--------|
| 15 Aug | Creditors | Balance Sheet | 10 | |
| 15 Aug | Purchase discount | Profit & Loss | | 10 |
| Discount received for early settlement of purchase invoice. | | | | |

# PURCHASES/ PROCUREMENT

## Chapter 22

Set out in this chapter is an overview of a procurement process, analysis of business transactions including controls to be used when purchasing goods and services.

## ❏ Procurement Process

The following is an outline of the procurement purchase process:

- A purchase order system should be in place to keep a record of all purchase orders made by a business.
- When goods/services are required, a purchase order form should be completed and a purchase order number assigned to the order.
- Two copies of the purchase order form should be signed, one sent to the supplier and the other kept by the business to be matched with the invoice.
- When the goods are delivered, check that the goods received match the goods stated on the delivery docket.
- The delivery docket should be signed.
- An invoice will be received from the supplier that should be recorded.

The following is an outline of the procurement payment process:

- The purchase order and delivery docket should be attached to the purchase invoice received.
- All the details on the purchase invoice, purchase order and delivery docket should be checked and all details, quantities and prices should match.
- A cheque requisition form should be completed, detailing the relevant information on the invoice and the cheque.
- The purchase order, invoice and delivery docket should be signed to acknowledge that the details are correct.
- A cheque should be drawn up for the relevant amount, signed by a cheque signatory and posted to the supplier.
- The cheque will be recorded and the creditor balance cleared; the cheque number should be filled in on the cheque requisition form and filed by cheque number.

# ❏ Procurement Process

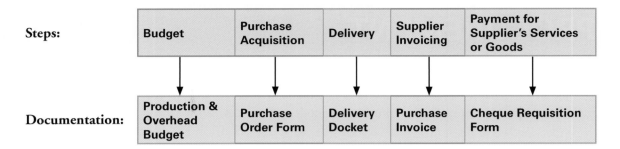

| Steps: | Budget | Purchase Acquisition | Delivery | Supplier Invoicing | Payment for Supplier's Services or Goods |
|---|---|---|---|---|---|

| Documentation: | Production & Overhead Budget | Purchase Order Form | Delivery Docket | Purchase Invoice | Cheque Requisition Form |
|---|---|---|---|---|---|

Set out in Figure 22.1 is an example of a purchase order form.

## Purchase Order Form

| To: ABC Ltd<br>Unit 12 Ashbourne Business Park<br>Ashbourne<br>Co Meath | | Order No.<br><br>**1563** | Date<br><br>**3/12/07** |
|---|---|---|---|

**Delivery Address:**
14 Main Street
Blackrock
Co Dublin

**Please supply the following:**

| Quantity | Description | Price Per Unit | Amount |
|---|---|---|---|
| | | € | € |
| 3 | XFJ3 Convertors | 150 | 450 |
| 1 | FL39 Adaptors | 100 | 100 |
| | | | |
| | | | |
| | | | |
| | | | |
| | | | |
| | | | |
| | | | |
| | | | |
| | | | |
| | VAT @ 21% | | 115.50 |
| | | | |
| **Total** | | | **€665.50** |

..........*Luke Reynolds*.....................
    Delivery Requested By

..............Marie Dowling.....................
    Purchasing Authority

Figure 22.1

## ❑ Analysing Business Transactions

Business transactions are economic events that affect a company's financial position. To measure a business transaction it is necessary to decide when the transaction occurred (recognition), what value to place on the transaction (valuation) and how the transaction should be categorised (classification). See Figure 22.2.

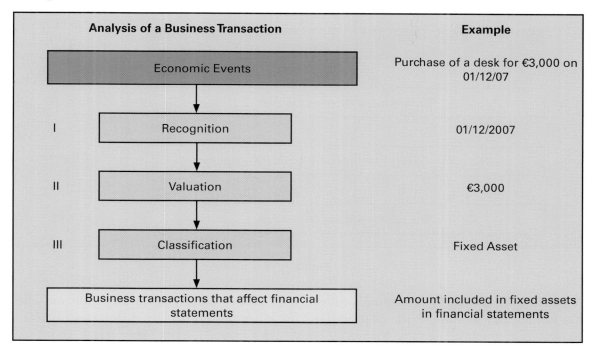

Figure 22.2

### I. Recognition

This refers to the difficulty of deciding when a business transaction should be recorded. The resolution of this issue is important because the date on which a transaction is recorded affects the amounts included in the financial statements. Set out in Figure 22.3 is an example.

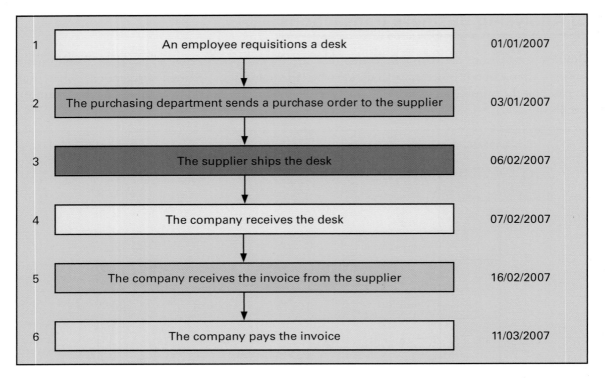

Figure 22.3

A purchase should not be recognised until title is transferred because up to that point the seller has not fulfilled its contractual obligation and the buyer has no liability. Many small businesses that have simple accounting systems do not record a transaction until they receive an invoice (stage 5) or pay for it (stage 6). Although purchase requisitions and purchase orders are economic events they do not affect a company's financial position and they are not recognised in the accounting records.

## II. Valuation

The valuation issue focuses on assigning a monetary value to a business transaction. Generally accepted accounting principles state that the original cost is the appropriate value to assign to all business transactions and therefore to all assets, liabilities, revenue and expenses.

## III. Classification

The classification issue has to do with assigning all the transactions in which a business engages to appropriate categories or accounts. Classification of debts can affect a company's ability to borrow money, and classification of purchases can affect its income. For example, the purchase of tools may be considered repairs (expense) or equipment (asset), depending on the amount of money spent on the tools.

Quick Tip

> Purchase invoices should be stamped when received so that there can be no dispute with suppliers in terms of the date stated on the invoice and when the business actually received the invoice. Credit terms may be 30 days from the date on the invoice; eg the invoice may state 1 January 2007 but it may only be received until 27 January 2007.

## Controls Over Procurement/Purchasing

- Expenditure should be properly planned, authorised and in line with the production and overhead budget.
- Purchases should be competitively priced, quality driven and sourced from reliable suppliers.
- Stocks should be kept to a workable minimum while satisfying customer demand.
- Existing suppliers should be used to obtain value for money and better quality and service. This should also lead to a reduction in the number of suppliers, thereby making savings in administrative time and costs.
- Only goods or services ordered should be accepted and recorded.
- Expenditure should be accurately recorded and allocated in the accounts system.
- Payments should be only made for goods and services that have been received.
- Creditors should be managed effectively, efficiently and reconciled on a regular basis.

The following should be considered when purchasing goods and services:

- Invite tenders and quotes from more than one supplier.
- Request and review any references for previous work carried out.
- Read the contract including the small print.
- Put any questions or specifications in writing and request a reply in writing.
- Ensure that the person who signs the contract has the authority to sign it.

# WAGES & PAYROLL/ PAYE/PRSI

## Chapter 23

This chapter covers the operation of the PAYE/PRSI system, calculation of tax, PRSI and submission of Forms P30, P45, P60 and P35.

## ❑ Registering as an Employer

When a business commences it must formally register with the Revenue Commissioners by completing Form TR1 (sole trader/partner) or TR2 (company). These forms includes details such as name, address, payroll system, number of staff, etc. Form TR1 and TR2 are used to register for many taxes such as income/corporation tax, VAT and PAYE. If an individual or company does not register as an employer, it can be done at a later date by completing form "PREM Reg".

## ❑ Registration of an Employee

When an employee comes into the employment system for the first time a **Form 12A** should be completed by the employee. This form is an application for a "Certificate of Tax Credits and Standard Rate Cut-off Point", which is a social insurance registration application. Form 12A requires personal details of the employee such as name, address and place of birth and details in relation to the new employer such as employer name, registration number and amount of pay. If an employee has already been in employment, he should give his/her new employer a **Form P45**. The Form P45 will have details of the pay, tax deducted and PRSI up to the date of leaving the previous employment. The new employer completes part 3 of Form P45 and sends it to the tax office to formally register the new employment of the employee.

### Payment of Wages Act 1991
Employers may not make deductions from wages or receive payment from their employees unless:

- Required by law, such as PAYE or PRSI.
- Provided for in the contract of employment, for example, pension contributions.
- Made with the written consent of the employee, for example health insurance payments or trade union subscriptions, saving scheme.
- Court order eg payment to a separated spouse.

The Act obliges employers to give to each employee, with every wage packet, a written statement (payslip) of gross wages itemising each deduction.

**The PAYE/PRSI system is**

- A method of tax deduction under which the employer calculates any tax due and deducts it each time a payment of wages is being made **(Pay As You Earn)**.
- A method of collecting Pay-Related Social Insurance contributions **(PRSI)**.

**The tax year starts on 1 January and finishes on 31 December.**

# ❏ PAYE

The PAYE system operates on the basis that an employer deducts tax at the appropriate tax rates on **gross pay** to calculate gross tax. The gross tax is then reduced by the **tax credits** due, to arrive at the net tax payable. Details of the tax credits, standard rate cut-off point and tax rate for each employee are sent to the employer by the tax office. Every year employers are issued with a leaflet advising them of any changes relevant to income tax for the year ahead, eg tax rates. This leaflet is essential for all employers and staff who have responsibility for payroll operation. An employer is issued with a certificate of tax credits and standard rate cut-off point for each employee each year. Both PAYE and PRSI must be deducted at the same time when processing payrolls.

## Tax Rates

The rates of income tax are outlined each year in the budget. Before the start of the new tax year, the tax office will send each employer a notice outlining the tax rates for the coming year. The tax rates for 2007 are 20% and 41% depending on the level of income.

## Certificate of Tax Credits and Standard Rate Cut-Off Point

This is calculated individually for each employee by the tax office and the employer will be issued with a certificate of tax credits and standard rate cut-off point and a tax rate to use in the calculation of tax for each employee. If an employer does not receive a certificate or a Form P45 for an employee, they should operate **emergency basis** and advise the employee to contact the tax office to arrange for the issue of a certificate.

To ensure that the correct amount of tax is deducted from an employee's pay, PAYE is normally computed on a **cumulative basis.** This means that when an employer computes the tax of an employee, the total tax due is calculated from the beginning of the tax year (January) to the date on which a payment is being made. The tax deducted in the particular week or month is the cumulative tax due to that date from the beginning of the tax year, reduced by the amount of tax previously deducted. It also ensures that refunds can be made to an employee, where a revised certificate of tax credits and standard rate cut-off point is received, increasing the employee's tax credits and standard rate cut-off point.

## Calculation of Tax

Under the tax credit system, tax is calculated at the appropriate rate on gross pay to arrive at gross tax in respect of the pay period. The gross tax figure is then reduced by the tax credits due for the period to arrive at the net tax payable. The appropriate rate of tax for 2007 is:

20% on gross pay up to the standard rate cut-off point for the pay period.

41% on gross pay over the standard rate cut-off point, see Figure 23.1.

## Calculation (Using 2007 Tax Rates)

**Gross Pay – Employee Pension = Taxable Pay**

PAYE is then calculated as follows:

  €34,000 @ 20% of taxable pay
+ Balance @ 41% of taxable pay
= Gross Tax

Gross Tax – Tax Credit = Tax Payable

Figure 23.1

## Pay

The following general guidelines apply in deciding whether a payment, benefit or expense should be regarded as pay and taxed under the PAYE system. All payments of wages, salaries, overtime, bonuses and holiday pay by an employer are regarded as pay.

## Holiday Pay

The tax credits and standard rate cut-off point to be used in the calculation of tax on "holiday pay" paid in advance of the usual pay day strictly relate to the income tax week or month in which it is paid. If, however, the effect of paying holiday pay in advance is that the employee receives the equivalent of two or three weeks' pay in the same week and no pay in the following week, or following two weeks, the tax credits and standard rate cut-off point for those weeks may be taken into account in the calculation of tax due on the normal pay and the holiday pay **except where the employee is being paid holiday pay immediately before leaving the employment.**

## Expenses

Leaflets issued by the Revenue called 'Employee's Motoring Expenses' (IT51)[11] and 'Employee's Subsistence Expenses' (IT54)[12] give further information about the payment of travel and subsistence expenses tax-free. (See Chapter 19.)

---

[11]  www.revenue.ie/leaflet IT51

[12]  www.revenue.ie/leaflet IT54

## Taxation on Different Types of Pay

| Types | Examples | Tax Treatment |
|---|---|---|
| **Pay** | • Wages<br>• Salaries<br>• Overtime<br>• Bonuses<br>• Commission<br>• Arrears<br>• Directors' fees<br>• Holiday pay | All taxed as pay |
| **Round Sum Pay** | • Tool money<br>• Travelling time<br>• Danger money<br>• Site allowance | All taxed as pay |
| **Benefits/Perks** | • Car<br>• Medical insurance<br>• Health club premiums | All taxed as benefits in kind (see the Revenue guide for treatment of different benefits in kind[13]) |
| **Expenses** | • Motor expenses<br><br>• Expenses<br>• Travelling to and from work<br>• Subsistence | • Not taxable if expenses are incurred in carrying out duties of the job<br>• Not taxable if receipts are retained<br>• Not allowable for tax purposes<br>• Not taxable if expenses are incurred in carrying out duties of the job |
| **Bus/Train Passes** | • Bus/train/Luas | Deducted from gross pay before PAYE is calculated |

Figure 23.2

# ❑ PRSI

In addition to the deduction of PAYE, employers are obliged to deduct PRSI on behalf of the Department of Social and Family Affairs. Employers will also have a liability to PRSI called employers' PRSI. The PRSI contribution is made up of a number of different components, including:

- A social insurance contribution that varies according to the earnings of the employee and the benefits for which the person is insured.
- A health contribution.

**Quick Tip**

PRSI is calculated on the reckonable earnings, ie gross pay less pension contributions and permanent health insurance contributions, so if an employee contributes to a pension scheme this will reduce the amount of PRSI that the employee and employer has to pay.

---

[13] www.revenue.ie/pdf/bikguide.pdf

# ❑ PAYE Definitions

## Reductions from Gross Salary

Tax relief on contributions to Revenue-approved permanent health benefit schemes and pension schemes will be given at source, by reducing the gross pay for tax and PRSI purposes, in the same way as gross pay is reduced for superannuation contributions.

## Cumulative System

The system operates on a cumulative basis for both tax credits and standard rate cut-off point. This means that tax credits and/or standard rate cut-off point which are not used in a pay period carry forward and are available for use in the calculation of tax due in the following pay period within the tax year.

## Week 1/Month 1

Sometimes an employer will receive a notice of determination of tax credits and standard rate cut-off point, which states that it has been issued on a "week 1" or "month" 1 basis. In such cases, PAYE is not operated on a cumulative basis and each pay period is looked at in isolation. If a week 1/month 1 basis applies neither the pay, tax credits nor standard rate cut-off point is accumulated for tax purposes. The tax credits and standard rate cut-off point for week 1/month 1 are used in the calculation of the tax due for each week/month. The employer is not permitted to make any refunds.

## Temporary Basis

This is when an employee has recently joined a company and presented the employer with a P45. The employee must be taxed on the week 1/month 1 basis until a new certificate of tax credits and standard rate cut-off point has been received. The temporary basis is essentially the same as the week 1/month 1 basis.

## Emergency Tax

Emergency tax is operated when:

- The employee has no certificate of tax credits and standard rate cut-off point.
- The employee has no tax deduction card for the current year.
- The employee has no Form P45 for the current year.
- The employee has given the employer a completed P45 without a PPS number and not indicated that the emergency basis applies.
- The employee's P45 indicates that emergency tax applies.

The emergency basis is non-cumulative and each week or month is looked at in isolation. See Figure 23.3.

| Employee does not provide a PPS number | | |
|---|---|---|
| Week/Month | Standard Rate Cut-Off Point | Tax Credit |
| Every Week or Month | €0 | €0 |
| **Employee provides a PPS number** | | |
| Weekly paid | Proportion Standard Rate Cut-Off Point | Proportion of Tax Credit |
| Week 1–4 | 1/52 | 1/52 |
| Week 5–8 | 1/52 | €0 |
| Week 9 onwards | €0 | €0 |
| | | |
| Monthly paid | Proportion Standard Rate Cut-Off Point | Proportion of Tax Credit |
| Month 1 | 1/12 | 1/12 |
| Month 2 | 1/12 | €0 |
| Month 3 | €0 | €0 |

Figure 23.3

### Example

| Employee provides a PPS number | | |
|---|---|---|
| Weekly paid | Standard Rate Cut-Off Point | Weekly Tax Credit |
| Week 1–4 | €654 (€34,000/52) | €34 (€1,760/52) |
| Week 5–8 | €654 | €0 |
| Week 9 onwards | €0 | €0 |
| | | |
| Monthly paid | Standard Rate Cut-Off Point | Monthly Tax Credit |
| Month 1 | €2,834 (€34,000/12) | €147 (€1,760/12) |
| Month 2 | €2,834 | €0 |
| Month 3 | €0 | €0 |

## Tax Credits

Under the tax credit system, an employee is entitled to tax credits depending on personal circumstances, eg married person's credit, employee (PAYE) tax credit etc. The amount of the employee's tax credits is adjusted to take account of any non-PAYE income such as benefits in kind and tax relief due at the higher rate of tax, eg expenses of employment.

| Tax Credits | |
|---|---|
| | € |
| Single Person's Allowance | 1,760 |
| Married Person's Allowance | 3,520 |
| PAYE Allowance | 1,760 |

**Note: Tax credits are non-refundable.**

Tax credits are used to reduce tax calculated on gross pay. Any unused tax credits are carried forward on a cumulative basis to subsequent pay periods within the tax year.

**Example:**

Where the gross tax on gross pay in a pay period is, say, €100 and the tax credit is €120, the difference of €20 is not refunded. The employee simply has no tax liability for that pay period. **The unused tax credit of €20 is carried forward and offset against tax due in the subsequent pay period(s).**

As mentioned, tax credits are non-refundable. Tax refunds will, of course, arise where cumulative tax for the last pay period exceeds cumulative tax for the current pay period.

**Example**

Where the cumulative tax at, say, week 20 is €1,400 and the cumulative tax at week 21 is €1,200, the difference of €200 is refunded.

## Standard Rate Cut-Off Point

A standard rate cut-off point is the amount of the personal standard rate tax band as adjusted for any non-PAYE income and tax relief due at the higher rate of tax. In each pay period an employee pays tax at the standard rate of tax (20%) up to the standard rate cut-off point. Any pay in a pay period over the cut-off point is taxed at the higher rate of tax (41%). Where an employee's standard rate cut-off point exceeds gross pay in a pay period, the unused amount is carried forward on a cumulative basis for use in the next pay period within the tax year.

|  | Standard Rate Cut-Off Point | Rate |
|---|---|---|
|  | € |  |
| Single/Widowed without dependent children | 34,000 | @20% |
|  | Balance | @41% |
|  |  |  |
| Single/Widowed qualifying for one-parent tax credit | 38,000 | @20% |
|  | Balance | @41% |
|  |  |  |
| Married couple | 43,000 | @20% |
| (one spouse with income) | Balance | @41% |
|  |  |  |
| Married couple | 43,000 | @20% |
| (both spouses with income). This may be increased by €25,000* | Balance | @41% |

Figure 23.4

* Note the increase in the standard rate cut-off point is restricted to the lower of €25,000 or the amount of the income of the spouse with the lower income. The increase is not transferable between spouses.

**Example**

Where the gross pay in a pay period is, say, €450 and the standard rate cut-off point is €500 the employee pays tax at the standard rate of tax (20%) on the €450. The unused amount of €50 (eg €500 less €450) carries forward on a cumulative basis to the next pay period.

## Non-PAYE Income and Non-Standard Rated Relief

Some employees have deductions that qualify for relief at the higher rate of tax. Some have tax collected on non-PAYE income (on which tax may be due at the higher rate of tax) through the PAYE system. To ensure that full entitlement is given for such deductions and the correct tax is collected in respect of such non-PAYE income, the tax office will make the necessary adjustments to the notification of tax credits and standard rate cut-off point issued to the employee.

The employer is issued with the bottom line figures only, ie the annual, monthly and weekly tax credits and standard rate cut-off point. The employer simply operates the system using the tax credits and standard rate cut-off point as advised by the tax-office. It is the employee's responsibility to ensure that his/her tax credits and standard rate cut-off point are correct.

## Tax Deduction Card

The Revenue will issue employers with a tax deduction card (TDC) for each employee unless the employer uses a payroll package. The TDC is a large spreadsheet that includes the employees' standard rate cut-off point, tax credits and rate of tax already pre-printed. The employer fills out the salary for the week or month and calculates the PAYE and PRSI using the instructions at the top of the TDC. Using TDC can be time-consuming if there is a large number of staff; a payroll software package is useful when there are several members of staff to be paid since all the PAYE and PRSI calculations will be automatic. See Figure 23.5 for an example of how to calculate salaries.

| Example of Salary Calculation Dermot Whelan | Steps | € | |
|---|---|---|---|
| Gross Pay | | 40,000.00 | |
| Less: Pension | | (2,000.00) | Pension contributions will reduce the amount of PAYE and PRSI, the employee has to pay. Employer's PRSI is also reduced. |
| Taxable Pay | 1 | 38,000.00 | |
| **PAYE** | | | |
| Standard rate Cut off point €34,000 @ 20% | 2 | 6,800.00 | |
| Balance €4,000 @ 41% (€38,000–€34,000) | 3 | 1,640.00 | |
| Gross Tax | 4 | 8,440.00 | |
| Less: Tax Credits | 5 | (3,520.00) | |
| Tax Payable | | 4,920.00 | |

(*Continued*)

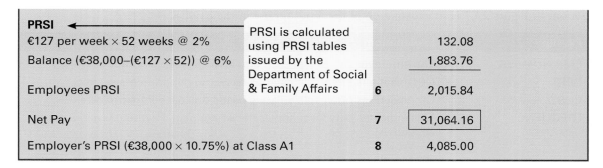

| PRSI | | |
|---|---|---|
| €127 per week × 52 weeks @ 2% | | 132.08 |
| Balance (€38,000–(€127 × 52)) @ 6% | | 1,883.76 |
| Employees PRSI | 6 | 2,015.84 |
| Net Pay | 7 | 31,064.16 |
| Employer's PRSI (€38,000 × 10.75%) at Class A1 | 8 | 4,085.00 |

PRSI is calculated using PRSI tables issued by the Department of Social & Family Affairs

Figure 23.5

## Steps

1. Calculate taxable pay.
2. Calculate tax due at 20%.
3. The balance of taxable pay is taxed at 41%.
4. Total tax at 20% and 41%.
5. Deduct tax credits; the net amount is tax payable.
6. Calculate employee's PRSI.
7. Taxable pay minus tax payable minus employees PRSI = Net pay.
8. Calculate employer's PRSI.

What will the figures look like on the payslip and the P60?

Set out in Figure 23.6 is an example of a payslip using the figures in Figure 23.5.

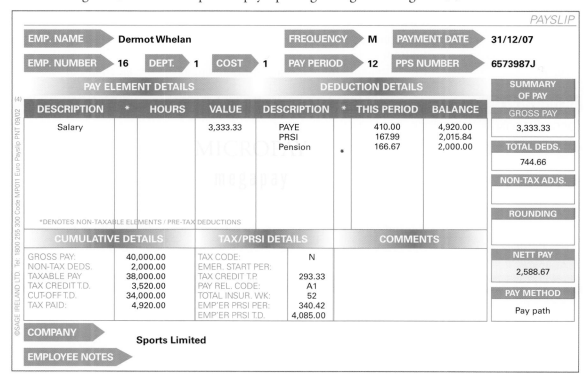

Figure 23.6

Set out in Figure 23.7 is an explanation of the headings use in the payslip.

| Payslip | Explanation |
|---|---|
| EMP. NUMBER | The employer will assign each employee payslip a number. |
| DEPT. | Organisations often split salaries based on departments or units. |
| COST | Organisations often split salaries based on cost centre/projects. |
| FREQUENCY | This indicates how frequently salaries are paid. Payments can be made as follows:<br>W= Weekly<br>M= Monthly<br>F= Bi-weekly |
| PAY PERIOD | This indicates what period the payslip relates to. If salaries are paid monthly then the number will correspond to the current month. If salaries are paid weekly then the number will range from 1 to 53. |
| PAYMENT DATE | This is the pay day. |
| PPS NUMBER | This is the employee's unique identifying number, used for all dealings with public service agencies; previously this was the RSI number. |
| **PAY ELEMENT DETAILS** | |
| DESCRIPTION | This may include the following:<br>Salary<br>Time $+ \frac{1}{2}$<br>Travel<br>Subsistence<br>Bonus |
| * | This indicates that the item included in "DESCRIPTION" is not taxable, eg travel expenses. |
| HOURS | If paid an hourly rate, the total number of hours will be included in this column. |
| VALUE | This is the amount of money attributed to each item listed under DESCRIPTION. |
| **DEDUCTION DETAILS** | |
| DESCRIPTION | This will include the following:<br>PAYE (Pay As You Earn)<br>PRSI (Pay Related Social Insurance)<br>Pension<br>Income protection<br>Life assurance<br>Union subscription |
| * | This indicates that the amount is deducted before PAYE/PRSI is calculated. |
| THIS PERIOD | This is the amount of PAYE, PRSI, pension deducted in this current payroll. |
| BALANCE | This is the total PAYE, PRSI, pension deducted since the start of the year. |
| **SUMMARY OF PAY** | |
| GROSS PAY | This is the total salary including overtime, bonuses, commission, etc. |
| TOTAL DEDS | This is the total of all deductions made, eg PAYE, PRSI, pension, etc. |
| NON-TAX ADJS | Non-tax adjustments are expenses that are not taxed and are added onto the pay cheque, eg travel and subsistence. |
| ROUNDINGS | Calculations may be rounded. |

(*Continued*)

| NETT PAY | This is the amount that should be transferred into the employee's bank account or the amount of the cheque they receive. |
| PAY METHOD | Pay path (direct into the employee's bank account) <br> Cheque <br> Cash |

| **CUMULATIVE DETAILS** | |
| --- | --- |
| GROSS PAY | This is the total pay before non-taxable deductions such as pension contributions. |
| NON-TAX DEDS. | This will include pension and income protection deductions, which are not taxable. |
| TAXABLE PAY | This will be GROSS PAY minus NON-TAXABLE DEDUCTIONS. |
| TAX CREDITS T.D. | This is the amount of tax credits used so far this year. Tax credits are deducted from gross tax to leave the actual amount of tax that has to be paid. |
| CUT-OFF T.D. | This is the amount of taxable salary that is taxed at the standard rate of tax (20%). Any income in excess of this is taxed at the higher rate of tax (41%). |
| TAX PAID | This is the total tax deducted from pay so far this year. |

| **TAX/PRSI DETAILS** | |
| --- | --- |
| TAX CODE | This indicates the basis that is used to calculate PAYE: <br> "N" indicates being taxed normally. <br> "E" would indicate being taxed on the emergency basis. <br> "W" would indicate being taxed on the week 1 basis. <br> "M" would indicate being taxed on the month 1 basis. |
| EMER. START PER | If taxed on the emergency basis, this indicates the first period in which emergency tax is operated. |
| TAX CREDIT T.P. | This is the tax credit entitlement for this pay period. It is deducted from gross tax to leave the actual amount of tax that has to be paid in this period. |
| PAY REL. CODE | This indicates the PRSI class for making contributions. "A1" is the standard PRSI class and provides cover for all social welfare benefits. |
| TOTAL INSUR. WK. | This is the number of weeks spent in insurable employment during the pay period. |
| EMP'ER PRSI PER: | This is the PRSI contribution made by the employer in this pay period. |
| EMP'ER PRSI T.D. | This is the total of all PRSI contributions made by the employer so far this year. |

Figure 23.7

**Quick Tip**

Use the above information to see if you are able to calculate all the figures that appear on your own payslip.

## ❑ What is a Form P60?

An employer issues a Form P60 to an employee certifying details of the employee's pay, tax and PRSI contributions for the tax year. The Form P60 must be given to each employee who is in employment at

31 December. This should be done before 15 February following the tax year. The figures on the form P60 should be copied from the TDC. The P60 is a summary of the TDC and certifies to the employee how much salary they have received for the year and how much tax they have paid. The document spans the full tax year and should incorporate any previous employment for the tax year. With regard to PRSI, it will show the value paid in the current employment only. A P60 is an important document as it is necessary if you are submitting a tax return, seeking mortgage approval or looking for a refund of PAYE/PRSI.

Set out in Figure 23.8 is an example of how the figures from the payslip would appear on the P60.

---

**P60** CERTIFICATE OF PAY, TAX AND PAY RELATED SOCIAL INSURANCE YEAR ENDED 31ST DEC. 2007

**PAYE-PRSI**

To be given to each employee in your employment on 31st December, whether or not tax was deducted.

| | | |
|---|---|---|
| **Name of Employee:** | Dermot Whelan | **Tax Credit €** 3,520 | **Standard Rate Cut Off € Point** 34,000 |

**Address:** 34 Pearse Park, Navan Road, Co Meath

"1" indicates that temporary basis applied **E9**

"2" indicates that emergency basis applied

**Personal Public Service No (PPS No.)** 6573987J

Enter "X" if there were 53 pay days in the year **F9**

Enter "W" if week 1/ month 1 applied          Enter "D" if employee was a director.

| (A) PAY | € | (C) PRSI in this employment | € |
|---|---|---|---|
| 1. Total pay (i.e. gross pay less any superannuation contributions allowable for income tax purposes) in the above year including pay in respect of previous employment(s), if any. | 38,000.00 | 1. EMPLOYEE'S PRSI | 2,015.84 |
| 2. Pay in respect of previous employment(s), if any, in above year. | 0 | 2. TOTAL (employer + employee) PRSI | 6,100.84 |
| 3. Pay in respect of THIS employment (i.e. gross pay less superannuation contributions allowable for income tax purposes). | 38,000.00 | 3. Total number of week's insurable employment. | 52 |
| **(B) TAX** | **€** | 4. Initial social insurance contribution class. | A1 |
| 1. Total net tax deducted in above year (including tax deducted by previous employer(s), if any) | 4,920.00 | 5. Subsequent social insurance contribution class. | |
| 2. Tax in respect of previous employment(s), if any, in above year | 0 | 6. No. of weeks at the class entered at line 5 above. | |
| 3. Net tax deducted (J7)/ refunded (H9) in this employment | J7  4,920.00 | 7. Date of commencement of employment. | |

I/We certify that the particulars given above include the total amount of pay (including overtime, bonuses, commission etc) paid to you by me/us in the above year, the total tax deducted by me/us less any refunds and the total pay-related social insurance contribution in respect of this employment.

**Employer's Name** Sports Limited          **Employer's Regd. No.** 9595342G          **Date** 19/1/07

TO THIS EMPLOYEE: THIS IS A VALUABLE DOCUMENT: You should retain it carefully as evidence of tax deducted. You may also require this document for production to the Collector General if you are claiming repayment of:
(a) PRSI contributions on the amount of pay in excess of pay ceiling for contribution purposes or
(b) The Health Contribution where income was below the relevant threshold for the year.

Figure 23.8

Set out in Figure 23.9 is an explanation of the headings use in the P60.

The P60 form includes two copies (top copy and bottom copy), both containing the same details.

| P60 TOP COPY | Explanation |
| --- | --- |
| "PAYE-PRSI" | If your tax liability for the year needs to be reviewed, you will have to send the top copy of your P60 to your local tax office. |
| PPS No. | This is a unique identification number, used for all dealings with public service agencies. |
| Tax Credit | This is the total tax credit entitlement for the year. It is deducted from gross tax to leave the actual amount of tax to be paid. |
| Standard Rate Cut-Off Point | The Standard Rate Cut-Off Point is the amount of income that is taxable at the standard rate of tax (20%). Any income in excess of this is taxed at the higher rate of tax (41%). |
| **(A) PAY** | |
| 1. Total Pay | This is your total pay for the year, ie:<br>– Your salary<br>– PLUS any taxable benefits you received during the year<br>– LESS any tax-deductible pension contributions made during the year<br>(BEFORE any tax or PRSI is deducted) |
| 2. Pay in respect of previous employment | This is total pay from any previous jobs that you had during the year. |
| 3. Pay in respect of THIS employment | This is total pay from the job that you held at the end of the year. |
| **(B) TAX** | |
| 1. Total net tax deducted | This is the total amount of tax deducted from your pay during the year. This figure depends on income level and tax credit entitlements. |
| 2. Tax in respect of previous employment(s) | This is the tax deducted in respect of any previous employments that you had during the year. |
| 3. Net tax deducted in this employment | This is the tax deducted in respect of the employment that you held at the end of the year. |
| **(C) PRSI in this employment** | |
| 1. EMPLOYEE'S PRSI | This is the PRSI (Pay Related Social Insurance) deducted from your pay during the year. |
| 2. TOTAL PRSI | This is the **total** PRSI contributed on your behalf during the year, ie<br>– The PRSI contributions deducted from your salary<br>– PLUS the PRSI contributions made by your employer |
| 3. Total number of week's insurable employment | This is the total number of weeks in the year for which you were employed in an insurable job. |
| 4. & 5. Social insurance contribution class | This indicates the PRSI class under which you made contributions. "A1" is the standard PRSI class. Contributions may be deducted under a number of classes depending on income levels. |

(*Continued*)

| 6. No. of weeks | This indicates the number of weeks where PRSI was calculated using a different class. |
| 7. Date of commencement | This will be the date the employee started the employment in the current year. |
| **P60 BOTTOM COPY** | |
| "Social Welfare Benefits" | If you wish to claim a social welfare benefit, you must send the bottom copy of your P60 to your local tax office as proof that you paid PRSI. |

Figure 23.9

## Calculation of PRSI

PRSI provides for a state old-age pension for an employee as well as benefits such as disability. There are different PRSI rates depending on the personal circumstances of the employee and the level of earnings. It is important that the employee is properly classified for PRSI to ensure that the correct deductions are made from the employee's pay. PRSI is calculated on gross pay less pension deductions, therefore both employer's PRSI and employee's PRSI will be lower if the employee is making pension contributions.

## PRSI Contributions

PRSI is payable by both employees and employers. The maximum rate of PRSI for employees is 6.5%, which is 4% PRSI and 2.5% health levy. The PRSI rates are set out in a leaflet issued by the Department of Social and Family Affairs[14], see Figures 23.10 and 23.12.

The most common PRSI class is Class A which is broken down into sub-classes depending on the level of income. PRSI is **not** calculated on a cumulative basis. If an employee's salary goes above €48,800 they will not be liable for PRSI (4%) but will be still liable for health levies at 2%. There is no income ceiling for employer's PRSI contributions.

---

[14] Leaflet SW14

| CLASS A | This covers employees under the age of 66 in Industrial, commercial and service-type employment who have reckonable pay of €38 or more per week from all employments, and Public Servants recruited from 6 April 1995. | | | | | | |
|---|---|---|---|---|---|---|---|
| **Weekly pay is the employee's money pay plus notional pay** | | | | | | | |
| Subclass | Weekly pay band | How much of weekly pay | First €48,800 | | | Balance over €48,800 | |
| | | | Employee | Employer | Employee | Employer | |
| AO | €38.00 – €339.00 inclusive | ALL | NIL | 8.5% | NIL | 8.5% | |
| AX | €339.01– €356.00 | First €127.00 | NIL | 8.5% | NIL | 8.5% | |
| | | Balance | 4.00% | 8.5% | NIL | 8.5% | |
| AL | €356.01– €480.00 inclusive | First €127.00 | NIL | 10.75% | NIL | 10.75% | |
| | | Balance | 4.00% | 10.75% | NIL | 10.75% | |
| A1 OR | More than €480.00 | First €127.00 | 2.00% | 10.75% | 2.00% | 10.75% | |
| | | €127.01– €1,925.00 | 6.00% | 10.75% | 2.00% | 10.75% | |
| | | Balance | 6.5% | 10.75% | 2.5% | 10.75% | |
| A2* | More than €480.00 | First €127.00 | NIL | 10.75% | NIL | 10.75% | |
| | | Balance | 4.00% | 10.75% | NIL | 10.75% | |

\* Subclass A2 applies to medical-card holders and people getting a social welfare widow's/widower's pension, one-parent family payment or deserted wife's benefit or allowance.

Figure 23.10

The PRSI allowance is €127 per week for the calculation of social insurance. It does not apply for the calculation of the health levy. PRSI may change on a weekly and annual basis depending on the value of reckonable income in the period in question. Weekly thresholds determine which subclass the employee falls into. A PRSI contribution week is each successive period of seven days starting on 1 January each year.

Examples of PRSI calculations for Class A, see Figure 23.11.

| Gross Pay | Class | Employee's PRSI Rate | € | Employer's PRSI | € | TOTAL PRSI |
|---|---|---|---|---|---|---|
| €216.00 | AO | All @ 0% | 0.00 | All @ 8.5% | 18.36 | 18.36 |
| €350.00 | AX | First €127 @ 0% | 0.00 | | | |
| | | Balance @ 4% | 8.92 | All @ 8.5% | 29.75 | 38.67 |
| €400.00 | AL | First €127 @ 0% | 0.00 | | | |
| | | Balance @ 4% | 10.92 | All @ 10.75% | 43.00 | 53.92 |
| €500.00 | A1 | First €127 @ 2% | 2.54 | | | |
| | | Balance (€500 – €127) @ 6% | 22.38 | | | |
| | | | 24.92 | All @ 10.75% | 53.75 | 78.67 |

Figure 23.11

Class S applies to directors of companies. Set out in Figure 23.12 are the PRSI rates for class S.

| CLASS S | This covers self-employed people, including certain company directors | | |
|---------|--------------------------------|-------------------|-------------|
| Weekly Limits | | | No Upper Ceiling |
| Subclass | Weekly Pay Band | How Much | All Income |
| SO | Up To €480.00 | ALL | 3.00% |
| S1 | More Than €480.00 | First €1,925.00 | 5.00% |
| | | Balance | 5.50% |
| S2* | More Than €480.00 | ALL | 3.00% |

\* Subclass S2 applies to medical cardholders and people getting a social welfare widow's or widower's pension, one-parent family payment or deserted wife's benefit or allowance.

Figure 23.12

## Controls for Operating Payroll

The purpose of this section is to outline guidelines for administering payroll.

- Salaries and overtime rates for staff must be agreed.
- Overtime should be approved in advance.
- Records should be kept of any amendments to pay and the overtime rates.
- Details of any new employees should be recorded.
- Employees who leave should be removed from the payroll and a P45 issued.
- Statutory and voluntary deductions should be correctly deducted.
- Payroll software should be updated annually to reflect any changes in the tax system after the budget.
- Third party payments should be timely and accurate.
- The P35 annual return must be submitted to the Revenue Commissioners by 15 February each year.
- A P30 return should be made monthly by the 14th of the following month.
- Overtime should be itemised as a separate amount from gross salary payments on the payslip and is subject to PAYE and PRSI deductions in the normal way.
- In order for the business to fulfil its statutory obligations to staff, Forms P45 and P60 must be issued promptly.
- Payslips must be issued to all employees.
- If using a payroll software package, it must be backed up to disk and stored off-site for security reasons.

# ❑ P30

## *When is Tax and PRSI Paid Over to the Revenue?*

The total PAYE deducted and the total PRSI contributions (employee and employer) should be sent to the Collector General **14 days after the month end;** eg PAYE/PRSI for January 2007 should be paid by 14 February 2007. Each month a Form P30 bank giro/payslip is issued by the Collector-General on which the employer's name, address, registration number and the relevant month are printed. Only forms showing the correct details should be used, otherwise payments made may not be correctly credited. The figures for total tax and total PRSI contributions should be entered on the form in addition to the gross total which will equal the amount of the payment. Where there is no PAYE/PRSI liability for a particular month, the Form P30 should be returned marked Nil. The Revenue will issue each monthly P30 form in advance of the 14$^{th}$ of the next month deadline. Payment may be made in the bank, by post, direct debit or using ROS.

Set out in Figure 23.13 is an example of a P30 form.

In all correspondence please quote:
Registration No:   1234567A

Notice No:   06350802-28115B

Collector-General
Sarsfield House
Francis Street
Limerick

V48   51015 132500 51015 132501 073105P30EE   Dist. 002

Enquiries: 1890 203070

ALPHABET LTD
56 FRANCIS STREET LOWER
DUBLIN 3

### INCOME TAX (PAYE), SOCIAL INSURANCE CONTRIBUTIONS and LEVIES (PRSI)

Please complete details of PAYE and PRSI deductions on the payslip below. Detach and return the payslip with your full payment in the enclosed prepaid envelope (see notes overleaf regarding completion and method of payment).

## Period:   1 Jun 2007 to 30 Jun 2007

## Payment due not later than:   14 Jul 2007

**Please do not photocopy this form or payslip or use it for any other period or customer. Always return the payslip even for nil returns.**

**BANK GIRO**
CREDIT TRANSFER

**Payslip   P30**

Revenue

| To: | BANK OF IRELAND COLLEGE GREEN DUBLIN 2. | **90-71-04** | For: | COLLECTOR-GENERAL PAYE/PRSI A/C No. 93288444 |
|---|---|---|---|---|

Name: ALPHABET LTD

I declare that the amounts shown below are the amounts I am liable to remit to the Collector-General for the above period(s).

Registration No:   1234567A

Notice No:   06350802-28115B

Period: 1 Jun 2007 to 30 Jun 2007

Signed:_____   Date:_____

Date Rec'd: ☐☐☐☐☐☐☐☐

PAYE  ☐☐☐,☐☐☐,☐☐☐.00

PRSI  ☐☐☐,☐☐☐,☐☐☐.00

TOTAL ☐☐☐,☐☐☐,☐☐☐.00

Receiving Cashier's Brand & Initials

| CHEQUES | | P30 A |
|---|---|---|
| TOTAL | | P30 A |

*Please do not fold this payslip or write or mark below this line.*

<063508022811504026      X      ⑲90⑲7104⑲ 93288444⑲ 71

Figure 23.13

## ❏ P35 End of Year Duties

Once proper records have been maintained during the year, completion of the end-of-year returns is relatively straightforward. It essentially involves transferring details from the TDC to the Form P35. The Form P35 must be returned before **15 February** each year to avoid penalties. Any PAYE or PRSI outstanding must be calculated and the payment sent with the completed P35 forms to The Employers P35 Unit, Collector General's Office, Government Offices, Nenagh, Co Tipperary.

- **What are Forms P35 and P35L?**
- **Form P35** is a declaration that the details being returned are correct. It is issued to all employers on record irrespective of the type of payroll system they use. This is the form on which the employer declares the overall amount of PAYE/PRSI deducted from employees during the tax year. It is important to ensure that all entries are legible and that the form is signed in the relevant places.
- **Form P35L** is pre-printed with the name and Personal Public Service (PPS) number of each employee. If any employee's name and PPS number are omitted from the list provided they should be added to the list.

The P35 lists the following:

- Employee's name.
- Employee's PPS number.
- Net tax deducted/refunded.
- Total PRSI contribution (Employer and Employee).
- Total number of insurable weeks.
- Initial PRSI class.
- Other PRSI classes.
- Number of weeks at other classes.
- Start date/finish date.
- Indication if employee is a director.
- Gross pay.
- Employee PRSI contribution.

## ❏ Form P35

Most computer payroll systems can now produce the P35 details that have to be submitted to the Revenue Commissioners using ROS or by filling out manual P35 forms. The advantage of using ROS is that it is quicker and there is less risk of transcribing figures incorrectly onto the P35 forms. The Revenue website has a useful section called frequently asked questions about the P35.

**Notes:**
Every person who was employed at any time during the tax year (even if no tax was deducted) must be detailed on the P35. All documents relating to pay, tax and PRSI **must** be retained by an employer for six years, after the end of a tax year.

Forms P30/P35/P35L can be filed through the Revenue On-Line Service (ROS).

## ❑ Year End

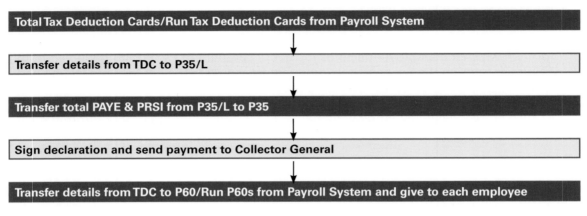

| |
|---|
| **Total Tax Deduction Cards/Run Tax Deduction Cards from Payroll System** |
| **Transfer details from TDC to P35/L** |
| **Transfer total PAYE & PRSI from P35/L to P35** |
| **Sign declaration and send payment to Collector General** |
| **Transfer details from TDC to P60/Run P60s from Payroll System and give to each employee** |

Figure 23.14

## ❑ P45

When an employee leaves employment it is the employer's responsibility to prepare a P45 which must be given to the employee. The employer sends Part 1 to the Revenue and gives Parts 2, 3 and 4 to the employee. The Form P45 will have details of pay, tax deducted and PRSI. The new employer completes Part 3 of the P45 and sends it to the tax office to formally register the new employment of the employee.

Set out in Figure 23.15 is an example of a completed P45 form.

| FORM P45 | CERTIFICATE NO.<br>U419833 | INCOME TAX - PAY AS YOU EARN - CESSATION CERTIFICATE<br>**Particulars of Employee Leaving** |
|---|---|---|

## PLEASE COMPLETE FORM IN BLOCK CAPITALS

Surname  `O'TOOLE`

First Name(s)  `STEPHEN`

Unit Number  ☐☐☐

**PPS Number**  `7 6 5 9 0 3 8 P`

Date of Leaving  `30/06/07`    Deceased ☐ (Tick ✔ if applicable)

Address  `14 RIVERVIEW AVENUE`
`NAVAN`
`Co. MEATH`

Employer Registered Number  `9 8 7 4 6 5 8 J`

Date of Birth  DD / MM / YY    Payroll/Works No.  `3`

Commencement  DD / MM / YY

◯ Weekly    (✔) Monthly (Please tick ✔ if you are paid weekly or Monthly)

Weekly/Monthly Tax Credit  € `293.33` c

Week/Month Number  `6`

Weekly/Monthly Standard Rate Cut-Off Point  € `2833.33` c

Tick ✔ if emergency tax operated ☐

(a) **TOTAL PAY & TAX** deducted from 1 January last to date of leaving

Total Pay  € `19,000.00` c         Total Tax Deducted  € `4220.00` c

(b) If Employment commenced since 1 January last enter Pay and Tax deducted for this period of employment only

Pay  € . c         Tax Deducted  € . c

(c) Amount of Taxable **LUMP SUM PAYMENT** on termination included in either pay figure above - if applicable  € . c

(a) Total amount of Taxable Disability Benefit included in Total Pay above  € . c

(b) Amount by which Tax Credits were reduced  € . c

Amount by which Standard Rate Cut-Off Point was reduced  € . c

(c) Indicate that Week 1/Month 1 basis was applied  ☐ (Tick ✔ if applicable)

Please complete **A, B,** or **C** across where an employee was in receipt of taxable Disability Benefit since 1st January last while employed by you

**PRSI - THIS EMPLOYMENT ONLY**

Total PRSI  € `3050.42` c

Employee's Share  € `1007.92` c

Total number of weeks of Insurable Employment  `26`

Total number of weeks at Class A or Subclass "A" in this period  `26`

PRSI Classes other than Class A or Subclass "A" in this period  `—`

I certify that the particulars entered above are correct.

Employer  `SPORTS LIMITED`       Trade name if different  `N/A`

Address  `11 GRAFTON STREET`
`DUBLIN 2`       Date  `30/06/07`

Phone No.  `7455551`

Fax No.  `7455552`

| Revenue On-Line Service | **Save Time File P45's on-line using the Revenue On-Line Service.** | www.revenue.ie |
|---|---|---|

**INSTRUCTIONS TO EMPLOYER**

(a)  Complete this form when an employee leaves your employment. Take care that all entries are in BLOCK capitals.

(b)  Copy PPS Number, Tax Credits, and Standard Rate Cut-Off Point from the latest Certificate of Tax Credits and Standard Rate Cut-Off Point.

(c)  If the employee commenced with you after 1st January last include pay and tax notified to you in respect of previous employment. Please insert date of commencement if after the start of this tax year.

(d)  Detach Part 1 and send it to your Tax Office immediately. Hand Parts 2, 3 and 4 (unseparated) to the employee when he/she leaves.

(e)  If employee has died please send ALL FOUR PARTS of this form (unseparated) to your Tax Office immediately.

(f)  A guide to PAYE / PRSI for small employers (IT 50) is available from our Forms & Leaflets Service 1890 306 706 or the Revenue Website.

PART 1

Figure 23.15

# ❑ Employee v Self-Employed

The distinction between whether an individual is an employee or is self-employed will have implications in terms of whether they are taxed under the PAYE system or are part of the self-assessment tax system. In recent years the Revenue have concentrated very much on this area. If someone is an employee they are not too concerned and accept this fact. However, is someone is self-employed and is receiving income from one person and carrying out their work at the "payer's" premises, their case will be looked at closely to see if that person is in fact an employee. To determine whether someone is an employee or is self-employed it is necessary to look at the facts of each case, as in Figure 23.16. It suits employers to have someone classified as self-employed as they will not have to pay employer's PRSI that is charged at either 8.5% or 10.75%. Holiday and sick pay do not have to be paid in respect of self-employed persons. The following factors should be considered when assessing whether someone is an employee or self-employed: it is important to distinguish between employees and independent contractors; employees are paid a wage or salary by the company and are under its direct supervision and control; independent contractors are not employees of the company and so are not accounted for under the payroll system. They offer services to the organisation for a fee, but they are not under its direct control or supervision.

Set out below are a list of questions that should be considered to determine if someone is an employee or self-employed.

|  | Employee | Self-Employed |
|---|---|---|
| Must do work during certain hours | Yes | No |
| Can be told how to do the work | Yes | No |
| Can be dismissed/made redundant | Yes | No |
| Entitled to holiday pay/bank holiday pay | Yes | No |
| Can be reprimanded for misconduct | Yes | No |
| Likely to incur financial risk | No | Yes |
| Can delegate work | No | Yes |
| Must register for VAT | No | Yes |
| Needs insurance (public liability, professional indemnity) | No | Yes |
| Must supply own tools/equipment | No | Yes |

Figure 23.16

It is not necessary for the contract to be in writing; eg if you engage the services of an electrician to rewire your home there may be no written contract. The relationship between you and the electrician is that of payer and self-employed contractor.

## ❑ **Benefits in Kind**

All taxable benefits and benefits in kind must be processed under the PAYE and PRSI systems. They are therefore subject to all the relevant taxes. All employees who currently have the use of any company asset or, if it is being used by a member of their family, may face a liability under the Benefit in Kind (BIK) scheme.

Employers are liable to deduct BIK tax from employees if they provide the following benefits to employees:

- A company car—tax will be based on 30% of the original market value of the car. The tax can be reduced if the employee has high annual business mileage. This is disadvantageous for the employee in that they are paying the tax based on the value of a new car but the car may be 10 years old and worth very little. The disadvantage for employers is that they have to pay employer's PRSI on this "deemed" benefit.
- If an employer provides an employee with a place to live free of charge, tax will be levied at 8% of the market value of the property.
- If an employer gives an employee a staff loan at preferential rates, there may be tax implications.
- If an employer pays club subscription or contribution to a health insurance scheme, it is taxable.

Employees who use bus/train or Luas services can avail of an annual or monthly travel pass; this is not a taxable benefit.

All cash payments, ie wages, salaries, bonuses etc, made to employees and directors must be paid under deduction of PAYE/PRSI. In addition, benefits in kind are subject to PAYE/PRSI. Employers are responsible for the calculation, recording and collection of PAYE and PRSI on the value of the taxable benefit, the total value of which is referred to as notional pay.

The value assigned to notional pay can be determined in one of several ways depending on the type of benefit in kind. The "best estimate" is based on the cost incurred by the employer or the market value less any contribution received from the employee.

The employer must calculate the benefit and this notional payment, which is added to wages to calculate PAYE/PRSI. An employer is responsible for ensuring that:

- The correct amounts of deduction are made from the employee's/director's pay.
- The amounts deducted are paid over on time to the tax office.
- The correct forms are completed.

Failure to comply with these requirements will result in the employer being charged penalties and interest. A useful guide issued by the Revenue is "PAYE/PRSI for small employers".[15]

---

[15] www.revenue.ie/publications

## ❑ Pension Contributions and PRSAs

Pension contributions to a Revenue-approved pension scheme will be allowed as a deduction from gross pay before calculating the tax due. The maximum relief available is restricted to 15%–40% of net relevant earnings depending on age (earnings from trade, professional, salary less capital allowances and losses). Any amounts that do not qualify for relief can be carried forward to the next year. Personal retirement saving schemes (PRSAs) are similar to pension contributions; employers must facilitate the deduction of PRSA contributions and pay the money over to the PRSA fund, and employers are not obliged to make a contribution on behalf of employees.

The amount of pension contributions that can be used for Income tax relief varies according to age.

|  | Net Relevant Earnings |
| --- | --- |
| Up to 30 years of age | 15% |
| 30–39 years of age | 20% |
| 40–49 years of age | 25% |
| 50–54 years of age | 30% |
| 55–59 years of age | 35% |
| 60 years and older | 40% |

## ❑ Pension Liability

A pension plan is a contract that requires the company to pay benefits to its employees after they retire. Some companies pay the full cost of the pension plan, but in many companies, employees share the cost by contributing part of their salaries or wages. The contributions from the employer and employee are usually paid into a pension fund which is invested on behalf of the employees and from which benefits are paid to pensioners. Pension benefits typically consist of monthly payments to retired employees and other payments upon disability or death. There are two types of pension plans, defined benefit and defined contribution.

- Defined contribution plans—the employer makes a fixed regular contribution (usually a percentage of the employee's gross pay). Retirement benefits depend on how much contributions are made to the employees pension fund and the investment returns on that fund. Employees may control their own investment account, can make additional contributions and can transfer funds if they leave the company.
- Defined benefit plans—the employer contributes an annual amount required to fund estimated future pension liabilities arising from employment in the current year. The exact amount of the liability will not be known until the retirement of the current employees. Although the amount of future benefits is fixed, the annual contributions vary depending on assumptions about how much the pension fund will earn. Companies prefer defined contributions plans because the employee assumes the risk that their pension assets will earn a sufficient return to meet their retirement needs.

# ❑ Duties of an Employer in Relation to Payroll

An employer must:

- Register with the Revenue Commissioners. The Revenue will issue the employer with a registration number.
- Check that there is a notice of determination of tax credits and standard rate cut-off point for each employee. Advise the Revenue of the name, address and PPS number of each employee for whom no notice of tax credits and standard rate cut-off point was received.
- Keep a register of employees and notify the Revenue of details of new employees.
- Deduct PAYE and PRSI on payments made to employees and keep all PAYE/PRSI records. Use tax deduction cards or a payroll package.
- Give each employee a payslip which should detail gross pay, PAYE, PRSI and net pay with each payment.
- Send a Form P45 to the Revenue whenever an employee leaves their employment. The employer must complete this form. Send Part 1 to the tax office and give Parts 2, 3 and 4 to the employee.
- Pay the PAYE deducted, employee's PRSI and employer's PRSI over to the Revenue on a monthly basis using Form P30.
- Send the Form P35 declaration at the end of the year to the Revenue together with any outstanding PAYE or PRSI for the tax year.
- Give each employee a P60 at the end of the tax year.
- Calculate the value of taxable benefits and charge the relevant amount of PAYE and PRSI.
- It is an employee's responsibility to sort out his/her own tax credits and standard rate cut-off point. If an employee's tax credits are incorrect it is not the employer's responsibility to sort it out.
- It is the employer's responsibility to allocate PRSI classes and calculation of PRSI.

**Quick Tip**

If possible, pay staff on a monthly basis rather than weekly or fortnightly or bi-monthly. This will reduce processing time and costs in terms of additional administration, cheques/bank transfers.

# NOMINAL LEDGER AND JOURNALS

## Chapter 24

This chapter sets out the control procedures that should be operated regarding the nominal ledger and journals.

Controls have to be in place so that the nominal ledger and journals are processed in a manner that ensures that:

- Data entry is authorised, accurate, complete, posted in the correct period and has adequate supporting documentation.
- All accruals and prepayments, particularly in respect of expenses/income, are reviewed and authorised on a monthly basis.
- Financial reports are prepared before closing the nominal ledger each month and adequate filing procedures are implemented to ensure completeness of physical records.
- All financial reports are reviewed for accuracy and completeness. This will make the preparation of the annual financial statements easier.
- All reconciling items between the nominal ledger and third party documentation are identified, documented, reviewed and authorised.
- Accounts comply with accounting standards and with accounting policies.
- Annual financial statements are reconciled to the year-end figures on the accounts system.
- All journals posted to the nominal ledger are documented and properly authorised.
- All journals are documented and authorised on standard journal forms with sufficient narrative and documentation to fully support each entry. These forms should be filed numerically for completeness.
- Standard journals that need to be made each month are set up.
- The chart of accounts is complete and all changes are authorised and accurate.
- The chart of accounts is set up in sufficient detail to comply with both management and financial statement reporting requirements.
- Management and control accounts are reconciled and reviewed monthly.
  The following list of nominal ledger accounts should be reconciled monthly:
  - Bank.
  - Creditors.
  - Debtors.
  - Prepayment and accrual accounts.
  - Other balance sheet control accounts, eg PAYE/PRSI.
- Access and security to the accounts software is controlled. Access control to the accounts software must be restricted to individuals responsible for processing accounting data.
- Back-up copies must be made of all the files. All the data information for the accounts software must be backed up on the network and externally. Data information for payroll software must also be backed up.
- All back-ups must be stored securely, preferably off-site.

# CHART OF ACCOUNTS Chapter 25

This chapter provides a description and example of the "chart of accounts" and provides an example. The chart of accounts is like a tree onto which each account has its own branch or leaf. When setting up accounts for the first time it is often a good idea to set up accounts on a manual system so that the basic accounting concepts are understood before transferring the information onto a computer system. Computer system accounts (nominals) will need to be set up. The descriptions used for the nominals should suit your type of business, so that similar items can be grouped together. In order to ensure that the nominals are set up in a logical manner there is a chart of accounts, which is a directory of accounting information. Each nominal account is usually allocated a four-digit account number. An accounting system has a separate account for each asset, each liability and each component of owner's equity, including revenue and expenses. Whether a company keeps records by hand or by computer, management must be able to refer to accounts in order to study the company's financial history and plan for the future. A very small company may only need a few dozen accounts. A multinational corporation may need thousands.

There is no standardised chart of accounts and therefore no requirement for all organisations to use a standardised numbering system. To set up a chart of accounts define the various accounts to be used by the organisation, each account should have a number to identify it. It is worthwhile to put thought into assigning the account numbers in a logical way. An example of how the digits might be coded is shown below:

## ❏ Account Numbering

1000–1499: Current Assets
1500–1999: Fixed Assets
2000–2499: Current Liabilities
2500–2999: Long Term Liabilities
3000–3999: Equity Accounts
4000–4999: Revenue Accounts
5000–5999: Cost of Goods Sold
6000–9999: Expense accounts

By separating each account by several numbers, many new accounts can be added between any two groups while maintaining the logical order.

## ❑ Defining Accounts

Different types of businesses will have different types of accounts. Accounting software packages often come with a selection of predefined account charts for various types of businesses. Keeping the number of accounts to a minimum has the advantage of making the accounting system simple. As certain accounts acquire significant balances they can be split into smaller, more specific accounts. However, following this strategy makes it more difficult to generate consistent historical comparisons. For example, if the accounting system is set up with a miscellaneous expense account that later is broken into property expenses, sundry expenses etc it then would be difficult to compare those detailed expenses with the previous year. In this respect, there is an advantage in organising the chart of accounts with a higher initial level of detail.

Set out in Figure 25.1 is an example of some of the accounts that might be included in a chart of accounts. The headings used are only for illustrative purposes.

| Classification | Account Number | Account Name | Description | Normal Balance |
|---|---|---|---|---|
| **Current Assets** | 1000 | Petty Cash | This should be use for recording petty cash received and petty cash paid. | Debit |
| | 1040 | Deposit Account | This represents the balance on the deposit account including any interest that has been earned. | Debit |
| | 1100 | Debtors | This represents the amount owed from customers who have purchased goods/services on credit. | Debit |
| | 1200 | Stock | This represents the amount of stock on hand. | Debit |
| | 1400 | Prepaid Expenses | This represents the amount of expenses that are paid in advance, eg rent. | Debit |
| | 1470 | Other Current Assets | This could include amounts paid to a supplier in advance. | Debit |
| **Fixed Assets** | 1500 | Fixtures & Fittings | Used to record assets such as desks, partitions and filing cabinets. | Debit |
| | 1510 | Equipment | Used to record computers, printers, projectors, etc. | Debit |
| | 1520 | Vehicles | Used to record cars, vans, trucks, etc. | Debit |
| | 1550 | Buildings | Used to record freehold buildings. | Debit |
| | 1560 | Leasehold Building | Used to record any improvements to a leasehold building, which the business has under a Lease agreement. | Debit |
| | 1690 | Land | Used to record the cost of land purchased. | Debit |
| | 1700 | Accumulated Depreciation Fixtures & Fittings | This account records all the depreciation recorded in relation to fixtures and fittings. | Credit |

(*Continued*)

| Classification | Account Number | Account Name | Description | Normal Balance |
|---|---|---|---|---|
| | 1710 | Accumulated Depreciation Equipment | This account records all the depreciation in relation to equipment. | Credit |
| | 1720 | Accumulated Depreciation Vehicles | This account records all the depreciation in relation to vehicles. | Credit |
| | 1740 | Accumulated Depreciation Buildings | This account records all the depreciation in relation to buildings. | Credit |
| | 1750 | Accumulated Depreciation Leasehold | This account records all the depreciation in relation to leasehold improvements. | Credit |
| *Current Liabilities* | 2000 | Creditors | This account represents the amounts due to suppliers for goods and services purchased on credit. | Credit |
| | 2300 | Accrued Expenses | This account represents estimates for invoices not yet received, eg electricity. | Credit |
| | 2310 | VAT | This account records all the VAT on sales less VAT claimed on purchases less the amount paid to Revenue. | Credit |
| | 2320 | Wages Payable | This account is used to record the amount of net wages due to staff; when cheques are written or bank transfers processed this account should be zero. | Credit |
| | 2410 | PAYE/PRSI | This account records all the PAYE/PRSI collected from staff wages and employer's contribution to PRSI, less money paid to Revenue. | Credit |
| | 2420 | Current Portion of Long-Term Debt | This represents the portion of a long-term loan that is due within one year (12 monthly repayments minus interest). | Credit |
| | 2480 | Other Current Liabilities | This represents other possible accounts such as staff loans, staff deductions not yet paid, etc. | Credit |
| *Long-term Liabilities* | 2500 | Bank Loans Payable | This represent the balance of a long-term loan that is payable after more than one year. It is the total loan minus the amount included in Current Portion of Long-Term Debt. | Credit |
| | 2740 | Other Long-Term Liabilities | This represents the balance on long-term liabilities > 1 year. | Credit |

(*Continued*)

| Classification | Account Number | Account Name | Description | Normal Balance |
|---|---|---|---|---|
| **Equity Accounts** | 3020 | Capital | This represents the amount of shares purchased by the owners of the business. | Credit |
| | 3030 | Retained Earnings | This represents profits/losses from prior years that are carried forward. | Credit/Debit |
| **Revenue Accounts** | 4000 | Sales | This represents total sales; it includes cash and credit sales. | Credit |
| | 4020 | Sales Returned | This represents sales returned by customers. | Debit |
| | 4040 | Sales Discount | This represents any discount that is allowed to customers. | Debit |
| | 4060 | Interest Income | Deposit interest received on deposit accounts. | Credit |
| **Costs of Sales** | 5000 | Purchases | This represents total purchases for resale; it includes cash and credit purchases. | Debit |
| | 5500 | Purchases Returned | This represents purchases returned to suppliers. | Credit |
| | 5600 | Purchases Discount | This represents any discount received from suppliers. | Credit |
| **Expenses** | 6010 | Advertising Expenses | This represents the amount spent on taking out advertisements. | Debit |
| | 6100 | Motor Expenses | This represents running costs relating to motor vehicles, eg petrol, diesel, repairs, car tax. | Debit |
| | 6150 | Bad Debt Expenses | This represents the amount of the provision for bad debts written off in the current year. | Debit |
| | 6200 | Bank Charges | This represents bank charges for certain transactions such as lodging money or writing cheques. | Debit |
| | 6400 | Depreciation Expenses | Amount of depreciation charged in respect of all assets. | Debit |
| | 6450 | Subscription Expenses | This represents any amount paid to be a member of a group/association. | Debit |
| | 6700 | Insurance | Amount of insurance premiums recorded. | Debit |
| | 6750 | Interest Expenses | Amount of interest incurred on overdrafts and term loan accounts. | Debit |
| | 6850 | Legal and Professional Fees | This account is used for legal fees paid, accountancy fees, architect fees, etc. | Debit |
| | 7000 | Maintenance Expenses | This represents the maintenance costs for equipment such as computer equipment. | Debit |
| | 7350 | Postage Expenses | This represents the cost of purchasing stamps, etc. | Debit |

*(Continued)*

| Classification | Account Number | Account Name | Description | Normal Balance |
|---|---|---|---|---|
| | 7400 | Rent or Lease Expenses | This represents the amount of rent payable; it can include service charges. | Debit |
| | 7450 | Repair and Maintenance Expenses | This represents repairs and maintenance to the buildings, eg fixing pipes, replacing a pane of glass, etc | Debit |
| | 7600 | Telephone Expenses | This represents the cost of landline, mobile phone and fax line costs. | Debit |
| | 7620 | Staff Training Expenses | This represents the cost of any training courses for staff. | Debit |
| | 7650 | Travel Expenses | This represents the cost of travel by train, bus, mileage paid, etc. | Debit |
| | 7700 | Salaries | This represents the gross salaries/wages paid. | Debit |
| | 7750 | Overtime | This represents the amount of overtime paid to staff. | Debit |
| | 7800 | Employer's PRSI | This represents the employer's contributions to PRSI. | Debit |
| | 8900 | Other Expenses | This can include any other relevant expenditure heading not already included. | Debit |
| | 9000 | Gain/Loss on Sale of Assets | This account is used when there is a disposal of an asset; the cost, depreciation and proceeds from the sales are netted and the balance is a gain or loss on disposal. | Debit/ Credit |

Figure 25.1

This chapter describes the budgeting process, provides an example of a budgeted profit & loss and balance sheet, together with budget control, reports and objectives.

Budgeting is the process of taking organisational objectives and converting them into short-term goals with a monetary value. Most organisational targets can be expressed in monetary terms. Overall, budgeting can be seen as a central feature of the strategic planning process that links planning to control and ensures that objectives are achieved. The three key aspects of this process are:

- Planning.
- Budgeting.
- Control.

**Planning**—Involves designing a desired future and establishing effective ways of bringing it about. The budget is a financial expression of that plan. It considers the desired position and how it can be achieved with the resources available to a business. It is important to note that the function of the budget is to integrate the long-term plan into the day-to-day operations of the business.

**Budgeting**—Is the process of planning for the future, which involves the quantification in monetary terms of proposed activity levels.

**Control**—Is the process of looking back over past performance to make sure that what was meant to happen, did happen. Where it did not the organisation can then make the necessary changes. To control the activity of a business, a comparison must be made between the budget on the one hand and the actual outcome on the other. This is called variance analysis. It is important that the system should provide quick and reliable information if full benefit is to be gained from it.

## ❏ Developing the Budget

There is no one correct method of budget preparation. In a small organisation, the responsibility for budget preparation may rest with an owner/manager who liaises with other parties to collect the relevant information. The detailed items will reflect past performance but more importantly take account of expected changes in prices and volume of activity in the future. The budget is usually based on the accounting year and is phased into shorter periods, eg monthly intervals.

In a medium-sized organisation, a more formal budgeting procedure is required. Top management should specify broad objectives to a budget committee comprising representatives of functional managers. Managers prepare outline plans and detailed proposals. This process may continue a number of times to integrate and coordinate the individual budget proposals. This is a "bottom up" approach with managers retaining ownership of the budgets as opposed to imposed or "top down" budgets. When finalised, functional budgets are incorporated into a master budget including

- A budgeted profit & loss account.
- A budgeted balance sheet.
- A budgeted cash flow statement.

Revenue forecasts are concerned with a forecast of sales income and operating costs feeding into the budgeted profit & loss account. A capital budget is concerned with plans for capital expenditure on individual projects or specific assets that need to be included in the budgeted balance sheet. Budgets and budgetary control are applicable in all organisations, whether manufacturing or service, whether profit seeking or not. The main purpose of budgetary control is to plan and control the firm's activities. Budgetary control is an expression of short-term financial plans to meet objectives in the coming accounting year.

## Functional Budgets

The functional budget forms the basis for preparing the master budget that will become the budgeted profit & loss account and projected balance sheet. The cash budget is a monthly budget of cash inflows and outflows, which are expected to arise from the plans expressed in the functional budgets.
Set out below is a list of the functional budgets.

1. Sales budget—the sales team will have to consider the present level of business, anticipate future trading conditions, and obtain feedback from sales representatives and market research.
2. Production budget—after specifying sales, the production budget comes next. The level of production must be linked to the sales budget. Production levels must fall within existing capacity.
3. Departmental overhead budget—these are prepared based on the level of service needed to allow the sales and production functions to meet their targets.

Set out in Figure 26.1 are the components of the budget process.

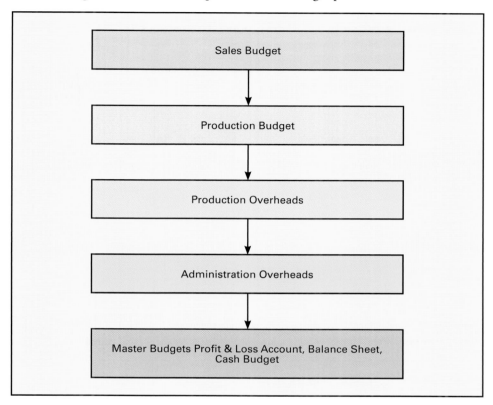

Figure 26.1

**Example**

Set out in Figure 26.2 is an example of a budget for the year January–December, setting out the budgeted profit & loss.

| Budget Profit & Loss | Jan | Feb | Mar | Apr | May | Jun | Jul | Aug | Sep | Oct | Nov | Dec | TOTAL |
|---|---|---|---|---|---|---|---|---|---|---|---|---|---|
| | € | € | € | € | € | € | € | € | € | € | € | € | € |
| *Sales Budget* | 6,000 | 9,000 | 11,000 | 14,000 | 7,000 | 9,000 | 9,000 | 12,000 | 9,000 | 8,000 | 11,000 | 24,000 | **129,000** |
| *Production Budget* | | | | | | | | | | | | | |
| **Cost of Sales** | | | | | | | | | | | | | |
| Opening Stocks | 0 | 1,000 | 1,500 | 750 | 2,000 | 1,000 | 500 | 500 | 500 | 500 | 2,000 | 4,000 | 0 |
| Purchases | 2,200 | 2,300 | 1,450 | 4,050 | 400 | 1,300 | 1,800 | 2,400 | 1,800 | 3,100 | 4,200 | 1,300 | **26,300** |
| Closing Stock | −1,000 | −1,500 | −750 | −2,000 | −1,000 | −500 | −500 | −500 | −500 | −2,000 | −4,000 | −500 | **−500** |
| | 1,200 | 1,800 | 2,200 | 2,800 | 1,400 | 1,800 | 1,800 | 2,400 | 1,800 | 1,600 | 2,200 | 4,800 | 25,800 |
| **Gross Profit** | 4,800 | 7,200 | 8,800 | 11,200 | 5,600 | 7,200 | 7,200 | 9,600 | 7,200 | 6,400 | 8,800 | 19,200 | 103,200 |

(*Continued*)

| Budget Profit & Loss | Jan | Feb | Mar | Apr | May | Jun | Jul | Aug | Sep | Oct | Nov | Dec | TOTAL |
|---|---|---|---|---|---|---|---|---|---|---|---|---|---|
| **Production Overheads** | | | | | | | | | | | | | |
| Salaries | 5,000 | 5,000 | 5,000 | 5,000 | 5,000 | 5,000 | 5,000 | 5,000 | 5,000 | 5,000 | 5,000 | 5,000 | 60,000 |
| Travel & Subsistence | 100 | | 100 | | 100 | | 150 | | 150 | | 100 | | 700 |
| **Administration Overheads** | | | | | | | | | | | | | |
| Advertising | | | | | | 2,000 | | | | | 5,000 | | 7,000 |
| Insurance | 7,500 | | | | | | | | | | | | 7,500 |
| Printing | | | | 1,000 | | | | | | | | | 1,000 |
| Postage | 100 | 100 | 100 | 100 | 100 | 100 | 100 | 100 | 100 | 100 | 100 | 100 | 1,200 |
| Telephone | 250 | 250 | 250 | 250 | 250 | 250 | 250 | 250 | 250 | 250 | 250 | 250 | 3,000 |
| Courier | 300 | 300 | 300 | 300 | 300 | 300 | 300 | 300 | 300 | 300 | 300 | 300 | 3,600 |
| Rent | 1,000 | | | 1,000 | | | 1,000 | | | 1,000 | | | 4,000 |
| Rates | 3,000 | | | | | | | | | | | | 3,000 |
| Repairs | | | | | 1,000 | | | | | | | | 1,000 |
| Audit | | | | | | | | | | | 3,000 | | 3,000 |
| Bank Interest | | | 1,500 | | | 1,500 | | | 1,500 | | | 1,500 | 6,000 |
| Depreciation | 250 | 250 | 250 | 250 | 250 | 250 | 250 | 250 | 250 | 250 | 250 | 250 | **3,000** |
| Total Expenditure | 17,500 | 5,900 | 7,500 | 7,900 | 7,000 | 9,400 | 7,050 | 5,900 | 7,550 | 6,900 | 14,000 | 7,400 | 104,000 |
| Profit/(Loss) | −12,700 | 1,300 | 1,300 | 3,300 | −1,400 | −2,200 | 150 | 3,700 | −350 | −500 | −5,200 | 11,800 | −800 |
| Accumulated Profit/(Loss) | −12,700 | −11,400 | −10,100 | −6,800 | −8,200 | −10,400 | −10,250 | −6,550 | −6,900 | −7,400 | −12,600 | −800 | |

Figure 26.2

## Assumptions

- Sales are based on a forecast of demand for the product.
- Cost of sales will be 20% of sales since the gross profit is 80%.
- Salaries will be €5,000 per month.
- Travel and subsistence are estimates based on the required amount of travel to generate sales.
- An advertisement will be put in a trade magazine in June and November.
- Insurance must be paid immediately.
- Printing is estimated to cost €1,000 for advertising brochures and flyers.
- Postage, telephone and courier: these figures are based on an estimate of monthly expenditure.
- Rent is payable at the beginning of each quarter.
- Rates are levied once a year.
- General repairs will be carried out during the year.
- The audit will cost €3,000.
- Bank interest on the loan will be €1,500 per quarter.
- Fixed assets costing €15,000 are depreciated at 20% straight line.
  The depreciation calculation is as follows:
  €15,000 × 20% = €3,000/12 months = €250 per month.

| Cash Budget | Jan | Feb | Mar | Apr | May | Jun | Jul | Aug | Sep | Oct | Nov | Dec | TOTAL |
|---|---|---|---|---|---|---|---|---|---|---|---|---|---|
| **Per Budget P+L** | € | € | € | € | € | € | € | € | € | € | € | € | € |
| Sales | 6,000 | 9,000 | 11,000 | 14,000 | 7,000 | 9,000 | 9,000 | 12,000 | 9,000 | 8,000 | 11,000 | 24,000 | 129,000 |
| **Cash Receipts in:** | | | | | | | | | | | | | |
| Cash within 30 days 50% | | 3,000 | 4,500 | 5,500 | 7,000 | 3,500 | 4,500 | 4,500 | 6,000 | 4,500 | 4,000 | 5,500 | **52,500** |
| Cash within 60 days 50% | | | 3,000 | 4,500 | 5,500 | 7,000 | 3,500 | 4,500 | 4,500 | 6,000 | 4,500 | 4,000 | **47,000** |
| Bank Loan | 50,000 | | | | | | | | | | | | 50,000 |
| **Total cash in** | 50,000 | 3,000 | 7,500 | 10,000 | 12,500 | 10,500 | 8,000 | 9,000 | 10,500 | 10,500 | 8,500 | 9,500 | 149,500 |
| **Per Profit & Loss** | | | | | | | | | | | | | |
| **Expenditure (credit taken)** | | | | | | | | | | | | | |
| Purchases | 2,200 | 2,300 | 1,450 | 4,050 | 400 | 1,300 | 1,800 | 2,400 | 1,800 | 3,100 | 4,200 | 1,300 | 26,300 |
| Advertising | | | | | | 2,000 | | | | | 5,000 | | 7,000 |
| Printing | | | 1,000 | | | | | | | | | | 1,000 |
| Telephone | 250 | 250 | 250 | 250 | 250 | 250 | 250 | 250 | 250 | 250 | 250 | 250 | 3,000 |
| Courier | 300 | 300 | 300 | 300 | 300 | 300 | 300 | 300 | 300 | 300 | 300 | 300 | 3,600 |
| Audit | | | | | | | | | | | 3,000 | | 3,000 |
| **Cash Payments out** | | | | | | | | | | | | | |
| Purchases paid after 30 days | | 2,200 | 2,300 | 1,450 | 4,050 | 400 | 1,300 | 1,800 | 2,400 | 1,800 | 3,100 | 4,200 | 25,000 |
| Advertising paid after 30 days | | | | | | | 2,000 | | | | | 5,000 | 7,000 |
| Printing paid after 60 days | | | | | 1,000 | | | | | | | | 1,000 |
| Telephone paid after 30 days | | 250 | 250 | 250 | 250 | 250 | 250 | 250 | 250 | 250 | 250 | 250 | 2,750 |
| Courier paid after 30 days | | 300 | 300 | 300 | 300 | 300 | 300 | 300 | 300 | 300 | 300 | 300 | 3,300 |
| Auditor paid after 30 days | | | | | | | | | | | | 3,000 | 3,000 |
| **Expenditure (no credit taken)** | | | | | | | | | | | | | |
| Salaries | 5,000 | 5,000 | 5,000 | 5,000 | 5,000 | 5,000 | 5,000 | 5,000 | 5,000 | 5,000 | 5,000 | 5,000 | 60,000 |
| Travel & Subsistence | 100 | | 100 | | 100 | 150 | | 150 | | | 100 | | 700 |
| Insurance | 7,500 | | | | | | | | | | | | 7,500 |
| Postage | 100 | 100 | 100 | 100 | 100 | 100 | 100 | 100 | 100 | 100 | 100 | 100 | 1,200 |
| Rent | 1,000 | | | 1,000 | | | 1,000 | | | 1,000 | | | 4,000 |
| Rates | 3,000 | | | | | | | | | | | | 3,000 |
| Repairs | | | | | | 1,000 | | | | | | | 1,000 |
| Bank Repayments | | | 2,500 | | | 2,500 | | | 2,500 | | | 2,500 | 10,000 |
| Fixed Asset | 15,000 | | | | | | | | | | | | 15,000 |
| **Total cash out** | 31,700 | 7,850 | 10,550 | 8,100 | 10,800 | 9,550 | 10,100 | 7,450 | 10,700 | 8,450 | 8,850 | 20,350 | 144,450 |
| **Summary** | | | | | | | | | | | | | |
| **Opening Balance** | **25,000** | 43,300 | 38,450 | 35,400 | 37,300 | 39,000 | 39,950 | 37,850 | 39,400 | 39,200 | 41,250 | 40,900 | 25,000 |
| Total cash in | 50,000 | 3,000 | 7,500 | 10,000 | 12,500 | 10,500 | 8,000 | 9,000 | 10,500 | 10,500 | 8,500 | 9,500 | 149,500 |
| Total cash out | −31,700 | −7,850 | −10,550 | −8,100 | −10,800 | −9,550 | −10,100 | −7,450 | −10,700 | −8,450 | −8,850 | −20,350 | −144,450 |
| Closing Balance | 43,300 | 38,450 | 35,400 | 37,300 | 39,000 | 39,950 | 37,850 | 39,400 | 39,200 | 41,250 | 40,900 | 30,050 | **30,050** |

Figure 26.3

## Assumption

- A loan of €50,000 has been obtained from the bank.
- 50% of customers will pay for sales after 30 days; 50% will settle their account within 60 days.
- 30 days' credit is taken to pay for goods purchased, advertising, couriers, telephone and audit fees.
- 60 days' credit is taken to pay for printing.
- The following expenses are paid for in the month that the expenditure is incurred: salaries, travel & subsistence, insurance, postage, rent, rates and repairs.
- Fixed assets costing €15,000 were purchased in January.
- The bank loan repayments are €1,000 capital and €1,500 interest per quarter, totalling €2,500.
- The amount invested by the owners is cash of €25,000.

**Note:** depreciation does not appear in the cash budget, as it is not a cash outflow; the purchase of the asset originally will be included in the cash budget as expenditure.

## Budgeted Balance Sheet

Set out in Figure 26.4 is the budgeted balance sheet, which is based on the figures included in the budgeted profit & loss and cash budget.

| Budgeted Balance Sheet | Account | € | € | Source of Information |
|---|---|---|---|---|
| **Fixed Asset** | Equipment Cost | 15,000 | | Cash Budget |
| | Accumulated Depreciation | (3,000) | 12,000 | Budget P&L |
| Cash Balance at year end | | | 30,050 | Cash Budget |
| **Current Assets** | | | | |
| Stock (closing stock december) | | | 500 | Budget P&L |
| Debtors | Sales | 129,000 | | Budget P&L |
| | Cash Received | (99,500) | 29,500 | Cash Budget |
| | (Total cash in less bank loan) | | | |
| **Current Liabilities** | | | | |
| Creditors | Purchases Cost of Sales | 26,300 | | Budget P&L |
| | Overheads (excl Depreciation) | 101,000 | | Budget P&L |
| | Cash Paid (excl Fixed Asset & Capital repayment of Loan) | (125,450) | (1,850) | Cash Budget |
| **Total Assets less Current Liabilities** | | | 70,200 | |
| **Finance by** | | | | |
| Capital Contributed | | | 25,000 | Cash Budget |
| Bank Loan (€50,000 less capital repaid €1,000 × 4) | | | 46,000 | Cash Budget |
| (Loss) for year | | | (800) | Budget P&L |
| | | | 70,200 | |

Figure 26.4

**Quick Tip**

Calculate all the costs as a percentage of turnover so that you can focus attention on those costs that will have the greatest impact on profits. Reduce/increase some of the variable costs to see the effect on net profit. This is called sensitivity analysis.

**Quick Tip**

It is often a good idea to include a figure for "contingency" in the budget to cover unforeseen eventualities, eg 5% contingency expense.

## ❑ Budget Control

The stages for managing the budget control process are set out in Figure 26.5.

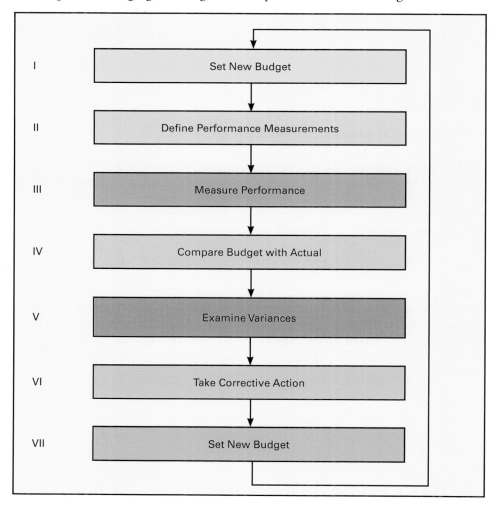

| | |
|---|---|
| I | Set New Budget |
| II | Define Performance Measurements |
| III | Measure Performance |
| IV | Compare Budget with Actual |
| V | Examine Variances |
| VI | Take Corrective Action |
| VII | Set New Budget |

Figure 26.5

# ❑ Budget Reports

The comparison of actual results to budget takes place at two levels. All managers gets information about the costs (and income) under their control and compare actual cost against budget for the month under review and for the cumulative months of the accounting year so far. Budget reports must be timely and contain information relevant to the recipient. If too much time elapses before a budget report is issued it will be too late to take corrective action.

## *Incremental or Zero-Based Budgets*

Thought must be given when setting budgets whether to base them on previous years' or to start with a clean sheet. The former approach is referred to as incremental budgeting. The previous year's figures are taken as a base and then adjusted for expected changes in price, costs and activity levels. The disadvantage of this approach is that it does not encourage fresh thinking and may perpetuate existing inefficiencies.

A more recent approach is to start with a clean sheet referred to as a zero base. This ignores previous experience and requires a manager to justify all the resource requirements expressed as costs in their budget. Each item of expense is therefore questioned. Every item of income and expense has to be justified in its own right.

# ❑ Budgeting Objectives

The objectives of the budgeting policies and procedures are to ensure that:

- Short and long-term strategies for the organisation are determined on a realistic basis. Budgets are central to the process of planning and control. Management should determine and prepare the long-term strategic plan for the organisation.
- Projects which run over budget are brought to the board's attention.
- Budgets are effectively planned, monitored and authorised for each section of the organisation.
- All assumptions are clearly stated and documented. This should include the background to each item of expenditure, activity description and financial summary.
- Budgets should be prepared in an efficient and timely manner. It should be the responsibility of each functional area of the organisation to prepare and sign off their respective budgets on time. It should be the responsibility of the accountant to complete the "final organisation budget" by an agreed date.
- A formal mid- and final-year review should take place to compare the budget against actual performance.

This chapter describes management reports and provides an example together with a checklist for preparing monthly management accounts.

A key element of the successful operation of any organisation is timely response on those areas that require action. This can only be done if there is sufficient, timely and accurate information available. Reporting on an annual basis is designed to provide information for external groups or individuals. However, the people working in the organisation and the members of the board will not have sufficient information to take action on particular issues if the only report available is the annual report.

## ❏ Management Accounting

In addition to keeping statutory records for reporting purposes, organisations also require internal reports on its areas of activity. The process of keeping financial information internally for use by the organisation is known as management accounting. Management accounts are produced for internal use within the organisation to assist management in running the company efficiently and effectively. They provide much greater detail than annual accounts and are normally produced on a monthly/ quarterly basis. Many decisions which managers take are based on financial information. Management accounts can be seen as a vital part of the wider management process. Managers and employees at all levels must be conscious of their responsibility in providing accurate financial information to the people who rely on it.

## ❏ Variance

A variance is the difference between the planned or budgeted outcome and the subsequent actual result. By analysing variances, it is possible to identify problem areas and take appropriate action. Variance analysis is often applied as part of the budgetary control process.

Set out in Figure 27.1 is an example of a management accounting report. The figures for the annual budget and the budget for January–March are taken from the example used in the Budgeting chapter, (Figure 26.2) ie sales for January, February and March are €6,000 + €9,000 + €11,000 = €26,000.

## Expenditure Report January–March

| Jan–March | Annual Budget | Budget Jan–Mar | Actual Jan–Mar | Variance | Reason | Action |
|---|---|---|---|---|---|---|
| **Income** | € | € | € | € | | |
| Sales | 129,000 | 26,000 | 20,000 | –6,000 | Loss of customer | Identify additional customers |
| Opening Stock | – | – | – | – | On target | None |
| Purchases | 26,300 | 5,950 | 4,550 | 1,400 | Purchases cost less than expected | Review supplier list |
| Closing Stock | –500 | –750 | –750 | – | On target | None |
| | 25,800 | 5,200 | 3,800 | 1,400 | | |
| **Gross Profit** | **103,200** | **20,800** | **16,200** | **–4,600** | | |
| **Expenditure** | | | | | | |
| Salaries | 60,000 | 15,000 | 15,000 | – | On target | None |
| Travel & Subsistence | 700 | 200 | 150 | 50 | On target | None |
| Advertising | 7,000 | – | – | – | On target | None |
| Insurance | 7,500 | 7,500 | 7,500 | – | On target | None |
| Printing | 1,000 | – | 300 | –300 | Trade magazine | Opportunity arose not in budget |
| Postage | 1,200 | 300 | 400 | –100 | Trade magazine | Opportunity arose not in budget |
| Telephone | 3,000 | 750 | 720 | 30 | On target | None |
| Courier | 3,600 | 900 | 1,000 | –100 | Special delivery | Use postal service more |
| Rent | 4,000 | 1,000 | 1,000 | – | On target | None |
| Rates | 3,000 | 3,000 | 3,000 | – | On target | None |
| Repairs | 1,000 | – | 150 | –150 | Broken window | None |
| Audit | 3,000 | – | – | – | On target | None |
| Bank Interest | 6,000 | 1,500 | 1,450 | 50 | On target | None |
| Depreciation | 3,000 | 750 | 750 | – | On target | None |
| **Total Expenditure** | **104,000** | **30,900** | **31,420** | **–520** | | |
| **Profit/(Loss)** | **–800** | **–10,100** | **–15,220** | **–5,120** | | |

Figure 27.1

Based on the figures, the expectation for the first quarter (January–March) was a budgeted loss of €10,100. The actual results were a loss of €15,220. By comparing the budget to the actual figures, the variance can be identified and action taken. The primary reason for the increase in the loss is because sales were €6,000 less than budgeted and expenditure was higher than expected for printing, postage, courier and repairs. The one positive variance was in relation to the purchase of goods for resale which were at a lower cost than budgeted.

If a business does not prepare a budget it should put last year's results on a page beside the current year's results. At least there will be some yardstick with which to compare this year's performance.

## ❑ **Management Accounts Checklist**

When preparing monthly/quarterly management accounts, a checklist should be used to ensure that all areas are covered. Set out in Figure 27.2 is an example.

| Management Accounts Checklist | | Month Ending: | |
|---|---|---|---|
| **Category** | **Task** | **Completed by** | **Tick** |
| **Bank** | Post all lodgements to bank account | | |
| | Post all cheques to bank account | | |
| | Post all direct debits to bank account | | |
| | Prepare bank reconciliation for all bank accounts | | |
| | Review and sign off all bank & petty cash reconciliations | | |
| **Petty Cash** | Reconcile petty cash | | |
| **Credit Card** | Analyse credit card statements and post expenses to the relevant nominals | | |
| **Creditors** | Post all invoices for month | | |
| | Review and reconcile list of creditor balances to accounts | | |
| | Agree creditors' balances to creditor statements | | |
| | Reconcile PAYE/PRSI liability | | |
| | Reconcile VAT liability | | |
| **Salaries** | Post salaries to accounts system from payroll system | | |
| | Ensure P45s received from new employees | | |
| | Ensure P45s issued to employees who are leaving | | |
| | Monthly P30 return sent to Revenue | | |
| | Overtime/subsistence expenses are approved and signed | | |
| | Annual P35 submitted to Revenue | | |
| **Fixed Assets** | Update fixed asset register | | |
| | Review and reconcile fixed asset register | | |
| **Income/ Expenditure** | Review income for month | | |
| | Ensure expenses coded correctly | | |
| | Complete filing for month | | |
| | Prepare list of accruals for month | | |
| | Prepare list of prepayments for month | | |
| | Review and print trial balance | | |
| | Review and print profit & loss account | | |
| | Review and print balance sheet | | |
| | Compare actual figures to budget | | |
| **Signature:** | | | |
| **Title:** | | | |
| **Date:** | | | |

Figure 27.2

This chapter sets out tools that can be used for business analysis which include ratios, horizontal analysis and vertical analysis.

When analysing financial statements, it is important to be able to judge whether the information in the financial statements is favourable or unfavourable. This can be achieved in a number of ways:

- Past performance—comparison of financial ratios or performance in the same company.
- Industry norms—using industry norms as a standard of comparison.

Limitation on the use of company norms:

1. Companies in the same industry may not be comparable.
2. Many large companies have multiple segments and operate in more than one market.
3. Companies may use different accounting policies.

## ❏ Ratios

Ratios provide an insight into a business by examining the relationship between pairs of figures extracted from the profit & loss account and the balance sheet. Ratios can be compared with last year's ratios, target ratios or competitors' ratios. Ratios can be expressed as a percentage or a multiple. Set out in Figure 28.1 is an extract from a profit & loss account and balance sheet. The figures below will be used in the next few examples. Ratios are useful tools for evaluating a company's financial position and operations and may reveal areas that need further investigation.

| *Extract from Profit & Loss Account year ended 31 December 2007* | | €|
|---|---|---|
| Sales | | 400,000 |
| Opening Stock | 80,000 | |
| Purchases | 300,000 | |
| Closing Stock | (30,000) | (350,000) |
| Gross Profit | | 50,000 |
| Profit Before Tax, Interest & Dividends | | 15,000 |

(*Continued*)

| Extract from Balance Sheet | 2007 € | 2006 € |
|---|---|---|
| Stock | 30,000 | |
| Debtors | 40,000 | 40,000 |
| Cash | 40,000 | |
| | | |
| Creditors | 45,000 | |

Figure 28.1

## Profitability Ratio

- Gross Profit Margin—this ratio measures the profit earned on sales and monitors buying and selling prices. It can be influenced by a change in the mix of items sold when different product lines have different gross margins.

$$\text{Gross Margin} = \frac{\text{Gross Profit} \times 100\%}{\text{Sales}}$$

### Example

| Gross Profit | 50,000 |
|---|---|
| Sales | 400,000 |

$$\frac{50,000}{400,000} \times 100\% = 12.5\%$$

In effect, every sale that the company makes will contribute 12.5% to the gross profit.

- Net Profit Margin—this ratio measures the net profit after all costs of sales and all overheads have been deducted from sales, it is expressed as a percentage of sales.

$$\text{Net Profit Margin} = \frac{\text{Net profit before tax, interest and dividends} \times 100\%}{\text{Sales}}$$

### Example

| Net profit before tax, interest and dividends | 15,000 |
|---|---|
| Sales | 400,000 |

$$\frac{15,000}{400,000} \times 100\% = 3.75\%$$

(Continued)

The Net Profit before tax, interest and dividends is 3.75% of sales. Tax and interest will have to be paid before the company can declare a dividend. Subtracting the gross profit margin and the net profit margin (15% − 3.75% = 11.25%) this implies that overheads are 11.25% of sales.

## Efficiency Ratios

These ratios relate to asset management and the business's efficiency.

- Debtor days—show on average how long it takes to collect money from debtors.

### Debtor Days

$$\frac{Debtors}{Sales} \times 365 \text{ days}$$

### Example

Debtors          40,000

Sales            400,000

$$\frac{40,000}{400,000} \times 365 \text{ days} = 36.5 \text{ days}$$

This implies that customers are taking 6.5 days longer to pay than the normal credit terms of 30 days. This could be for a variety of reasons.

- Creditor days—this ratio is used to determine how long it takes the business to pay suppliers.

### Creditor Days

$$\frac{Creditors}{Credit\ Purchases} \times 365 \text{ days}$$

### Example

Creditors                45,000

Credit Purchases         300,000

$$\frac{45,000}{300,000} \times 365 \text{ days} = 55 \text{ days}$$

(Continued)

This implies that the business is taking 25 days longer to pay over and above the normal credit terms of 30 days. This could be for a variety of reasons, such as cash flow problems or a dispute over goods delivered.

## Stock Turnover

- Stock Turnover identifies the number of days' stock being carried by the business.

**Stock Turnover**

$$\frac{\text{Stock}}{\text{Cost of Sales}} \times 365 \text{ days}$$

**Example**

| | |
|---|---|
| Stock | 30,000 |
| Cost of Sales | 350,000 |

$$\frac{30,000}{350,000} \times 365 \text{ days} = 31 \text{ days}$$

This implies that the business holds 31 days of stock.

## Solvency Ratios

In order to survive, companies must maintain cash to pay short-term debts. Companies go out of business when they are unable to pay debts as they fall due.

- The acid test or quick ratio is crucial to a company's survival. It measures current assets as a percentage of current liabilities. Current assets are debtors, cash and short-term investments. Where a company has a ratio of 1:1 this means that the company has sufficient liquid assets to pay its debts.

**Acid Test/Quick Ratio**

$$\frac{\text{Debtors} + \text{Cash}}{\text{Current Liabilities}}$$

**Example**

| | |
|---|---|
| Debtors | 40,000 |
| Cash | 40,000 |
| Current Liabilities | 45,000 |

$$\frac{40,000 + 40,000}{45,000} \quad 1.77 : 1$$

This implies that the company has sufficient liquid assets to pay its debts.

## *Current Ratio*

This is another liquidity ratio, which includes stock in current assets based on the assumption that stock will be turned into debtors and then into cash. Current assets are compared to current liabilities. A ratio of 2:1 is considered the norm.

- The current ratio is closely related to working capital. Many bankers and other creditors believe it is a good indicator of a company's ability to pay its debts on time.

**Current Ratio**

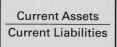

**Example**

| Debtors | 40,000 |
| Cash | 40,000 |
| Stocks | 30,000 |
| Current Liabilities | 45,000 |
| | |
| $\dfrac{40,000 + 40,000 + 30,000}{45,000}$ | 2.44 : 1 |

These ratios are often used to ask a further question. Is the ratio too high because there are large unused cash resources or slow stock turnover?

Although companies in the same industry may have comparable earnings, their quality of earnings may not be comparable. To assess the quality of a company's earnings, you must know the estimates and the methods, it uses to compute income. Generally accepted accounting principles allow several methods, each yielding a difference result. The accounting policies a firm uses will affect its operating income eg depreciation or stock valuation. Reviewing the financial statements of a business for a number of years can identify trends.

## ❑ Horizontal Analysis

This looks at changes in figures from the previous year to the current year.

$\dfrac{\text{Amount of change} \times 100\%}{\text{Base year amount}}$

The base year is always the first year to be considered in any set of data.
Set out in Figure 28.2 and 28.3 is the profit and loss account and balance sheet for Murphy Limited using horizontal analysis.

**Murphy Limited**
**Profit & Loss Account**
**Year ended 31 December 2007**

| | € | € | € | % |
|---|---|---|---|---|
| **Income** | **2007** | **2006** | **Change** | **Percentage** |
| Subscription | 120,000 | 111,000 | 9,000 | 8% |
| Sales | 424,000 | 375,000 | 49,000 | 13% |
| Sponsorship | 17,000 | 6,500 | 10,500 | 162% |
| Other Income | 15,000 | 6,500 | 8,500 | 131% |
| | 576,000 | 499,000 | 77,000 | 15% |
| | | | | |
| Opening Stock | 1,000 | 1,500 | (500) | −33% |
| Purchases | 285,000 | 246,000 | 39,000 | 16% |
| Closing Stock | (800) | (1,000) | 200 | −20% |
| | 285,200 | 246,500 | 38,700 | 16% |
| | | | | |
| Gross Profit | 290,800 | 252,500 | 38,300 | 15% |
| | | | | |
| **Expenditure** | | | | |
| Salaries | 198,000 | 157,500 | 40,500 | 26% |
| Travel & Subsistence | 5,500 | 6,000 | (500) | −8% |
| Advertising | 4,000 | 3,000 | 1,000 | 33% |
| Insurance | 12,000 | 10,000 | 2,000 | 20% |
| Printing | 6,000 | 4,500 | 1,500 | 33% |
| Postage | 4,000 | 3,000 | 1,000 | 33% |
| Telephone | 5,000 | 4,500 | 500 | 11% |
| Courier | 3,600 | 3,000 | 600 | 20% |
| Rent | 16,000 | 15,000 | 1,000 | 7% |
| Depreciation | 16,750 | 12,117 | 4,633 | 38% |
| Rates | 3,000 | 3,000 | – | 0% |
| Repairs | 1,100 | 2,100 | (1,000) | −48% |
| Bank Interest | 600 | 600 | – | 0% |
| Bank Charges | 300 | 300 | – | 0% |
| | | | | |
| | 275,850 | 224,617 | 51,233 | 23% |
| | | | | |
| Net Profit | 14,950 | 27,883 | (12,933) | −46% |
| | | | | |
| Retained Profit 1/1/07 | 42,733 | 14,850 | | |
| | | | | |
| Retained Profit | 57,683 | 42,733 | | |

$$\frac{9{,}000}{111{,}000} \times 100\%$$

Figure 28.2

**Murphy Limited**
**Balance Sheet**
**as at 31 December 2007**

| | € | € | € | % |
|---|---|---|---|---|
| **Fixed Assets** | **2007** | **2006** | **Change** | **Percentage** |
| Tangible Assets | 41,383 | 38,133 | 3,250 | 9% |
| | | | | |
| **Current Assets** | | | | |
| Stock | 800 | 1,000 | (200) | −20% |
| Trade Debtors | 7,500 | 2,500 | 5,000 | 200% |
| Prepayments | 1,255 | 800 | 455 | 57% |
| Cash at bank and in hand | 38,245 | 19,750 | 18,495 | 94% |
| | 47,800 | 24,050 | 23,750 | |
| | | | | |
| **Creditors Due Within 1 year** | | | | |
| Bank Loan & Overdraft | 2,000 | 1,500 | 500 | 33% |
| Trade Creditors | 20,500 | 15,000 | 5,500 | 37% |
| PAYE/PRSI | 1,500 | 1,200 | 300 | 25% |
| Other accruals | 6,500 | 750 | 5,750 | 767% |
| | (30,500) | (18,450) | (12,050) | |
| | | | | |
| **Net Current Assets** | 17,300 | 5,600 | 11,700 | 209% |
| | | | | |
| **Net Assets** | 58,683 | 43,733 | 14,950 | 34% |
| | | | | |
| **Represented by** | | | | |
| Share Capital | 1,000 | 1,000 | – | 0% |
| Reserves | 57,683 | 42,733 | 14,950 | 35% |
| | | | | |
| | 58,683 | 43,733 | 14,950 | |

3,250/38,133 × 100%

Figure 28.3

Trend analysis is a variation of horizontal analysis. With this tool, the percentage changes for several successive years are calculated instead of just for two years. Trend analysis uses an index number to show changes in related items over time. For index numbers, the base year is equal to 100. Set out in Figure 28.4 is trend analysis for income for Murphy Limited 2003–2007.

| Murphy Limited | | | | | |
| --- | --- | --- | --- | --- | --- |
| | € | € | € | € | € |
| **Income** | **2007** | **2006** | **2005** | **2004** | **2003** |
| Subscriptions | 120,000 | 111,000 | 105,000 | 101,000 | 85,000 |
| Sales | 424,000 | 375,000 | 315,000 | 316,000 | 250,000 |
| Sponsorship | 17,000 | 6,500 | 6,000 | 5,500 | 5,000 |
| Other Income | 15,000 | 6,500 | 6,000 | 5,500 | 5,000 |
| | 576,000 | 499,000 | 432,000 | 428,000 | 345,000 |
| | | | | | |
| **Percentages** | **2007** | **2006** | **2005** | **2004** | **2003** |
| Subscriptions | 141.2 | 130.6 | 123.5 | 118.8 | 100.0 |
| Sales | 169.6 | 150.0 | 126.0 | 126.4 | 100.0 |
| Sponsorship | 340.0 | 130.0 | 120.0 | 110.0 | 100.0 |
| Other Income | 300.0 | 130.0 | 120.0 | 110.0 | 100.0 |

Figure 28.4

## ❑ Vertical Analysis

Vertical analysis shows how the different components of the financial statements relate to the total figures. The income and net asset figures are set at 100 and each component's percentage of that total is calculated. See Figures 28.5 and 28.6. This method is used to compare the importance of specific components in the operation of a business and to identify important changes in the components from one year to the next.

**Murphy Limited**

**Profit & Loss Account**

**Year ended 31 December 2007**

| Income | € 2007 | € 2006 |
|---|---|---|
| Income | 100% | 100% |
| Cost of Sales | (49%) | (49%) |
| Gross Profit | 51% | 51% |
| | | |
| **Expenditure** | | |
| Salaries | 34% | 32% |
| Travel & Subsistence | 1% | 1% |
| Advertising | 1% | 1% |
| Insurance | 2% | 2% |
| Printing | 1% | 1% |
| Postage | 1% | 1% |
| Telephone | 1% | 1% |
| Courier | 1% | 1% |
| Rent | 3% | 3% |
| Depreciation | 3% | 2% |
| Rates | 0% | 0% |
| Repairs | 0% | 0% |
| Bank Interest | 0% | 0% |
| Bank Charges | 0% | 0% |
| | 48% | 45% |
| Net Profit | 3% | 6% |

€285,200/€576,000 × 100%

Figure 28.5

**Murphy Limited**
**Balance Sheet**
**as at 31 December 2007**

€41,383/€58,683
× 100%

| | € | € |
|---|---|---|
| **Fixed Assets** | **2007** | **2006** |
| Tangible Assets | 71% | 87% |
| | | |
| **Current Assets** | | |
| Stock | 1% | 2% |
| Trade Debtors | 13% | 6% |
| Prepayments | 2% | 2% |
| Cash at bank and in hand | 65% | 45% |
| | 81% | 55% |
| | | |
| **Creditors Due Within 1 year** | | |
| Bank Loan & Overdraft | 3% | 3% |
| Trade Creditors | 35% | 34% |
| PAYE/PRSI | 3% | 3% |
| Other accruals | 11% | 2% |
| | (52%) | (42%) |
| **Net Current Assets** | 29% | 13% |
| | | |
| **Net Assets** | 100% | 100% |
| | | |
| **Represented by** | | |
| Share Capital | 2% | 2% |
| Reserves | 98% | 98% |
| | | |
| | 100% | 100% |

Figure 28.6

Working capital is the value of all current assets, less the value of current liabilities. It includes the cost of stocks of raw materials, work in progress and finished goods, together with the amount owed by customers, less the amount owed to suppliers and other creditors.

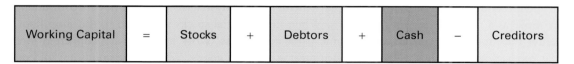

The total assets of a business are made up of fixed assets and working capital (stock, debtors, cash and creditors). Set out in Figure 29.1 is a diagram of how the capital employed in a business is either invested in fixed assets or working capital.

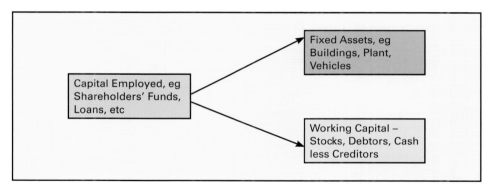

Figure 29.1

## ❑ Managing Working Capital

The key to managing working capital successfully is to find the right balance between liquidity and profitability. A firm needs to have enough cash to pay the wages and other bills when required, but on the other hand it needs to carry sufficient stocks so that production is not unduly disrupted or customers dissatisfied if the item they wish to purchase is unavailable. Both of these requirements can be met given unlimited working capital, but much of the stock would be idle for long periods of time. Idle stock means that profits would be lost due to the extra holding costs of large volumes of stock. A balance needs to be struck between profitability and liquidity, recognising that they pull in opposite directions. How much working capital is needed is related to the volume of business and the level of sales. Annual sales is divided by the amount of working capital to find out how many times the working capital circulated during the year.

## Profitability Management

As a goal, profitability competes with liquidity for managerial attention because liquid assets are not the best profit-producing resources. Cash gives purchasing power, but a satisfactory profit can only be made if purchasing power is used to buy profit-producing assets such as stocks.

## Liquidity Management

Working capital requirements can be determined from the length of the operating cycle. This term refers to the length of time between the company paying out cash on materials, wages and overheads, and the eventual receipt of cash from the sales of the goods and services provided. In basic terms, the longer the operating cycle, the more working capital that will be required and the lower the return on capital achieved.

Current assets are not intended to be held permanently or for any lengthy period. They are continually on the move as a result of trading operations. When raw material stocks are issued to the shop floor, they enter the production process and become work in progress. Work in progress is converted into saleable goods, which are shown in the balance sheet as finished goods. When these goods are sold on credit, they are delivered to a customer who is then listed as a debtor. As soon as the debtor settles his account, cash flows to the company—the current asset "cash" replacing the current asset "debtor"—and the cycle of business operation is almost complete. See Figure 29.2. Some of the money will be used to pay creditors who supply the company with raw materials, components and services necessary for its business. Some will be used to buy new fixed assets or to increase the amount of the firm's working capital, but the continuous movement of current assets results in this being called "circulating" assets.

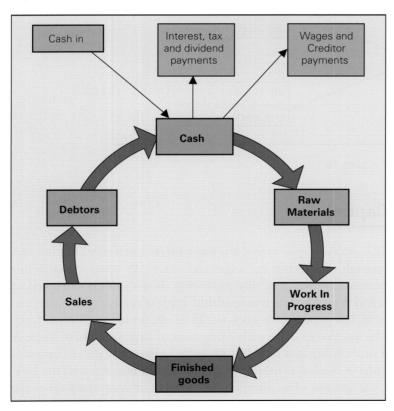

Figure 29.2

## *Operating Cycle*

The transactions that make up the operating cycle are as follows:

1. Purchase of stock for cash or on credit from creditors.
2. Payments for purchases made on credit.
3. Sales of stock for cash or on credit to debtors.
4. Collection of cash from debtors.

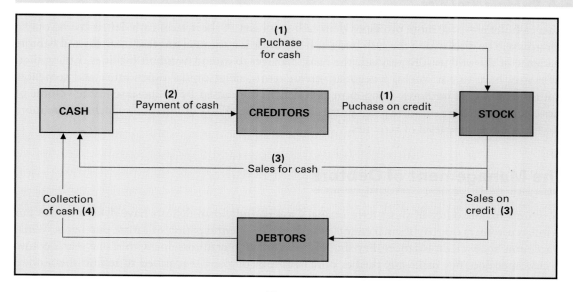

Figure 29.3

When retailers purchase stock on credit, they have a period of time before payment is due. However, this period is usually shorter than the time it takes to sell the goods. To finance the stock until they sell it and collect payment for it, retailers must rely on cash flows from within the company or from borrowing. If they lack the cash to pay bills when they become due, they can be forced out of business.

Cash flow management involves planning a company's receipts and payments of cash. If a company is not able to pay its bills when they are due, it may be forced out of business. This is particularly true for retail businesses, which differ from service businesses in that they must have goods on hand so that they are available for sale to customers.

## ❏ The Management of Cash

Cash is the lifeblood of a business. It is central to the operating cycle because all operating transactions use or generate cash. Most companies experience seasonal cycles of business activity. During some periods, sales are weak, during others they are strong. There are periods when expenditures are high and others when they are low. Seasonal cycles require careful planning of cash inflows, cash outflows and borrowings.

There are a number of factors that have a bearing on the amount of cash a company needs to hold at any one time. Foremost will be its forecast of future cash inflows and outflows compiled in the cash budget.

Cash is the asset most readily available to pay debts, but at times a company may have more cash on hand than it needs to pay its debts. Excess cash should not remain idle, especially during periods of high interest rates. Management may decide to invest the excess cash in short-term interest deposit accounts.

### Cash Surplus/Deficits

Forecast cash deficits pose more problems than cash surpluses. A short-term cash deficit lasting only a few months will be disclosed in the cash budget. If the cause is a seasonal increase in stocks and debtors the evidence of this will usually persuade the bank manager to extend overdraft facilities. Failing that, the firm may have to cut stocks, renegotiate credit terms, defer capital expenditure and somehow level out the peak cash outflows. Long-term cash deficits are caused by an increase in the volume of business, large capital expenditure programmes or simply the effects of inflation, which require more cash to finance the same level of activities.

## ❏ The Management of Debtors

Debtors are a major source of short-term financial assets. Individual debtors have debit balances but sometimes customers overpay their accounts by mistake or in anticipation of future purchases. When these accounts show credit balances they should be included in creditors due within one year, because if the customer does not make any further purchases the company is required to refund the money. Companies that sell on credit do so to remain competitive and to increase sales. In setting credit terms, companies must keep in mind the credit terms of its competitors and the needs of its customers. Any company that sells on credit wants customers who will pay their bills on time. To increase the likelihood of selling only to customers who will pay on time, most companies develop control procedures and maintain a credit department. The credit department examines every person or company that seeks credit and approves or rejects it. The credit department will normally ask for details of the person's debts and financial resources.

Credit management is a balancing act where the gain from extending credit to customers is offset by the cost of interest, discounts, administration and bad debts. When a customer applies for credit it would be rash to agree without checking his or her creditworthiness. This can be done by employing a suitable credit agency. Checks should include talking to other suppliers who have been quoted as trade references and checking bank referees. A copy of the client's annual accounts can be requested from the Companies Registration Office and reviewed using ratio analysis to review liquidity and profitability.

### Terms of Sale

A company must decide the terms on which it will make sales, being the length of the credit period and whether it offers cash discounts for early payment. The length of the credit period will often be settled by the normal terms for that particular industry, eg 30 days. Early collection has the advantage of reducing the probability of a customer defaulting.  In some industries it is customary to give a discount for early payment. This discount is called sales discount. It is intended to increase the seller's liquidity by reducing the amount of money tied up in debtors.

### *Follow-Up Procedures*

Having sold to credit customers and specified the payment terms, businesses must consider what follow-up procedures to adopt with late payers. Many firms use a monthly statement both as a reminder and for the customer to check the balance against their own records. If payment is not forthcoming in the stipulated time, a reminder letter should be sent, followed by a more strongly worded letter. If payment is still not received, consideration should be given to terminating supplies and instituting legal action, and the customer informed accordingly. Legal action for the recovery of the debt may not be appropriate where the debt is small or where the sale was subject to an unresolved dispute and the client's ability to pay is in doubt.

## ❏ The Management of Creditors

Trade creditors are debts owed to suppliers of goods and services in whose books they appear as debtors. The policy for dealing with creditors is very straightforward and mirrors that of debtors. If no cash discounts are offered, the full credit period should be taken.

This chapter provides an overview of what is involved when Financial Statements are audited, a description of the auditors report and an example of a set of Financial Statements.

Companies/businesses whose turnover is less than €7.3 million are not required to carry out an audit, but may choose to have a full audit carried out. All companies must prepare accounts in accordance with the companies acts.

*How do I prepare my financial statement/accounts?*
A bookkeeper/accountant can prepare the financial statements from your books and records. It is essential for businesses to maintain good accounting records.

*Once I have the accounts prepared, how do I get them audited?*
A qualified auditor will have to be selected to conduct the audit of your business. The auditor must be registered with a professional body of accountants, eg The Institute of Chartered Accountants in Ireland.

*Can an auditor prepare the financial statements and carry out the audit at the same time?*
Yes, an auditor can prepare the financial statements and audit the financial statements. This has the advantage that they will be familiar with the transactions that the business has carried out.

## ❑ Auditing Accounts

The term "audited accounts" means that the financial records of the business have been independently verified by a registered auditor as showing a "true and fair" view of the financial operations and position of the business at that time. Directors or employees of the company or a parent, spouse, brother or sister of a director are disqualified from being appointed as an auditor under the companies acts.

**Quick Tip**

Allow sufficient time to have your accounts prepared/audited. There are certain times of the year when accountancy firms are very busy.

Whether your business is having accounts prepared or an, audit carried out the accountant/auditor will require access to the business books and records. The accountant's job will be to check what stage the preparation of accounts is at and to convert this into finalised financial statements. The auditor's job is to report on whether the financial statements give a "true & fair" view of what has happened and the financial position at the accounting date. To do this they need to examine records and understand how the organisation works, and the kind of controls in place to prevent things going wrong.

The accountant will need to ensure that the following information is correct in order to prepare the financial statements:

- All sales invoices and credit notes have been recorded.
- All lodgements have been recorded in the correct nominal.
- All cheques paid have been recorded in the correct nominal.
- All purchase invoices and credit notes have been recorded.
- Petty cash has been recorded and reconciled at the year-end.
- All bank accounts have been reconciled.
- A list of debtors at the year end has been drawn up and agreed to the debtor nominal.
- A list of the creditors at the year end has been drawn up and agreed to the creditor nominal and creditor statements.
- A file of bank statements is available.
- Payroll records have been reconciled.
- A physical stock count has been undertaken, costs have been allocated to each item and a stock value calculated.

An audit file should be prepared in advance of the auditor commencement the audit, which should contain the following:

- A copy of last year's signed accounts.
- A copy of the current years draft accounts.
- A schedule for each part of the financial statements with a breakdown of all the relevant figures.
- A printout of the trial balance.
- A printout of the profit & loss account.
- A printout of the balance sheet.
- A printout of the nominals.
- Any relevant working papers with a copy of supporting correspondence.
- Copies of bank statements in sequence.

During the course of the audit, the auditor will ask questions and request information. The auditor may carry out the audit at their own office; this type of audit may suit some small businesses, as they may not have room at the office for an auditor to work. The disadvantage of this type of audit is that the business will not have access to the books and records for several weeks. If any queries arise during the audit it will not be easy to answer them as quickly.

The auditor may suggest changes to the financial statements due to errors found. Additional information may have to be disclosed or certain omitted transactions may have to be included. Once the financial statements have been cleared by the auditor, then two directors will have to sign and date them if they are company accounts. If the accounts are those of a sole trader, then the individual will have to sign and date the accounts.

The auditor will issue a management letter, highlighting any issues noticed during the audit. They will also request the business to sign a letter of representation, covering areas such as the valuation of stock, petty cash balance, any legal cases outstanding, disputes, etc.

**Quick Tip**

> At the end of the accounts preparation/audit ask the accountant/auditor for a list of adjustments made to the financial statements, in order to reconcile your books and records to the final signed financial statements.

## ❏ Auditor's Report

Limited companies whose turnover exceeds €7.3 million must submit their annual accounts for audit by an independent qualified auditor. The audit report is an independent report made to the shareholders about whether the accounts give a "true and fair" view of the company's state of affairs. This means that adequate records have been kept and that the accounts comply with the companies acts and professional accounting standards.

The companies acts require that the company's balance sheet shall give a "true and fair" view of the state of affairs of the company as at the end of the financial year. Furthermore, every profit & loss account must similarly give a "true and fair" view of the profit and loss of the company for the financial year. The "true and fair" view concept is the overriding principle, which supersedes all other policies and conventions in deciding what is to be reported and how it is to be presented. Yet nowhere in the legislation is a definition given for what "true and fair" means. It is generally accepted as meaning that the accounts are:

1. Prepared and presented in accordance with recognised accounting principles and practices in general use throughout the profession.
2. Contain figures which are as accurate and objective as possible, judged by the above common principles and practices throughout the accounting profession.
3. Not biased or drawn up to conceal material facts about the company's actual state of affairs.
4. Reasonably comparable to previous years enabling fair judgments to be undertaken.

### *Auditor's Report*

The first paragraph of the auditor's report identifies the financial statements that have been audited. It also identifies responsibilities. The company is responsible for preparing the financial statements and the auditor is responsible for expressing an opinion on the financial statements.

The second paragraph is the scope section, which states that the audit was carried out in accordance with auditing standards and company law. The third paragraph is the opinion section, which states the result of the auditor's work. The words used are very important because the auditor does not certify or guarantee that the statements are absolutely correct.

In addition to the "true and fair" requirement, there are a number of accounting conventions:

## Accounting Conventions

- Going concern—this assumes that the company being reported on has an indefinite life, that it has an expected continuity of existence and is not intended to be liquidated in the foreseeable future.
- Consistency—this requires that the accounting treatment of items in separate reporting periods should be followed consistently.
- Prudence—conservative basis of accounts preparation leads to the following rules:
  - Profits will not be recognised until they are realised.
  - Losses will be recognised as soon as they are apparent even though they have not at the time of reporting been realised into cash.
- Accrual—this convention has as its basic principle that income and the costs of earning that income should be identified with one another when calculating the net profit of the period. Costs and income are to be recognised as incurred or earned not when the money is paid or received but when the liability or benefit can reasonably be anticipated.

## An Auditor's Report May Be Qualified or Unqualified

- An unqualified report is an opinion by the auditor that a "true and fair" view is given by the state of the company's affairs at the end of its financial year and the company's profit & loss for the financial year.
- A qualified report would be one in which the auditor states any or all of the following:
  - Proper books of account have not been kept by the company.
  - The balance sheet is not in agreement with the books of account.
  - They have not received all the information and explanations which they consider necessary for their audit.

To help interpretation, accountants use five conventions:

1. Comparability means that the information is presented in such a way that a decision-maker can recognise similarities, differences and trends over time periods or between different companies.
2. Consistency convention requires that once a company adopts an accounting procedure, it remains in use from one period to the next unless the users of financial statements are informed of a change.
3. Materiality refers to the relative importance of an item or event. If an item or event is material, it is probably relevant to users of the financial statements. An item is material if users would have acted differently had they not know about the item.
4. Conservatism means that when accountants face major uncertainties about which accounting procedure to use, they generally choose the one that is least likely to overstate assets and income, eg the use of the lower of cost and realisable value in accounting for stock. Under this method, if the realisable value falls below the cost, the more conservative realisable value is used.
5. Full disclosure requires that financial statements and their notes present all the information that is relevant to the user's understanding of the statements.

# ❑ Cash Flow Statements

In addition to the profit & loss account and the balance sheet, some companies are required to include an additional statement called the cash flow statement. This statement analyses the change in the cash position of the business and looks at the causes. An increase in the bank balance could be caused by a reduction in money being tied up in stock and debtors or an increase in the amount of credit taken from suppliers. The main areas analysed in a cash flow statement are changes in working capital, capital investment and income received from financial assets, eg interest received.

Companies do not have to provide a cash flow statement in their financial statements unless they satisfy two or more of the following criteria:

| | |
|---|---|
| Average number of employees | exceeds 50 |
| Balance sheet | €1,904,607 |
| Turnover | €3,809,214 |

The following is an example of how the financial statements may be presented; it is only included for illustrative purposes as the company used in the example would not be required to have the financial statements audited as the turnover is less than €7.3m.

**SPORTS LIMITED**

**FINANCIAL STATEMENTS**
**YEAR ENDED 31 DECEMBER 2007**

**SPORTS LIMITED**

**FINANCIAL STATEMENTS
YEAR ENDED 31 DECEMBER 2007**

## CONTENTS

**SPORTS LIMITED**

**DIRECTORS AND OTHER INFORMATION**

| | |
|---|---|
| Board of Directors: | John Murphy |
| | Mary Smyth |
| Secretary: | James Lyons |
| Company Number: | 123456 |
| Registered Office: | 11 Grafton Street |
| | Dublin 2 |
| Bankers: | Bank of Ireland |
| | Main Street |
| | Blanchardstown |
| | Dublin 15 |
| Solicitors: | Ryan & Co |
| | 48 Main Street |
| | Blackrock |
| | Co Dublin |
| Auditors: | Lynch & Co |
| | Chartered Accountants & |
| | Registered Auditors |
| | 12 Main Street |
| | Blanchardstown |
| | Dublin 15 |

**SPORTS LIMITED**

**REPORT OF THE DIRECTORS**

The directors submit their report together with the audited financial statements for the year ended 31 December 2007. In preparing the financial statements, the directors have exercised the options available to a small private company under the Companies (Amendment) Act, 1986.

### Principal Activities and Review of the Business

The company's principal activity during the year was the promotion and advertising of sportswear throughout Ireland.

### Results and Dividends

The profit for the year ended 31 December 2007 was €77,200 (2006—Profit €76,800).

### Research and Development

The company did not engage in any research and development activities during the year.

### Events since the Year End

There have been no significant events affecting the company since the year end.

### Directors

James McDonnell resigned during the year. Mary Smyth was appointed during the year. All other directors listed on page 1 held office throughout the year.

### Safety Health and Welfare at Work Act 1989

The company has prepared a safety statement as required by Section 12 of the Safety Health and Welfare at Work Act 1989. The safety policy contained therein has been fulfilled for the year.

### Books and Records

The directors believe that they have complied with the requirements of Section 202 of the Companies Act 1990 with regard to books of account by employing accounting personnel with appropriate expertise and by providing adequate resources to the financial function. The books of account of the company are maintained at 11 Grafton Street, Dublin 2.

**SPORTS LIMITED**

**REPORT OF THE DIRECTORS CONTD**

**Auditors**

The auditors Lynch & Co, Chartered Accountants & Registered Auditors are to continue in office in accordance with Section 160(2) of the Companies Act 1963.

On behalf of the directors.

*John Murphy*
_____

                              Directors

*Mary Smyth*
_____

Date: *3 March 2008*

**SPORTS LIMITED**

**STATEMENT OF DIRECTORS' RESPONSIBILITIES**

The directors are responsible for preparing the annual report and the financial statements in accordance with applicable Irish Law and Generally Accepted Accounting Practice in Ireland including the accounting standards issued by the Accounting Standards Board and published by the Institute of Chartered Accountants in Ireland.

Irish company law requires the directors to prepare financial statements for each financial year which give a true and fair view of the affairs of the company and of the profit and loss of the company for that year. In preparing the financial statements, the directors are required to:

- Select suitable accounting policies and then apply them consistently.
- Make judgments and estimates that are reasonable and prudent.
- Prepare the financial statements on the going concern basis unless it is inappropriate to presume that the company will continue in business.

The directors confirm that they have complied with the above requirement in preparing the financial statements.

The directors are responsible for keeping proper accounting records that disclose with reasonable accuracy at any time the financial position of the company and to enable them to ensure that the financial statements are prepared in accordance with accounting standards generally accepted in Ireland and with Irish statutes comprising the Companies Acts 1963 to 2006.

They are also responsible for safeguarding the assets of the company and hence for taking reasonable steps for the prevention and detection of fraud and other irregularities.

On behalf of the directors.


*John Murphy*
_____

                                    Directors

*Mary Smyth*
_____

Date: *3 March 2008*

## SPORTS LIMITED

## INDEPENDENT AUDITORS' REPORT TO THE MEMBERS OF SPORTS LIMITED

We have audited the financial statements on pages 7 to 15, which have been prepared under the historical cost convention and the accounting policies.

### Respective Responsibilities of Directors and Auditors

The directors' responsibilities for preparing the Directors' Report and the financial statements in accordance with applicable Irish law and Accounting Standards issued by the Accounting Standards Board and published by the Institute of Chartered Accountants in Ireland (Generally Accepted Accounting Practice in Ireland) are set out in the Statement of Directors' Responsibilities on page 4.

Our responsibility is to audit the financial statements in accordance with relevant legal and regulatory requirements and Auditing Standards promulgated by the Auditing Practices Board in Ireland. This report, including the opinion, has been prepared for and only for the company's members as a body in accordance with section 193 of the Companies Act 1990 and for no other purpose. We do not, in giving this opinion, accept or assume responsibility for any other purpose or to any other person to whom this report is shown or into whose hands it may come save where expressly agreed by our prior consent in writing.

We report to you our opinion as to whether the financial statements give a true and fair view, in accordance with Generally Accepted Accounting Practice in Ireland, and are properly prepared in accordance with Irish statute comprising the Companies Acts 1963 to 2006. We state whether we have obtained all the information and explanations we consider necessary for the purpose of our audit and whether the financial statements are in agreement with the books of account. We also report to you our opinion as to:

- Whether the company has kept proper books of account; and
- Whether the Directors' Report is consistent with the financial statements.

We also report to you if, in our opinion, any information specified by law regarding directors' remuneration and directors' transactions is not disclosed and, where practicable, include such information in our report.

We read the Directors' Report included and consider the implication for our report if we become aware of any apparent misstatement within it.

**SPORTS LIMITED**

**INDEPENDENT AUDITORS' REPORT TO THE MEMBERS OF SPORTS LIMITED**

**Basis of Audit Opinion**

We conducted our audit in accordance with Auditing Standards issued by the Auditing Practices Board. An audit includes examination, on a test basis, of evidence relevant to the amounts and disclosures in the financial statements. It also includes an assessment of the significant estimates and judgments made by the Directors in the preparation of the financial statements, and of whether the accounting policies are appropriate to the company's circumstances, consistently applied and adequately disclosed.

We planned and performed our audit so as to obtain all the information and explanations which we considered necessary in order to provide us with sufficient evidence to give reasonable assurance that the financial statements are free from material misstatement, whether caused by fraud or other irregularity or error. In forming our opinion we also evaluated the overall adequacy of the presentation of information in the financial statements.

**Opinion**

In our opinion the financial statements

- Give a true and fair view in accordance with Generally Accepted Accounting Practice in Ireland, of the state of the company's affairs as at 31 December 2007 and of its profit for the year ended.
- Have been properly prepared in accordance with the requirement of the Companies Acts, 1963 to 2006.

We have obtained all the information and explanations we consider necessary for the purpose of our audit. In our opinion, proper books of account have been kept by the company. The company's financial statements are in agreement with the books of account.

In our opinion, the information given in the Directors' Report is consistent with the financial statements.

*Lynch & Co*
Chartered Accountants & Registered Auditors
12 Main Street
Blanchardstown
Dublin 15

Date: *4 March 2008*

**SPORTS LIMITED**

**PROFIT & LOSS ACCOUNT
YEAR ENDED 31 DECEMBER 2007**

| | Note | 2007 €| 2006 € |
|---|---|---|---|
| **Income** | | 890,000 | 785,000 |
| Administration Expenses | | (798,800) | (701,200) |
| **Operating Profit** | | 91,200 | 83,800 |
| Interest payable | 5 | (4,000) | (4,500) |
| **Profit on ordinary activities before taxation** | 3 | 87,200 | 79,300 |
| Tax on profit on ordinary activities | 6 | (10,000) | (2,500) |
| **Profit for the financial year** | | 77,200 | 76,800 |
| Balance at beginning of year | | 106,200 | 29,400 |
| **Balance at end of year** | | **183,400** | **106,200** |

This is analysed on Page 18

This is analysed on Page 19

This figure is included in the Balance Sheet

A separate statement of total recognised gains and losses is not presented, as there are none except as reflected above.

On behalf of the directors.

*John Murphy*
_____

                          Directors

*Mary Smyth*
_____

Date: *3 March 2008*

**SPORTS LIMITED**

**BALANCE SHEET
AS AT 31 DECEMBER 2007**

| | Note | 2007 € | 2006 € |
|---|---|---|---|
| **Fixed Assets** | | | |
| Tangible Assets | 7 | 24,200 | 36,800 |
| | | This must agree to the bank reconciliation | |
| **Current Assets** | | | |
| Debtors | 8 | 152,500 | 164,000 |
| Cash at bank and on hand | | 129,800 | 19,000 |
| | | 282,300 | 183,000 |
| **Creditors: amounts falling due within one year** | 9 | (114,000) | (99,500) |
| **Net current assets** — This is current assets minus creditors falling due within one year | | 168,300 | 83,500 |
| **Total assets less current liabilities** | | 192,500 | 120,300 |
| **Creditors: amounts falling due after more than one year** | 10 | (9,000) | (14,000) |
| **Net assets** — This is net current assets plus fixed assets | | 183,500 | 106,300 |
| **Capital and Reserves** | | | |
| Called up share capital | 13 | 100 | 100 |
| Profit & loss account | 14 | 183,400 | 106,200 |
| **Shareholders' funds** | | 183,500 | 106,300 |

On behalf of the directors.

*John Murphy*
_____

Directors

*Mary Smyth*
_____

Date: *3 March 2008*

**SPORTS LIMITED**

**NOTES TO THE FINANCIAL STATEMENTS
YEAR ENDED 31 DECEMBER 2007**

1) **Accounting Policies**

   (a) **Basis of Preparation of Financial Statements**

   The financial statements are prepared in accordance with Accounting Standards generally accepted in Ireland and Irish Statue comprising the Companies Acts, 1963 to 2006. Accounting Standards generally accepted in Ireland in preparing financial statements giving a true and fair view are those published by the Institute of Chartered Accountants in Ireland and issued by the Accounting Standards Board.

   (b) **Turnover**

   Turnover represents amounts receivable for promotion and advertising provided within the Republic of Ireland net of VAT.

   (c) **Tangible Assets**

   Fixed assets are stated at cost less accumulated depreciation. Depreciation is calculated in order to write off fixed assets on a straight-line basis at the following annual rates.

   | | |
   |---|---|
   | Fixtures and Fittings | 20% |
   | Office Equipment | 20% |
   | Computer Equipment | $33\frac{1}{3}$% |
   | Motor Vehicle | 20% |

   (d) **Leased Assets**

   Assets held under leasing arrangement that transfer substantially all the risks and rewards of ownership to the company are capitalised. The capital element of the related rental obligations is included in creditors. The interest element of the rental obligations is charged to the profit & loss account so as to produce a constant periodic rate of charge.

   (e) **Foreign Currencies**

   Transactions denominated in foreign currencies relating to revenues and costs are translated into euro at the rates of exchange ruling on the dates on which the transactions occurred. Monetary assets and liabilities denominated in foreign currencies are translated into euro at the rates of exchange at the balance sheet date.

   (f) **Pension**

   The company operates a defined contribution pension scheme for the benefit of its employees.

**SPORTS LIMITED**

**NOTES TO THE FINANCIAL STATEMENTS CONTD**

2) **Turnover and Business**

The financial statements comply with FRS 3—"Reporting Financial Performance". The turnover and operating profit relate to continuing operations as no businesses were acquired or discontinued in 2007 or 2006.

3) **Profit on ordinary activities before taxation**

|  | 2007 | 2006 |
|---|---|---|
|  | € | € |
| Staff costs |  |  |
| Wages and salaries (see note below) | 341,000 | 274,000 |
| Social welfare costs | 6,000 | 4,000 |
| Pension costs (see note below) | 24,000 | 20,000 |
|  | 371,000 | 298,000 |
| Auditors' remuneration | 4,000 | 4,000 |

This is gross salary for all employees

This is the company's contribution to the pension scheme

This is employer's PRSI

**Note** included under staff costs are the following amounts in respect of directors:

| | | |
|---|---|---|
| Directors' fees | 276,000 | 230,000 |
| Pension costs | 24,000 | 20,000 |

4) **Employees**

The average number of employees employed by the company (including Directors) during the year was as follows:

|  | 2007 | 2006 |
|---|---|---|
|  | No. | No. |
| Staff | 3 | 3 |

This is the average number of staff employed by the company

**SPORTS LIMITED**

**NOTES TO THE FINANCIAL STATEMENTS CONTD**

### 5)  Interest Payable

|  | 2007 € | 2006 € |
|---|---|---|
| Borrowing wholly repayable within five years |  |  |
| Bank Interest and Charges | 1,500 | 2,000 |
| Lease Charges | 2,500 | 2,500 |
|  | 4,000 | 4,500 |

### 6)  Taxation

|  | 2007 € | 2006 € |
|---|---|---|
| Tax Charge for the year  *This is 12.5% of the tax adjusted profit* | 10,000 | 2,500 |
|  | 10,000 | 2,500 |

### 7)  Tangible Fixed Assets

|  | Computer Equipment € | Fixtures & Fittings € | Office Equipment € | Motor Vehicles € | Total € |
|---|---|---|---|---|---|
| **Cost** |  |  |  |  |  |
| At 1 January 2007 | 6,000 | 16,000 | 22,000 | 20,000 | 64,000 |
| Additions | 1,500 | – | – | – | 1,500 |
| Disposals | – | – | – | – | – |
| At 31 December 2007 | 7,500 | 16,000 | 22,000 | 20,000 | 65,500 |
| **Depreciation** |  |  |  |  |  |
| At 1 January 2007 | 4,000 | 6,400 | 8,800 | 8,000 | 27,200 |
| Charge for the year | 2,500 | 3,200 | 4,400 | 4,000 | 14,100 |
| Disposals | – | – | – | – | – |
| At 31 December 2007 | 6,500 | 9,600 | 13,200 | 12,000 | 41,300 |
| **Net Book Value** |  |  |  |  |  |
| At 31 December 2007 | 1,000 | 6,400 | 8,800 | 8,000 | 24,200 |
| At 31 December 2006 | 2,000 | 9,600 | 13,200 | 12,000 | 36,800 |

Included above are the following amounts in respect of assets which are financed by Finance Leases and which remain in the legal ownership of the lessors:

**SPORTS LIMITED**

**NOTES TO THE FINANCIAL STATEMENTS CONTD**

|  | 2007 | 2006 |
|---|---|---|
|  | € | € |
| Net Book Value | 8,000 | 12,000 |
| Depreciation | 4,000 | 4,000 |

**8) Debtors**

|  | 2007 | 2006 |
|---|---|---|
|  | € | € |
| Debtors | 120,000 | 140,000 |
| Prepayments | 32,500 | 24,000 |
|  | 152,500 | 164,000 |

**9) Creditors—amounts falling due within one year**

|  | 2007 | 2006 |
|---|---|---|
|  | € | € |
| Trade Creditors | 75,000 | 65,000 |
| Other Creditors and Accruals | 12,000 | 19,000 |
| Finance Lease (see note 11) | 5,000 | 5,000 |
| Other Taxes and Social Welfare | 12,000 | 8,000 |
| Corporation Tax | 10,000 | 2,500 |
|  | 114,000 | 99,500 |

This is the VAT and PAYE/PRSI liability

**SPORTS LIMITED**

**NOTES TO THE FINANCIAL STATEMENTS CONTD**

10) **Creditors—amounts falling due after one year**

|  | 2007 € | 2006 € |
|---|---|---|
| Finance Lease (see note 11) | 9,000 | 14,000 |
|  | 9,000 | 14,000 |

11) **Finance Leases**

These leases finance certain tangible assets, which remain in the legal ownership of the lessors (see note 7).

|  | 2007 € | 2006 € |
|---|---|---|
| The lease instalments falling due in the following years after 31 December |  |  |
| Within one year | 5,000 | 5,000 |
| Between one and five years | 9,000 | 14,000 |
|  | 14,000 | 19,000 |

12) **Related Party Disclosures**

The company has no related party transactions that require disclosure under Financial Reporting Standard 8 – Related Party Transactions.

**SPORTS LIMITED**

**NOTES TO THE FINANCIAL STATEMENTS CONTD**

13) **Share Capital**

|  | 2007 € | 2006 € |
|---|---|---|
| This is the maximum number of shares that can be issued | | |
| Authorised | | |
| 100,000 ordinary shares of €1 each | 100,000 | 100,000 |
| This is the actual number of shares that have been issued to the shareholders | 100,000 | 100,000 |
| Allotted and fully paid | | |
| 100 ordinary shares of €1 each | 100 | 100 |
|  | 100 | 100 |

14) **Reconciliation of Movements in Shareholders' Funds for the year ended**

|  | 2007 € | 2006 € |
|---|---|---|
| Profit for the year | 77,200 | 76,800 |
| Opening Shareholders' funds | 106,200 | 29,400 |
| Closing Shareholders' funds | 183,400 | 106,200 |

15) **Commitments**

|  | 2007 € | 2006 € |
|---|---|---|
| Capital Commitments | | |
| Expenditure contracted for | – | – |
| Authorised by the directors but not contracted for | – | – |

**SPORTS LIMITED**

**NOTES TO THE FINANCIAL STATEMENTS CONTD**

16) **Pension Information**

|  | 2007 | 2006 |
|---|---|---|
|  | € | € |
| Contribution to pension scheme | 24,000 | 20,000 |

The company operates a defined contribution pension scheme. The assets of the scheme are held separately from those of the Company in an independently administered fund. The pension charge represents contributions payable by the Company to the scheme. Pension Costs amounted to €24,000 (2006: €20,000). At the year end the full liability for the year had been discharged.

17) **Cash Flow Statement**

Under FRS 1 Cash Flow Statements, the company is exempt from the requirement to prepare a cash flow statement because of its size.

18) **Approval of financial statements**

The directors approved the financial statements on *3 March 2008.*

**SPORTS LIMITED**

**FINANCIAL STATEMENTS**
**YEAR ENDED 31 DECEMBER 2007**

**SUPPLEMENTARY INFORMATION**

**SPORTS LIMITED**

**DETAILED PROFIT & LOSS ACCOUNT
YEAR ENDED 31 DECEMBER 2007**

**Schedule I**

|  | 2007 € | 2006 € |
|---|---|---|
| Income (Schedule II) | 890,000 | 785,000 |
| Administration Expenses (Schedule III) | (798,800) | (701,200) |
| **Operating Profit** | 91,200 | 83,800 |
| Interest Payable | (4,000) | (4,500) |
| **Net Profit for the year** | 87,200 | 79,300 |

**SPORTS LIMITED**

**INCOME**
**YEAR ENDED 31 DECEMBER 2007**

**Schedule II**

|                       | 2007<br>€ | 2006<br>€ |
|-----------------------|----------:|----------:|
| Promotional Income    | 850,000   | 750,000   |
| Sponsorship Income    | 5,000     | 10,000    |
| Advertising Income    | 35,000    | 25,000    |
|                       | 890,000   | 785,000   |

**SPORTS LIMITED**

**ADMINISTRATIVE EXPENSES**
**YEAR ENDED 31 DECEMBER 2007**

**Schedule III**

|                              | 2007 € | 2006 € |
|------------------------------|-------:|-------:|
| Directors' Remuneration      | 300,000 | 250,000 |
| Wages and Salaries           | 65,000 | 44,000 |
| Employer's PRSI              | 6,000 | 4,000 |
| Rent and Rates               | 30,000 | 30,000 |
| Promotions Costs             | 250,000 | 220,000 |
| Advertising                  | 42,000 | 43,000 |
| Website Costs                | 5,000 | 8,000 |
| Telephone                    | 12,000 | 13,000 |
| Postage                      | 11,000 | 14,000 |
| Stationery                   | 5,000 | 4,000 |
| Light and Heat               | 2,000 | 1,500 |
| Insurance                    | 6,000 | 6,500 |
| Entertainment                | 5,000 | 10,000 |
| Travel and Subsistence       | 25,000 | 19,000 |
| Depreciation                 | 14,100 | 13,600 |
| Legal and Professional Fees  | 6,500 | 9,000 |
| Audit and Accountancy Fees   | 5,000 | 5,000 |
| Foreign Exchange Loss        | 5,000 | 2,000 |
| Bank Charges                 | 200 | 300 |
| Miscellaneous Expenses       | 4,000 | 3,500 |
| Bad Debts                    | – | 300 |
| Loss on Disposal             | – | 500 |
|                              | 798,800 | 701,200 |

# GLOSSARY OF TERMS

**Account** – An account is a structured record of monetary transactions, held within an accounting system, relating to a customer, supplier, income, expenditure, asset or liability.

**Accrual** – If goods or services have been received but no invoices received by the period end, then an accrual is used to include the cost in the financial statements.

**Accumulated Depreciation** – An annual allowance is made for the wear and tear of capital items. Each fixed asset is depreciated annually.

**Annual General Meeting** – The meeting that a company is required to hold every year. Shareholders attend to consider various aspects of the running of the company. Company law requires certain topics to be discussed including the election of directors, review of the annual report and accounts, payment of dividends and appointment of auditors.

**Asset** – Assets can be fixed assets or current assets; fixed assets include buildings or computers that will be used in a business for a number of years. Current assets are consumed by the business in the current year, eg debtors, stock, cash.

**Balance Sheet** – A statement of all assets and liabilities of a business at a point in time.

**Breakeven Point** – The level of sales at which total costs equal total sales.

**Budget** – A plan expressed in financial terms for a specific future period.

**Budgetary Control** – A term used to describe controlling a business through a clearly defined structure of budgets. Management are responsible for ensuring that the budgeted results are achieved, while individual budget holders are held responsible for specific areas and departments in the business.

**Budget Holder** – A person or manager in charge of a department for which a budget is prepared. The budget holder is normally involved in preparing the budget and will be held responsible for ensuring that the financial results of the department are close to the budgeted levels.

**Capital Allowances** – Taxation allowances are allowed for the write-off of fixed assets over the life of the asset.

**Capital Employed** – The permanent and longer term capital used by a company comprising share capital, reserves and borrowings.

**Capital Expenditure** – Some expenditure lasts for several years such as buildings and equipment. This is deemed to be capital expenditure and is included in the balance sheet.

**Consistency Concept** – One year's accounts should be prepared on the same basis as the next; a fair comparison should be made between one year's accounts and the next.

**Corporation Tax** – Is taxation levied on companies, different taxation rules apply depending on the source of profits.

**Cost of Goods Sold** – Cost of Goods Sold = Opening Stock + Purchases − Closing Stock.

**Credit** – A credit entry to an account is recorded on the right-hand side of an account and covers the following types of transactions:
Reduction in value of an asset
Incurring or recognition of a liability
Introduction of capital by the owners
Receipt of income
Reduction of an expense

**Creditor** – Someone owed money by the business.

**Current Assets** – Any asset the business owns that can be turned into cash within one year, eg stocks, debtors, cash.

**Current Liabilities** – The total of debts owing by the business that are due and payable within one year. These include bank overdrafts, short-term loans, creditors, VAT, PAYE/PRSI, payroll deductions, trade creditors, tax etc.

**Debit** – A debit entry to an account is recorded on the left-hand side of an account and covers the following types of transactions:
Receipt or recognition of an asset
A liability reduction
Withdrawal of capital or profits by owners
Recording of an expense or loss

**Debtor** – Those who owe money to the business.

**Depreciation** – Depreciation is the term used to describe the wearing out of a fixed asset over a period of time, usually several years. The amount that is estimated to have worn out in the particular year is deducted from the profit as a depreciation charge and the value of the asset after deducting depreciation is recorded in the books as the net book value of the fixed asset.

**Directors** – A director is someone appointed by the shareholders to manage a company on a day-to-day basis.

**Dividend** – A periodic profit distribution to shareholders in proportion to the amount of shares they own.

**Double-Entry Bookkeeping** – The method of recording financial transactions whereby every item is entered as a debit in one account and a corresponding credit in another account.

**Emergency Tax** – When a new employee starts employment without a P45 or tax credits, tax is calculated on a non-cumulative basis and taxed separately for each week/month.

**Equity** – The amount of money the business owes the owner. In the case of a sole trader, this will be the amount of money put into the business, plus or minus profits or losses less drawings. In the case of a company, this will be share capital plus or minus reserves.

**Fixed Assets** – Assets purchased that are used for the business eg land and buildings, plant & machinery, computers that are used by the business for a number of years. They are necessary for the business to produce goods and services, but are not directly consumed or used up in the process. They have a life of several years and are recorded in the books of account in the fixed asset register.

**Going Concern** – Means that the accounts are prepared on the basis that the organisation is going to continue. The assumption of continuity is made unless information is available to the contrary.

**Goodwill** – Value that a purchaser would pay to acquire a business, over and above the values of the net assets.

**Gross Pay** – The total pay due to the employee before any deductions are made.

**Gross Profit** – This is the measure of profit calculated by deducting the cost of goods sold from sales. It is the profit before taking account of overheads. This is a vital area to monitor because gross profit pays for the overhead expenses and wages.

**Gross Profit Margin** – Gross profit expressed as a percentage of sales.

**Income Tax** – Taxation levied on sole traders/partnerships and PAYE employees.

**Leasehold Improvements** – A permanent addition to a structure. These assets remain in the building if the business closes or moves, eg carpets, lighting and renovations to the building.

**Ledger** – A collection of accounts grouped into a particular category.

**Liabilities** – The total of all debt owing by a business broken down between "within one year" and "more than one year". Amounts that are due to be repaid within one year of the accounting date are current liabilities. Amounts to be repaid later than one year from the accounting date are creditors due after one year.

**Liquid Assets** – Those assets which can be turned into cash quickly.

**Long-Term Liabilities** – A debt due and payable over a number of years. Examples include equipment loans, leases, mortgages and shareholder's loans.

**Matching** – This principle requires that accountants match the cost of sales against the value of those same sales in the same time period when determining the profit or loss.

**Material** – This usually means something significant in the context of the size of the business. If an item is mistaken or omitted, would the accounts still given a true and fair view?

**Net Book Value** – The difference between the purchase price of a fixed asset less accumulated depreciation.

**Net Pay** – Gross pay after all the deductions have been made.

**Net Profit** – Net profit is often referred to as the bottom line. It is calculated by deducting the overhead costs from the gross profit. Net profit is the yardstick by which the financial success of the business is measured.

**Net Profit Margin** – Net profit expressed as a percentage of sales.

**Net Tax** – Gross tax less the value of the tax credits.

**Notional Pay** – The value attributable to taxable benefits/benefits in kind that is added to reckonable earnings for the purposes of calculating PAYE and PRSI.

**Ordinary Shares** – The class of share that entitles the owner to all remaining profits after interest and preference dividends have been paid. The owner is also entitled to all residual assets once other claimants have been repaid on liquidation.

**Owners' Equity** – The part of the net worth of the business that is due to the owners of the business. It is normally calculated as the sum of the owners' investment in the business plus profit in the business.

**Pay As You Earn (PAYE)** – A method of taxation where the pay is taxed at source.

**Personal Public Service (PPS) Number** – a number issued by the Department of Social and Family Affairs and unique to each employee.

**Preference Shares** – A class of capital entitling the holders to a fixed rate of dividend prior to any ordinary share dividend. On liquidation they are also entitled to the repayment of their capital before ordinary shareholders are repaid.

**Prepayment** – Expenses paid ahead of the financial statements date which relate to the following period; examples include rent, rates and insurance.

**Profit Forecast** – This is a detailed statement of the expected income of the business less expected expenditure.

**Profit & Loss Account** – Often referred to as the "P&L Account". This is the most important financial statement in any business. It provides a statement of the total income less all of the costs of the business for the accounting period. The difference between the income and the costs is the profit or loss for the period.

**PRSI-Pay Related Social Insurance** – This is deducted at source; it includes Social Insurance and Health Contribution Levies.

**Prudence** – If income is expected and it becomes clear that it will not be received, prudence will state that it is not counted as part of income.

**Reckonable Pay** – Gross pay less pension deductions.

**Reserves** – Revenue reserves are the retained profits which can be distributed as dividends. Capital reserves are not available for distribution as they have not arisen from normal trading activities.

**Revaluation** – Adjusting the value of an asset in the books to reflect its latest market value.

**Separate Entity** – Every business is regarded as an entity on its own. Financial transactions for each business need to be kept separate and personal transactions of the owner should not be included with the business.

**Share Capital** – Money subscribed by shareholders in a limited company for ordinary or preference shares. Issued share capital is the amount of money actually received while authorised capital is the total amount the company is allowed to issue.

**Shareholders** – Shareholders of the company are its legal owners and are entitled to a share of its profits.

**Standard Rate Cut-off** – This is the value at which point the standard rate changes to the higher tax rate.

**Statutory Deductions** – Legal deductions required by law under the PAYE and PRSI systems.

**Stock** – The value of unsold materials and products. These include raw materials, goods purchased for resale and finished goods.

**Tax Credits** – The amount of credits generated by the employee's tax allowances, as determined by the individual's circumstances.

**Temporary Basis** – If an employee starts a new job with only their P45 details, they are put on the week 1/ month 1 basis until the business receives a copy of their tax details.

**Trial Balance** – This is a list of all the debit and credit balances on the various accounts. The total of debits must equal the of total credits.

**Turnover** – This term is often used instead of sales. It is the total income generated by a business from selling its goods or services.

**Variance** – The difference between a budgeted figure and the actual income or expenditure.

**Week 1/Month 1** – The monthly or weekly salary is taxed in isolation; there is no accumulation of tax credits from the previous week/month.

**Work in Progress** – Partially completed contracts, services or goods being produced but not yet billed to the customer.

**Working Capital** – The money required to conduct the day-to-day operations of a business. It takes into account money that is needed to pay for stocks and money owed to the business by a customer; it is offset by the amounts that are owed by the business to its suppliers.